ADVANCING CRITICAL CRIMINOLOGY

Critical Perspectives on Crime and Inequality

Critical Perspectives on Crime and Inequality presents cutting edge work informed by these schools of thought: feminism, peacemaking criminology, left realism, Marxism, cultural criminology, and postmodernism. In an age of instrumental reason and increasing state control, the need for critical and independent analysis of power and social arrangements has never been more acute. Books published in this series will be monographs for scholars and researchers, as well as texts for course use.

Titles in Series:

The Politics of Organized Crime and the Organized Crime of Politics, by Alfredo Schulte-Bockholt

Advancing Critical Criminology: Theory and Application, edited by Walter S. DeKeseredy and Barbara Perry

ADVANCING CRITICAL CRIMINOLOGY

Theory and Application

Edited by
Walter S. DeKeseredy
and
Barbara Perry

LEXINGTON BOOKS

A division of
ROWMAN & LITTLEFIELD PUBLISHERS, INC.
Lanham • Boulder • New York • Toronto • Oxford

LEXINGTON BOOKS

A division of Rowman & Littlefield Publishers, Inc.
A wholly owned subsidiary of The Rowman & Littlefield Publishing Group, Inc.
4501 Forbes Boulevard, Suite 200
Lanham, MD 20706

PO Box 317
Oxford
OX2 9RU, UK

British Library Cataloguing in Publication Information Available

Library of Congress Cataloging-in-Publication Data

Advancing critical criminology : theory and application / edited by Walter S. DeKeseredy and Barbara Perry.
p. cm.
Includes index.
ISBN-13: 978-0-7391-1252-6 (cloth : alk. paper)
ISBN-10: 0-7391-1252-X (cloth : alk. paper)
ISBN-13: 978-0-7391-1253-3 (pbk. : alk. paper)
ISBN-10: 0-7391-1253-8 (pbk. : alk. paper)
1. Critical criminology. I. DeKeseredy, Walter S., 1959– II. Perry, Barbara, 1962– III. Title.
HV6019.A38 2006
364—dc22 2006002937

Printed in the United States of America

∞ ™ The paper used in this publication meets the minimum requirements of American National Standard for Information Sciences—Permanence of Paper for Printed Library Materials, ANSI/NISO Z39.48–1992.

Contents

Preface

THE SEEDS OF THIS BOOK were sown in the early summer of 2003 shortly after Lexington Books published *Under Siege: Poverty and Crime in a Public Housing Community*. Written by Walter S. DeKeseredy, Shahid Alvi, Martin D. Schwartz, and E. Andreas Tomaszewski, this book played a key role in influencing Jason Hallman, their acquisitions editor, to consider publishing a series of books on topics of major concern to critical criminologists. In the late summer of 2003, Jason called Walter DeKeseredy when he was then affiliated with Ohio University and asked him whether such a series would generate much interest in the criminological community and whether Walter would be willing to serve as series editor. Walter immediately agreed to take on this responsibility and to edit what Jason referred to as a "flagship book" consisting of timely chapters on various issues covered by critical criminologists.

The series was then titled the Lexington Series on Critical Criminology and this book was to be the first one in the series. However, life is complicated and Alfredo Schulte-Bockholt's *The Politics of Organized Crime and the Organized Crime of Politics: A Study in Criminal Power* was released before ours and the title of the series is now Critical Perspectives on Crime and Inequality. Further, Jason has moved on to work for AltaMira Press. And, given the great amount of time and effort required to successfully produce a book like this one, Walter sought the assistance of Barbara Perry, who is the coeditor of this anthology.

Indeed, this book is the product of collective effort. Obviously, it would not exist without the important contributions made by the authors of each chapter. We greatly appreciate their friendship, collegiality and patience. We also thank them for producing work that meets the highest disciplinary standards in a timely fashion. Special thanks also go to the series editorial board: Shahid Alvi, Meda Chesney-Lind, Mark Israel, Claire Renzetti, and Martin D. Schwartz.

The staff at Lexington Books were instrumental in figuring out ways to quickly get *Advancing Critical Criminology* published. We are especially indebted to Joseph Parry, our acquisitions editor. He was a pleasure to work with and his many contributions to this project went well beyond the call of duty. Of course, our families, too, helped us in many ways and were constantly there to remind us that there is more to life than doing scholarly and political work. Needless to say, without the support of Patricia and Andrea DeKeseredy, Eva Jantz, Michael Groff, and Keith and Joanne Perry, we would not have been able to muster up the energy required to edit this book.

Last, but certainly not least, we thank the support staff at the University of Ontario Institute of Technology's (UOIT) Faculty of Social Science. Emma Aquilino and Christina Vanderlee did many things to help us edit *Advancing Critical Criminology*, and we will never forget their patience and good humor.

Introduction

The Never-ending and Constantly Evolving Journey

Walter S. DeKeseredy and Barbara Perry

Radical criminology . . . has since proliferated, developed and flourished. The various currents that form its past, whether Marxist, radical feminist or anarchist, continue in fierce dispute but have in common the notion that crime and the present-day processes of criminalization are rooted in the core structures of society, whether it is class nature, its patriarchal form or its inherent authoritarianism (Walton and Young 1998, vii).

WHAT PAUL WALTON and Jock Young stated in their preface to *The New Criminology Revisited* still holds today. Indeed, there is ample evidence that critical criminology is even stronger than it was when these British scholars published their seminal collection of readings. For example, the American Society of Criminology's (ASC) Division on Critical Criminology (DCC) now has approximately four hundred members, many of whom are based outside the birthplaces of critical criminology: the United States and the United Kingdom. Further, with the assistance of thirty editorial board members from around the world, the DCC publishes *Critical Criminology: An International Journal*, and this progressive collective produces a quarterly newsletter titled *The Critical Criminologist*. A website (<www.critcrim.org>) is also an important source of information for DCC members and others interested in topics covered in this book.

The DCC is one of only five divisions of the ASC and overlaps with three of the ASC's strongest divisions: the Division on Women and Crime, the Division of International Criminology, and the Division on People of Color and Crime. Consider, too, that one of the pioneers of critical criminology,

William Chambliss, was the President of the ASC and the Society for the Study of Social Problems (SSSP), arguably the second most important organization in sociology (DeKeseredy and Schwartz 1996). Stephen Pfhol, a postmodern criminologist and deviance theorist, succeeded him as President of the SSSP in the early 1990s. Moreover, Robert Bohm, another widely cited critical criminologist, served as President of the Academy of Criminal Justice Sciences (the national association for criminal justice scholars and practitioners), and at the time of writing this chapter, Jeffery Walker held this position.

There are dozens of other examples of critical criminologists who have held key positions, such as annual meeting or major committee chairs. Further, critical criminologists routinely serve on the editorial boards of major "mainstream" journals, such as *Criminology*, *Justice Quarterly*, and *Crime and Delinquency*. The main point is this: critical criminologists are a major part of the broader academic criminological community.

Definition of Critical Criminology

What is critical criminology and what do critical criminologists do? These are fair and important questions, given that although the term critical criminology has been around since the early 1970s, many criminologists today are not sure what the words *critical criminology* mean (DeKeseredy and Schwartz 1996). Perhaps this is a function of not being able to keep up with all the new and exciting developments in the field. For example, each year, criminology as a whole is responsible for generating thousands of new books, articles, studies, and so on. Thus, one cannot be expected to read everything. On the other hand, many people are politically opposed to critical criminology and purposely ignore the work produced by critical scholars. Then, there are people who are actually part of this tradition who still have problems defining critical criminology.

As Schwartz and Hatty (2003, ix) remind us, another problem students and faculty alike face when challenged by the task of defining critical criminology is "that there are as many types of critical criminology as there are writers and teachers in the area," and one of the key objectives of this book is to provide readings that reflect this diversity. While the chapters in this anthology may at first appear at odds with each other, they are, like other critical scholarly publications, complementary (MacLean and Milovanovic 1991). They are also included here because they fit with our definition of critical criminology, which, guided by Young's (1988) definition of radical criminology, views the major sources of crime as the class, ethnic, and patriarchal relations that control our society. Further, critical criminology rejects as solutions to crime short-term measures such as tougher laws, increased incarceration, coercive counseling therapy, and the like. Rather, critical criminologists regard major structural and cultural changes within society as essential steps to reduce criminality and to promote social justice.

However, just because critical scholars call for major political, economic, social, and cultural transformations does not mean that they disregard criminal justice reform, an issue that is of central concern to conservative scholars. After all, every society requires a combination of formal and informal processes of social control. Still, the types of criminal justice reforms called for by left realists (see chapter 1) and other critical criminologists such as Barbara Perry (see chapter 7) do not include harsher punishment or draconian means of psychological treatment (e.g., shock therapy).

In addition to proposing criminal justice reforms, critical criminologists call for what William Julius Wilson (1996) refers to as short-term policies that reflect a "broader vision." This involves developing strategies that target the key social, cultural, and economic forces that propel people into crime, such as family violence, poverty and unemployment. Of course, critical criminologists are not the only ones who call for such strategies. For example, some initiatives informed by the work of strain theorists such as Merton (1938) and Cloward and Ohlin (1960) are also designed to maximize people's educational and job opportunities. Consider the following solutions advanced by left realists and described in chapter 1 by Walter S. DeKeseredy, Shahid Alvi and Martin D. Schwartz:

- A higher minimum wage.
- Job rationing.
- Meaningful jobs.
- State-sponsored, affordable, and quality child care.
- Housing subsidy and refurbishment programs.
- Improved public transportation.

To give you even more information on what critical criminologists do, below are some of the questions to which they seek answers (Lynch and Groves 1989, viii; Lynch, Michalowski, and Groves 2000, 12–13). Some scholars outside the tradition ask some of these questions, and the list omits some very important questions for critical criminologists. Nevertheless, the following taken together should give readers an idea of the central direction that critical criminologists take:

- Who has the real power in society?
- What are the deeper social forces that shape the definition, commission and punishment of crime?
- What do race/ethnicity, class, and gender have to do with crime and its control?
- Why do affluent people and politicians commit so many crimes?
- Is our criminal justice system fair?
- What are the popular images of crime and of criminals, and where do these images come from?
- Are people well informed or deluded about the nature of crime?

Many critical criminologists are interested in the same questions as other criminologists: Why do some people rape, commit robbery, beat up their intimate female partners, and steal cars? The most important difference is that critical criminologists are not likely to seek answers to such questions by examining flaws in the makeup of the individual actor, or studying the "inherent" pathologies of particular groups, but rather they focus on the flaws in the makeup of a society that breeds, creates, and sustains such people (DeKeseredy and Schwartz 1996). Moreover, as noted by Henry and Lanier (2006, 183), the critical perspectives described in this book and elsewhere are:

> macro-level theories in that they assume that forces external to the individual, resulting from the organization of society as a whole, shape the nature of social institutions, and within these, channel the behavior of humans and their interactions. Thus they look to society's organizational structure, particularly in its divisions or inequalities as the cause, and as an indicator, of the type and level of crime that society will experience. These theories each view humans as potentially active creative entities who have the ability to shape their social world, but who also recognize that the world, in the form of hierarchical power structures, shapes them. Thus, although recognizing a degree of individual human agency, these theories ultimately see humans as pressed, co-opted, and manipulated for the benefit of dominant powerful interests.

Purpose of This Book

Since the history of critical criminology is described in great detail elsewhere (e.g., Lynch et al. 2000), it will not be given much attention in this anthology. Rather, the main objective of this book is twofold:

(1) to provide in-depth reviews of the extant literature on several major branches of critical criminology and

(2) to provide readers with examples of how critical criminologists apply their theoretical perspectives to substantive topics, such as drugs, interpersonal violence, and rural crime.

Accordingly, the book is divided into two main sections:

(1) overviews of theories and
(2) applications.

Readers who heavily immerse themselves in critical criminological literature will immediately detect that some major variations of critical scholarship are conspicuously absent from this book. Further, by the time you finish reading the eleven chapters, even more important variations will have been developed and this is why we selected the title of this chapter. Indeed, critical criminology involves participating in a never-ending and constantly evolving journey, and as Lynch et al. (2000, 1) remind us, any attempt to review critical or radical criminology is "incomplete due to the field's rapidly developing character." That it is impossible to cover every strand of critical criminology in a single book is a powerful statement on the field and on the proliferation of scholarship that has occurred in the last thirty-five years.

This is not to say, however, that the chapters included in this book do not look to the future. All of the contributors are fully aware that more work on their topics is necessary and that their own views on one or more areas are subject to revision due to demographic, political, economic, technological and other types of changes we will witness in the near and distant future. Note, too, that just because the contributors identify themselves as critical criminologists does not mean that they totally reject the work done by mainstream scholars. Consider left realists Walter S. DeKeseredy, Shahid Alvi and Martin D. Schwartz (see chapter 1). In addition to embracing contributions made by social and economic exclusion theorists (e.g., Young 1999) and those made by feminist criminologists discussed in chapter 2 by MaDonna R. Maidment, they draw heavily upon elements of Merton's (1938) anomie theory and Cohen's (1955) subcultural analysis of delinquent boys. A key point to keep in mind here is that contemporary critical criminologists are dedicated to developing integrated theories and often borrow from mainstream perspectives. The difference, however, between "pure" mainstream theories such as Hirschi's (1969) social bond theory and integrated critical theories is that the latter do not consign "wider critical social, political, and cultural reflections to the margins" (Yar and Penna 2004, 537).

Integrative theoretical work done by critical criminologists often also involves engaging in another form of what Schwartz and Hatty (2003) refer to as "mixing and matching." For example, in addition to frequently borrowing from mainstream theories, critical criminologists "create for themselves identities that cross over several of the subfields" of critical thought and research (x), and these identities change according to the topics studied. For example, Walter S. DeKeseredy and Martin D. Schwartz draw upon left realism to explain predatory street crime and are guided by feminist and male peer support theories in their work on woman abuse in a variety of intimate and public settings. In sum, then, rather than strictly adhere to one position, contemporary criminologists such as those who contributed to this book "are able to balance more than one belief at the same time" and often find that "an amalgam of two or more theories satisfies them best intellectually" (Schwartz and Hatty 2003, x).

One of the key strengths of part I of this book is that readers are given in-depth reviews of various strands of critical criminological theory. Still, rather than simply describe various perspectives, contributors to part I sensitize readers to the limitations of left realism, feminist criminology, cultural criminology, restorative justice, and the new penology in a critical context, and they suggest new directions in these schools of thought. Hopefully, others will take their suggestions into account and build upon their recommendations.

Like other criminologists, critical scholars are also deeply committed to applying theories to substantive topics of major concern to researchers, practitioners, policy makers, and the general population, such as those covered in part II. Nevertheless, their application of theory is not simply a mechanical process. In other words, the work presented in part II is based on years of in-depth research using a variety of empirical techniques, including ethnography, biography, narrative and deconstruction (Lynch et al. 2000). Still, readers unfamiliar with critical criminological research should not assume that all critical scholars use only these methods. In fact, some use mainstream methods, such as surveys and the analysis of government data (e.g., police statistics). Consider the study of poverty and crime in public housing conducted by DeKeseredy, Alvi, Schwartz and Tomaszewski (2003). Heavily informed by Jock Young's (1999) theoretical work on social and economic exclusion, feminist perspectives on woman abuse, and other critical schools of thought, this project involved administering a victimization survey, in-depth interviews with public housing residents, and the analyses of available Canadian census tract and enumeration area data. Similarly, "card carrying" critical criminologists such as Walter S. DeKeseredy and Martin D. Schwartz routinely use quantitative methods to uncover the pain and suffering experienced by woman who are abused by intimate male partners.

Another important point to keep in mind as you read the material presented in this book is that theories and methods are tools that can be used in a variety of ways and to achieve a variety of goals. Consider something as simple as a shovel. It can be used to build a battered women's shelter and a correctional facility that houses and punishes socially and economically disenfranchised victims of the U.S. government's "war on drugs." Obviously, critical criminologists prefer using a shovel to build a shelter and use research methods to reveal how broader social forces contribute to crime and draconian means of social control. Similarly, when they borrow concepts from conservative or mainstream theories, they do so to help explain how various types of inequality propel people to commit crimes or leave them vulnerable to victimization.

As partially reflected in this book, scholars from around the world have made, and continue to make, many important contributions to critical understandings of crime and its control. Further, new information technologies make it easier for critical criminologists to exchange ideas with their peers based outside their respective countries and to develop collaborative theoretical and empirical projects. Nevertheless, an in-depth review of the extant literature reveals that much more work needs to be done to develop a more inclusive critical criminology, one that consistently involves including scholarly work produced outside primarily English-speaking countries in readers such as this one. This, too, will eventually happen, given that critical criminology is a never-ending and constantly evolving way of "doing criminology" (Lynch et al. 2000). The project will always be incomplete, which we view as a blessing rather than as a curse. Critical criminologists fully recognize that resisting change, or advancing standardization of theory and methodology, "is the parent of stagnation" (Jacobs 2004, 119).

References

Cloward, R. A., and L. E. Ohlin. 1960. *Delinquency and Opportunity: A Theory of Delinquent Gangs*. New York: Free Press of Glencoe.

Cohen, A. 1955. *Delinquent Boys: The Culture of the Gang*. New York: Free Press.

DeKeseredy, W. S., S. Alvi, M. D. Schwartz, and E. A. Tomaszewski. 2003. *Under Siege: Poverty and Crime in a Public Housing Community*. Lanham, MD: Lexington Books.

DeKeseredy, W. S., and M. D. Schwartz. 1996. *Contemporary Criminology*. Belmont, CA: Wadsworth.

Henry, S., and M. M. Lanier. 2006. "Conflict and Radical Theories." Pp. 183–84 in S. Henry and M. M. Lanier, eds., *The Essential Criminology Reader*. Boulder, CO: Westview Press.

Hirschi, T. 1969. *Causes of Delinquency*. Berkeley: University of California Press.

Jacobs, J. 2004. *Dark Age Ahead.* Toronto: Vintage.
Lynch, M. J., and W. B. Groves. 1989. *A Primer in Radical Criminology.* 2nd ed. New York: Harrow & Heston.
Lynch, M. J., R. Michalowski, and W. B. Groves. 2000. *The New Primer in Radical Criminology: Critical Perspectives on Crime, Power and Identity.* 3rd edition. Monsey, NJ: Criminal Justice Press.
MacLean, B. D., and D. Milovanovic. 1991. "On Critical Criminology." Pp. 1–8 in B. D. MacLean and D. Milovanovic, eds., *New Directions in Critical Criminology.* Vancouver: Collective Press.
Merton, R. K. 1938. "Social Structure and Anomie." *American Sociological Review* 3: 672–82.
Schwartz, M. D., and S. E. Hatty. 2003. "Introduction." Pp. ix–xvii in M. D. Schwartz and S. E. Hatty, eds., *Controversies in Critical Criminology.* Cincinnati: Anderson.
Walton, P., and J. Young. 1998. "Preface." Pp. vii–viii in P. Walton and J. Young, eds., *The New Criminology Revisited.* London: St. Martin's Press.
Wilson, W. J. 1996. *When Work Disappears: The World of the New Urban Poor.* New York: Knopf.
Yar, M., and S. Penna. 2004. "Between Positivism and Post-modernity?: Critical Reflections on Jock Young's *The Exclusive Society.*" *British Journal of Criminology* 44: 533–49.
Young, J. 1988. "Radical Criminology in Britain: The Emergence of a Competing Paradigm. *British Journal of Criminology* 28: 159–83.
———. 1999. *The Exclusive Society.* London: Sage.

Part I

Overviews of Theoretical Perspectives

Introduction to Part I

Walter S. DeKeseredy and Barbara Perry

In the introduction, we noted that critical criminology has gone through a number of significant changes since its birth and that it will continue to change. Again, critical criminologists advocate progress. Still, just because something is deemed "old" does not mean that it is no longer valuable. For example, ten years ago, in the introduction to their reader *Thinking Critically about Crime*, Brian MacLean and Dragan Milovanovic (1997, 15) observed that "far from being 'hegemonic,' and far from being monolithic in its thinking, critical criminology is a discipline characterized by a rich theoretical diversity." Fortunately, this is still the case today, and the chapters featured in the first section of this book reflect an ongoing, deep-rooted commitment to embrace multiple ways of thinking critically about crime, law and justice. And, like the authors who contributed to MacLean and Milovanovic's anthology, what the contributors to this book have in common, among other things, is "their opposition to conventional regimes of power that give rise to particular forms of criminal-justice delivery systems" (MacLean and Milovanovic 1997, 15).

We cannot emphasize enough that the order in which each author's chapter appears does not reflect a hierarchy of importance. All of the chapters in this section are equally important and are explicitly designed to provide readers with overviews of various schools of critical thought and to suggest new directions in theoretical, empirical, and political work. Similarly, the chapters in part II of this book suggest "ways forward." It is to a summary of left realism's contributions to the ongoing journey identified in the Introduction that we turn to first.

Left Realism

Elliott Currie offers one of the best summaries of this school of thought, which is not surprising, given that he is a left realist. According to him, left realism "is an approach that links variations in serious crime to variations in key structural conditions and policies, and that is distinguished by its activist and ameliorative implications" (2006, 303). Born during the years that Ronald Reagan and Margaret Thatcher governed their respective countries, left realism is now seen by many scholars as a marginal subdiscipline of critical criminology. For Walter S. DeKeseredy, Shahid Alvi and Martin D. Schwartz, nothing can be further from the truth, and one of the key objectives of their chapter is to demonstrate that left realism is still important today.

Rather than simply respond to widely read and cited criticisms of left realism, DeKeseredy and his colleagues focus on its often overlooked theoretical and empirical contributions, and they suggest new directions in theory, research and policy. One of their key points is that, contrary to what many criminologists claim, left realism offers rich insights into the causes and control of crime. Rarely will you find a textbook that devotes this much attention to left realist theories, and we are sure that readers who are unfamiliar with these offerings will agree with Schwartz and Hatty's (2003, xii) assertion that left realism is "[o]ne of the most important critical criminologies in the English-speaking world."

Feminist Criminology

Feminist criminology has much in common with left realism. In fact, as pointed out in chapter 1, left realists were among the first critical criminologists to recognize the importance of feminist inquiry (Thomas and O'Maolchatha 1989). Informed readers, however, are likely to ask, "What type of feminism guides left realism?" The same question can be directed at other schools of thought that claim to be driven in part by feminist contributions. As noted in chapter 2 by MaDonna R. Maidment, and by other feminist scholars elsewhere, there are at least twelve variants of feminist criminological theory, but space limitations confine Maidment to addressing six of the most widely cited perspectives: liberal, Marxist, socialist, radical, postmodern, and standpoint.

In addition to doing a comprehensive review of the extant literature on feminist contributions to a social scientific understanding of crime and its control, Maidment raises several important issues at the forefront of discussions and debates about the relationship between gender and a host of social phenomena. For example, many readers have probably noticed surveys and other documents that ask people to report their gender. Such requests equate gender with sex, but, following the path-breaking work done by Kathleen Daly and Meda Chesney-Lind (1988), Maidment reminds us that there are major differences between these two factors. As Daly and Chesney-Lind (1988, 502) correctly point out, "Gender is not a natural fact but a complex social, historical, and cultural product; it is related to, but not simply derived from, biological sex differences and reproductive capacities."

Maidment's chapter also shows that feminist work on crime and its control involves much more than critiquing criminological contributions that ignore women or simply pay lip service to them. Clearly, there is a rapidly growing body of feminist theoretical work on topics such as woman abuse, female gangs, prostitution, and gender inequality in the law and criminal justice system. Moreover, like other critical criminologists, feminists are taking a constantly evolving and never-ending journey, and Maidment suggests a few new paths to take along the way. One path in particular that stands out in her chapter involves a journey for both men and women. This journey has begun because we are witnessing a growing number of male scholars who publicly identify themselves as feminists and who put gender at the center of their theoretical and empirical work on a broad range of criminological issues.

Cultural Criminology

Although they study different topics and are guided by different theoretical approaches, cultural criminologist Stephen L. Muzzatti and feminist scholar MaDonna R. Maidment have at least four things in common. First, they are young Canadian scholars who have quickly made several significant contributions to their fields of inquiry. Second, a rich sociological understanding of how culture shapes crime and its control is part and parcel of their research. Third, they both use qualitative methods and are heavily influenced by critical work done in their own country, in the U.S., in the U.K., and in other parts of the world.

Another thing Muzzatti and Maidment have in common is that their approaches to understanding crime and its control are partly rooted in labeling theory, as are other variants of critical criminology. However, there are some key factors that differentiate Muzzatti and Maidment. Again, Muzzatti is a cultural criminologist and he is working in a tradition that is younger than feminism. Invented by U.S. scholars Ferrell (1999) and Ferrell and Saunders (1995), cultural criminology, as described by one of its pioneers:

> critically investigates the ways in which the dynamics of media and popular culture, the lives and activities of criminals, and the operations of social control and criminal justice come together in everyday life. Cultural criminologists

> emphasize the role of image, style, and symbolic meaning among criminals and their subcultures, in the mass media's representation of crime and criminal justice, and in public conflicts over crime and crime control. (Ferrell 2003, 71)

In addition to tracing the history of cultural criminology and its intellectual roots, Muzzatti, like his close colleague Jeff Ferrell (2003), provides a compelling and effective response to criticisms of cultural criminology and sensitizes us to the fact that cultural criminologists are taking new directions, such as studying genocide, corporate crime, and terrorism. Obviously, cultural criminology is "here to stay," and it is attracting an international cadre of scholars who constantly generate new and timely publications. In the words of Muzzatti, "the publication of edited collections such as *Cultural Criminology Unleashed*, the launch of new journals such as *Crime, Media, Culture*, and special editions of established journals such as *Theoretical Criminology* devoted to the works of cultural criminology all attest to this growing orientation."

Restorative Justice

Critical criminologists "wear many hats," and Kimberly J. Cook and Chris Powell are prime examples of this. Consider that Cook has a long history of doing exciting feminist work on social problems such as woman abuse and the death penalty, and Powell has published scholarly work on topics such as humor, animal abuse, feminist methodology, drunk driving, and so on. Simultaneously, they are heavily involved in advancing a rich interdisciplinary understanding of restorative justice, as described in chapter 4.

Restorative justice is closely related to another variant of critical criminology: peacemaking criminology (Schwartz and Hatty 2003). Peacemaking criminology is informed by anarchism, humanism, Christian socialism, liberation theology, Eastern meditative thought, penal abolitionism, feminism, and Marxism (Pepinsky and Quinney 1991). As outlined by Richard Quinney (1991, 11–12), one of the pioneers of peacemaking criminology, its basic principles are:

- Crime is suffering, and crime can only be eliminated by ending suffering.
- Crime and suffering can only be ended through the achievement of peace.
- Human transformation will achieve peace and justice.
- Human transformation will occur if we change our social, economic, and political structure.

Like peacemaking criminology, restorative justice is not motivated primarily by punishment and blame, which divide people, but by collaboration and healing. Used extensively in Australia, New Zealand, and increasingly in Canadian Aboriginal communities, restorative justice initiatives are based on the goal of restoring or creating individual, family, and community health. Following the World Health Organization (2005, 1), health is defined here "as a state of complete physical, mental and social well-being and not merely the absence of disease or infirmity." Diversionary conferences, such as those observed by Cook in Australia and described by her and Powell in their chapter, are key community-based mechanisms specifically designed to achieve this goal. Obviously, such conferences are not popular among neoconservatives because they reject draconian societal reactions to crimes (e.g., imprisonment).

Of major concern to Cook and Powell are the emotional dynamics and bureaucratic pressures affecting diversionary conferences. Their chapter is rich with ethnographic data and it sensitizes us to the importance of carefully examining progressive means of dealing with crime that exist beyond the narrow confines of North America, a continent dominated by "get tough" responses to violations of social and legal norms such as the criminalization of incivilities like public drunkenness. Note, too, that thinking critically about crime and its control also involves thinking critically about one's own position on these issues, which is why Cook and Powell recommend that "one should adopt a sound dose of scepticism when confronted with the apparent differences between restorative justice and more conventional processes of justice." Their scepticism is not only based on rigorous research, but also on being an integral part of the restorative justice process. For example, Cook is a certified facilitator and has been very active in local community restorative justice programs. She, Powell, and the other contributors to this book are major examples of scholars who integrate theory and practice and do so in a variety of progressive ways. They are part of what Lynch et al. (2000, 15) refer to as "social movements that confront social inequality and seek to liberate oppressed peoples."

The New Penology in a Critical Context

The U.S. is experiencing an "imprisonment binge" (Irwin 2005). For example, as noted in chapter 5 by postmodern theorist Michelle Brown, at the end of the last century, the U.S. incarcerated more people than any other country in the world with a total prison/jail population of over 2 million people. Critical criminologists, among others, question the value of such punitive measures, given that the U.S. is currently experiencing a drop in crime. Moreover, there is ample evidence showing that prison, the death penalty, or other "get tough" approaches do little, if anything, to reduce crime. So, why do they continue to exist and expand? According to Malcolm Feeley and Jonathan Simon (1992), the answer to this question is the emergence of a new penology.

Put simply, the new penology is actuarial. In other words, mass incarceration, zero-tolerance policing, and the like are not concerned with individual guilt, deterrence, offender motivation, and rehabilitation. Rather, the goal is to manage populations who are considered dangerous or at high risk of committing crime. In the words of Feeley and Simon (1998, 375), the new penology is:

> concerned with techniques for identifying, classifying and managing groups assorted by levels of dangerousness. It takes crime for granted. It accepts deviance as normal. It is skeptical that liberal interventionist crime control strategies do or can make a difference. Thus its aim is not to intervene in individuals' lives for the purpose of ascertaining responsibility, make the guilty "pay for their crime" or charging them. Rather it seeks to regulate groups as part of a strategy of managing danger.

In chapter 5, Brown carefully reviews Feeley and Simon's thesis and critiques of it. Regardless of whether you agree with Feeley and Simon's analysis, Brown's insightful chapter compels us to think critically about actuarialism and its impact on our everyday lives. As stated in her conclusion, "The new penology . . . maps a possibility that extends far beyond immediately apparent penal contexts into a fundamental reconfiguration of social life."

Brown is yet another example of a critical criminologist who has multiple research interests and who is influenced by diverse progressive schools of thought. Further, she has much in common with other contributors to this book, given her expertise in cultural theory, media studies, and the sociology of punishment and risk. There is another thing that unites her with the other contributors and critical criminologists around the world. In all of her work, she provides an alternative vision and places on the floor of public debate the idea that there are other ways of looking at crime and other ways to work with those who offend against us.

References

Currie, E. 2006. "Inequality, Community, and Crime." Pp. 299–306 in S. Henry and M. M. Lanier, eds., *The Essential Criminology Reader*. Boulder, CO: Westview.

Daly, K., and M. Chesney-Lind. 1988. "Feminism and Criminology." *Justice Quarterly* 5: 497–538.

Feeley, M., and J. Simon. 1992. "The New Penology: Notes on the Emerging Strategy of Corrections and Its Implications." *Criminology* 30: 449–74.

———. 1998. "Actuarial Justice: The Emerging New Criminal Law." In P. O'Malley, ed., *Crime and the Risk Society*. Brookfield, VT: Ashgate.

Ferrell, J. 1999. "Cultural Criminology." *Annual Review of Sociology* 25: 395–418.

———. 2003. "Cultural Criminology." Pp. 71–84 in M. D. Schwartz and S. E. Hatty, eds., *Controversies in Critical Criminology*. Cincinnati: Anderson.

Ferrell, J., and C. Sanders, eds. 1995. *Cultural Criminology*. Boston: Northeastern University Press.

Irwin, J. 2005. *The Warehouse Prison: Disposal of the New Dangerous Class*. Los Angeles: Roxbury.

Lynch, M. J., R. Michalowski, and W. B. Groves. 2000. *The New Primer in Radical Criminology: Critical Perspectives on Crime, Power and Identity*. 3rd edition. Monsey, NJ: Criminal Justice Press.

MacLean, B. D., and D. Milovanovic. 1997. "Thinking Critically about Criminology." Pp. 1–16 in B. D. MacLean and D. Milovanovic, eds., *Thinking Critically about Crime*. Vancouver: Collective Press.

Pepinsky, H., and R. Quinney, eds. 1991. *Criminology as Peacemaking*. Bloomington: Indiana University Press.

Quinney, R. 1991. "The Way of Peace: On Crime, Suffering and Service." Pp. 3–13 in H. Pepinsky and R. Quinney, eds., *Criminology as Peacemaking*. Bloomington: Indiana University Press.

Schwartz, M. D., and S. E. Hatty. 2003. "Introduction." Pp. ix–xvii in M. D. Schwartz and S. E. Hatty, eds., *Controversies in Critical Criminology*. Cincinnati: Anderson.

Thomas, J., and A. O'Maolchatha. 1989. "Reassessing the Critical Metaphor: An Opportunistic Revisionist View." *Justice Quarterly* 2: 143–72.

World Health Organization. 2005. WHO definition of Health [Online]. <www.who.int/about/definition/en/>.

1

Left Realism Revisited

Walter S. DeKeseredy, Shahid Alvi, and Martin D. Schwartz

Since its inception in the mid-1980s, left realism has been sharply attacked from the right and the left. For example, mainstream criminologist Don Gibbons (1994, 170) contends that it "can be best described as a general perspective centered on injunctions to 'take crime seriously' and to 'take crime control seriously' rather than as a well-developed theoretical criminological perspective." Similarly, critical criminologist Stuart Henry (1999a, 139) claims that left realists offer a "limited conception of criminal etiology." Note, too, that it is often said at academic conferences and elsewhere that left realism has "nothing new to say" and that it is no longer a major subdiscipline of critical criminology (DeKeseredy and Schwartz 2005a; Young 1991). Of course, as is the case with criticisms of other major criminological schools of thought, some of those directed at left realism are valid, especially ones offered by some feminist theorists (e.g., Carlen 1992; Schwartz and DeKeseredy 1991). However, what Jock Young (1991, 15) said fourteen years ago is still relevant today: "Yet many of the criticisms encountered are based on a limited and distorted reading of this work."

Contrary to what some critics assert, left realism is not dead and is just as important now as it was during the Reagan and Thatcher years when it was born. Further, left realism offers progressive complex theories and a set of "best practices" that are given selective inattention by conservatives seeking to preserve the status quo and by left-wing scholars who inaccurately portray this relatively new direction in critical criminology as little more than "an exercise in dubious politics and the cult of personality" (O'Reilly-Fleming 1996, 5). Rather than respond again to the standard criticisms of left realism published elsewhere,[1] the main objective of this chapter is twofold: (1) to describe its often-overlooked contributions and (2) to suggest new directions in theoretical, empirical, and political work.

What Is Left Realism?

An in-depth review of many popular criminology textbooks and journals supports Wright and Friedrichs' (1998, 227) claim that "most mainstream criminologists seem to have little awareness of the scholars and the work that are credible and influential in critical criminology." Consider what Adler, Mueller and Laufer (2004) say about left realism in their widely used text *Criminology*. Only one short paragraph is devoted to this perspective, and little is said about theoretical and empirical contributions. Even some texts written by U.S. critical criminologists pay little, if any, attention to left realism,[2] and their brief summaries focus mainly on British left realist policies advanced in the mid-1980s, such as democratic or community control of the police.[3] The intent here is not to complain about the problematic information disseminated about what Rock (1992) refers to as the "criminology that came in out of the cold," but rather to highlight that many criminologists socially construct left realism as lacking rich insight into the causes and control of crime.[4] Nothing can be further from the truth and it is to left realists' theoretical contributions that we turn next.

Left Realist Theories

Left realists take crimes of the powerful seriously and have published scholarly materials on this topic,[5] but the bulk of their theoretical work focuses on street crime, "zero-tolerance policing" (Dennis 1997), and woman abuse in intimate heterosexual relationships. The main reason for this is that prior to the 1980s, most critical criminologists focused primarily on harms such as white collar and corporate crime, as well as on the influence of class and race relations on definitions of crime and the administration of justice. Obviously, these are important topics and warrant much more social scientific scrutiny. Still, the "abstentionist position" of failing to acknowledge crimes committed by the powerless allows right-wing politicians in several countries to manufacture ideological support for "law and order" policies that are detrimental to the socially and economically disenfranchised and that preclude the development of a socialist society (Boehringer, Brown, Edgeworth, Hogg and Ramsey 1983; Taylor 1992). Moreover, the left's ongoing failure to take working-class victimization seriously contributes to the right's hegemonic control over knowledge about crime and policing (DeKeseredy and Schwartz

1991a; MacLean 1988). Consider, too, as U.S. left realist Elliott Currie reminds us, neglecting to address the pain and suffering caused by crimes in impoverished communities and in domestic settings only serves to:

> help perpetuate an image of progressives as being both fuzzy-minded and, much worse, unconcerned about the realities of life for those ordinary American who are understandably frightened and enraged by the suffering and fear crime brings to their communities and families. (1992, 91)

There are left realists based in the U.K., Australia, Canada, and the U.S., but most of the theoretical work on crime in socially and economically excluded inner-city communities was, and continues to be, done by British scholars. The early stages of British left realist theorizing, although clearly recognizing the criminogenic effects of capitalism and patriarchy, focused heavily on the concepts of relative deprivation and subculture. For example, John Lea and Jock Young (1984, 88) argued that it is not poor people's inability to buy Apple iPods or other "glittering prizes of capitalism" that motivates people commit crime. Rather, it is:

> poverty experienced as unfair (relative deprivation when compared to someone else) that creates discontent; and discontent where there is no political solution leads to crime. The equation is simple: relative deprivation equals discontent: discontent plus lack of political solution equals crime.

The relation between one's position in the broader social structure and crime is, according to left realists, mediated by subjective experiences. For example, as strain theorist Robert Merton (1938) pointed out decades ago, in advanced capitalist societies, many people lack the legitimate means to achieve culturally defined goals (e.g., cars, houses, and other symbols of material success). Some people respond to the strain induced by the disjunction between these goals and means by becoming "innovators" (Merton 1938). In other words, they deal drugs or steal from their neighbors for material gain.

Left realists also contend that people lacking legitimate means of solving the problem of relative deprivation may come into contact with other frustrated disenfranchised people and form subcultures, which, in turn, encourage and legitimate criminal behaviors. For example, receiving respect from peers is highly valued among ghetto adolescents who are denied status in mainstream, middle-class society. However, respect and status is often granted by inner-city subcultures when one is willing to be violent, such as using an assault rifle (DeKeseredy and Schwartz 2005b; Messerschmidt 1993).

Interestingly enough, the above theory receives harsher criticism from the left than from the right. Perhaps this is because the right holds Merton's (1938) anomie theory and Cohen's (1955) subcultural theory in much higher regard than do most critical criminologists. For example, recently Jock Young was labeled a positivist by Yar and Penna (2004) for his continued application of strain and subculture to an understanding of crime and its control in this period of late modernity. In critical criminological circles, such a label is generally seen as an insult because it situates you as an ally of mainstream criminology. Other critical criminologists, however, do not see "borrowing a theoretical analysis from the mainstream" as wrong (Henry 1999b), but contend that doing so should not involve consigning "wider critical social, political, and cultural reflections to the margins" (Yar and Penna 2004, 537).

Other progressive scholars are critical of the above left realist theory for only paying lip service to gender-related issues, such as the role of familial and social patriarchy (DeKeseredy and Schwartz 1991a). Certainly, feminist concerns, such as violence against women, influence left realist thinking. In fact, left realists were among the first critical criminologists to recognize the importance of feminist inquiry (Thomas and O'Maolchatha 1989). The impact of feminism on left realism is articulated by two of its main proponents, Matthews and Young (1986, 2): "The limits of the romantic conception of crime and the criminal were brought home forcibly by the growing feminist concern during the 1970s. Discussions around the issue served to introduce into radical criminology discourse neglected issues of aetiology, motivation and punishment." True, prior to start of this century, this influence never penetrated to the deeper levels of discourse. However, today, British and North American left realists are taking important steps to develop theories of woman abuse that integrate key realist concepts with feminist concerns. Further, as evident in Young's (1999) *Exclusive Society* and DeKeseredy, Alvi, Schwartz and Tomaszewski's (2003) *Under Siege: Poverty and Crime in a Public Housing Community*, left realism now devotes considerable attention to the ways in which broader social, political, and cultural forces shape interpersonal crimes and their control.

For example, as described in figure 1.1, DeKeseredy and Schwartz (2002) integrate an economic exclusion/left realist argument with a feminist/male peer support model to explain woman abuse in public housing. Heavily informed by sociological perspectives offered by Sernau (2001), DeKeseredy and Schwartz (1993), Wilson (1996) and Young (1999), this model argues that recent major economic transformations in North America (e.g., the shift from a manufacturing to a service-based economy) displaces working-class men and women who often end up in public housing or other "clusters of poverty" (Sernau 2001). Unable to economically support their families and

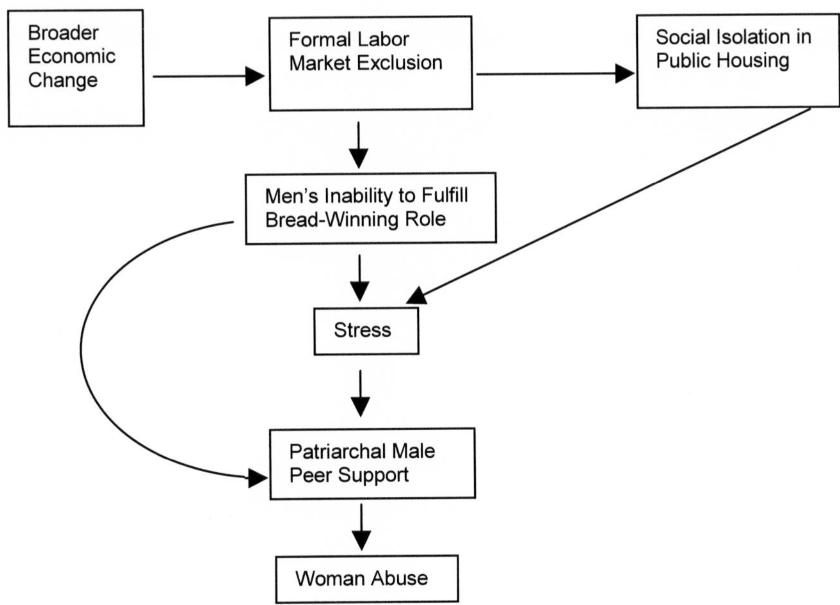

FIGURE 1.1.
DeKeseredy and Schwartz's Economic Exclusion/Male Peer Support Model

live up to their culturally defined role as bread winner, socially and economically excluded men experience high levels of life events stress or strain because "their normal paths for personal power and prestige have been cut off" (Raphael 2001). Such stress prompts men to seek social support from peers with similar problems. Such support may help men resolve intimate relationship problems or facilitate the management of their stress, "but there are no guarantees that such a resolution is free of cost" (Vaux 1985, 102). As demonstrated by studies of woman abuse in courtship (e.g., DeKeseredy 1988a; Schwartz and DeKeseredy 1997), male peer support may alleviate dating life events stress, but it can also have negative consequences for the health and safety of women. For instance, DeKeseredy (1988a) found that for men with high levels of dating life events stress, social ties with abusive peers were strongly related to woman abuse in Canadian college dating. Similarly, patriarchal male peer support in public housing promotes sexual assault and other highly injurious "macho activities" (Raphael 2001).

Thus far, this section only touched on pieces of the complex theoretical background of left realism. For example, the *square of crime* presented in figure 1.2 is also a major component of left realism. The square consists of

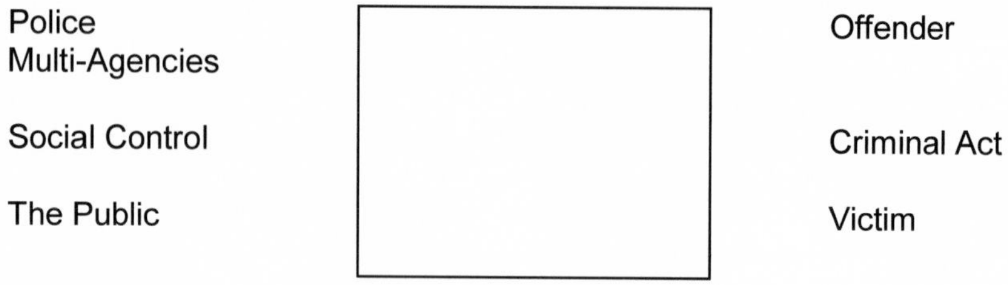

FIGURE 1.2.
The Square of Crime

four interacting elements: victim, offender, state agencies (e.g., the police), and the public. Young describes the social relationships between each point on the square:

> It is the relationship between the police and the public which determines the efficacy of policing, the relationship between the victim and the offender which determines the impact of crime, the relationship between the state and the offender which is a major factor in recidivism. (1992, 27)

Apparently, many critics of left realism are either unaware of or choose to ignore the square of crime and modified versions of it (e.g., DeKeseredy 1996). For example, in his critiques of left realism, Henry devotes most of his attention to realists' "largely strain theory analysis of the cause of working class predatory crime" (1999a, 140). Further, as Yar and Penna (2004) note in their critique of Young's (1999) *Exclusive Society*, several scholars take issue with realists' apparent dismissal of the role of the state. Conspicuously absent from these and other criticisms is that fact that left realists offer a square of crime that focuses simultaneously on the criminal behavior or action and on societal, including state, reactions to it. Indeed, the square of crime shows that crime rates are outcomes of four interrelated causes: (1) the causes of offending (e.g., relative deprivation); (2) factors that make victims vulnerable (e.g., lifestyles/routine activities); (3) the social conditions that influence public levels of social control and tolerance; and (4) the social forces that propel agents of social control (e.g., police) (Young 1992, 30).

It is also said that left realists "rarely offer new propositions or hypotheses that are testable" (Schmalleger and Volk 2005, 300). Here, again, we find an example of an inadequate or limited understanding of left realist theory (Young 1991). For example, below Young (1992, 55–56) lists five testable hypotheses derived from figure 1.3, which is a modified square of crime that reflects the realist view of the world as an "open system *par excellence*" (Young 1992, 55):

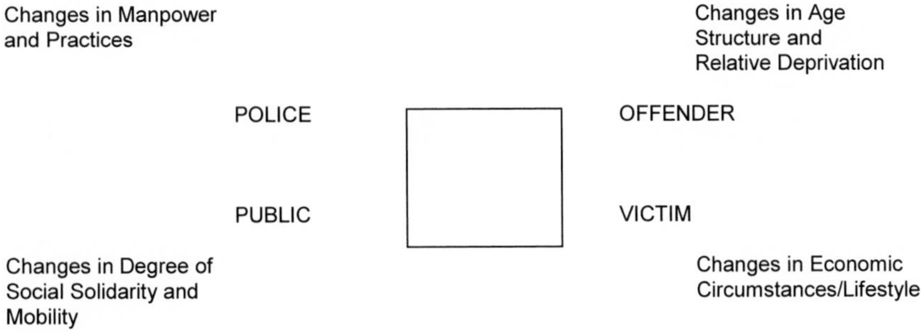

FIGURE 1.3.
Modified Square of Crime

1. Increased gentrification affects the number of victims and also by increasing relative deprivation, the number of offenders.
2. Increased population mobility affects the social solidarity of the area and hence the strength of public control of crime.
3. Changes in the age structure, particularly of young males, affects the number of offenders.
4. Changes in employment and economic marginalization affects the number of offenders.
5. Changes in lifestyles by increasing, for example, the number of evenings out made by members of the public would affect the victimization rate, both in terms of risks in public space and the risks of homes unattended.

Some readers might argue that the square of crime is a dated contribution and has little relevance to current criminal activities and societal reactions to them. Of course, this is an empirical issue that can only be addressed empirically, given that left realists have thus far not specifically set out to test the above hypotheses. Still, Kelling and Coles's (1997) "fixing broken windows" approach to crime control is in vogue today, and as described in figure 1.4, left realists offer a timely, but not widely cited, theoretical model that directs attention to the negative outcomes of criminalizing incivilities, such as public drunkenness in urban public housing communities. Clearly, this model focuses heavily on the role of the state.

Left realists and other progressives assert that social and physical disorders do not always need to be dealt with by a massive police presence (Alvi, Schwartz, DeKeseredy and Maume 2001). In fact, as described in figure 1.4, many disenfranchised inner-city residents view police "crackdowns" on public drinking, panhandling, and other minor offenses in the public housing community as grossly unfair with regard to the seriousness of these offenses and the degree to which the police monitor some sections of the city instead

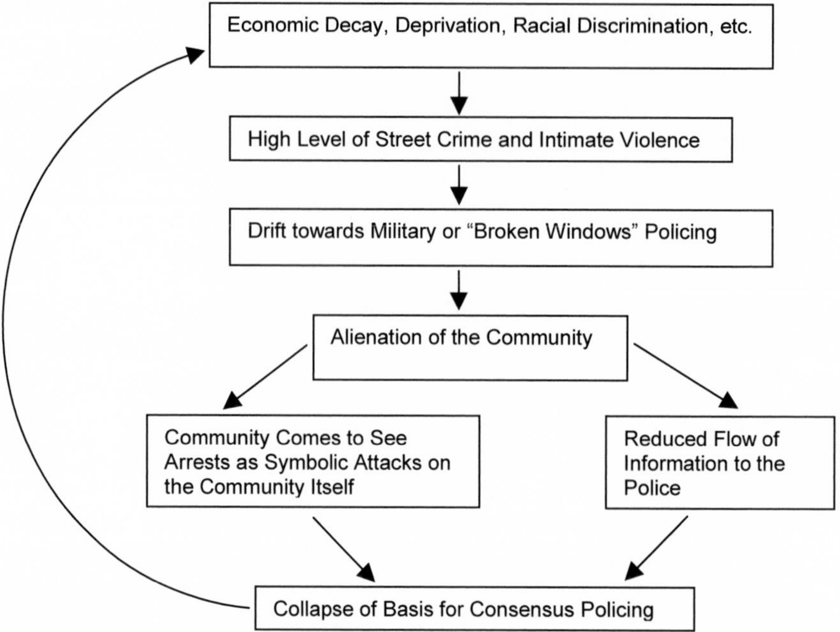

FIGURE 1.4.
The Vicious Circle of Broken Windows Policing in Socially and Economically Marginalized Communities

of others (Sampson and Raudenbush 2001; Young 1999). "Hard" police tactics, such as stopping and searching people who are publicly drunk only serve to alienate socially, economically, and politically excluded urban communities (DeKeseredy, Alvi, Schwartz and Tomaszewski 2003; Getlin 2002). These tactics also influence many people to withhold support and information the police need to solve more serious crimes (DeKeseredy 1988b; Kinsey, Lea and Young 1986). In turn, the police respond with more "military tactics," which in turn lead to further community alienation from the police (Ismaili 2001).

This process depicted in figure 1.4 is DeKeseredy et al.'s (2003) slightly modified rendition of a model developed by British left realists Kinsey et al. (1986, 42) to explain the "vicious circle of the collapse of consensus policing" in the U.K. during Margaret Thatcher's tenure as Prime Minister. Following Kinsey et al. (1986, 39), consensus policing is defined here as "police working to control crime with the bulk of the community supporting, or at least tolerating, their activities."

In sum, then, given the theoretical work described here, it is wrong to portray left realism as "representing more of an ideological emphasis than a theory" (Schmalleger and Volk 2005, 300). Note, too, that left realism is not just a theoretical enterprise. Rather, as described in the next section, left realists in the U.K. and Canada use local victimization surveys to challenge mainstream interpretations of crime and official conservative statistics.

Left Realist Research

Left realist local crime surveys include quantitative and qualitative questions that elicit data on social problems generally considered irrelevant by the police, conservative politicians, and most middle- and upper-class members of the general public, such as woman abuse; sexual harassment and the verbal harassment of gays, lesbians and people of color in public places; and corporate crime. Even when government agencies decide to gather data on one or more of these topics, left realists typically elicit higher incidence and prevalence rates because they define criminal harms much broadly and in ways that more accurately reflect the pain and suffering caused by them. Consider the Quality of Neighborhood Life Survey (QNLS) conducted in a Canadian public housing community. DeKeseredy, Alvi, Schwartz and Perry (1999) uncovered an annual rate of physical violence against women in intimate relationships (19.3 percent) that is markedly higher than the national estimate (3 percent) generated by Statistics Canada's (1993) Violence against Women Survey. The QNLS figure is also higher than that (1.3 percent) elicited by the U.S. National Violence against Women Survey (Tjaden and Thoennes 1998).

Some could argue that the much higher QNLS figure stems from the fact that DeKeseredy et al.'s (1999) survey was administered to a population at very high risk of being abused. This point is well taken. However, mainstream government surveys, such as the National Crime Victimization Survey, typically ignore the plight of "nontraditional populations" and thus their voices are rarely heard, which, in turn, results in limited state resources being devoted to alleviate their pain and suffering. Note, too, that although national surveys are claimed to be antithetical to the main objectives of left realism (MacLean 1992), some North American critical criminologists have conducted a national survey of woman abuse heavily influenced by left realist discourse that generated incidence and prevalence rates significantly higher than those obtained by the two government surveys cited above (DeKeseredy 1996; DeKeseredy and Schwartz 1998).[6]

Some progressives (e.g., Brickey 1989) raise legitimate concerns about state-sponsored criminological research and see it as social control science that takes two forms: "it is related either to defense against potential external enemies, or the development of techniques for the pacification, manipulation and control of the indigenous population" (Rose and Rose 1976, 14–15). Of course, much government-funded mainstream criminological research contributes to the maintenance of what Feely and Simon (1992) refer to as the "new penology" (Savelsberg, King and Cleveland 2002). Nevertheless, left realists such as us receive government funding for some of our work and produce results that challenge the status quo. Further, there is some evidence that state-sponsored left realist surveys occasionally make a major difference. Consider Basran, Gill, and MacLean's (1995) Canadian local survey of corporate violence against Punjabi farmworkers and their children. This study influenced Kwantlen University College and the British Columbia government to provide suitable and affordable childcare for Punjabi farmworkers. This is definitely not a means of strengthening inequality so that people can continue working under capitalism. Rather it is one of several empirically informed "realistic solutions to distorted social conditions" (Devine and Wright 1993).

In addition to conducting state-sponsored research specifically designed to identify people who suffer in silence and to promote social change, some left realists serve as consultants to state agencies, such as the U.S. National Institute of Justice. Does this mean that their empirical guidance and their research are simply means of buttressing an oppressive regime? Have they simply been co-opted by the ruling class? Contrary to what the late Ian Taylor (1992) argued, left realists do not see criminal justice research agencies as simply "more or less autonomous" and they are deeply concerned about their work being used to further victimize disenfranchised people. Still, as Lea and Young (1984: 103) remind us, although any capitalist state represents ruling-class interests, "gains can be wrung from it; reforms, however difficult, are possible and, in fact, relate to the state as in essence a site of contradicting interests."

As one of our close feminist friends and colleagues who chooses to remain anonymous once said to Walter DeKeseredy when he expressed his reluctance to review a set of proposals submitted to a state agency, "It is important that progressives serve on government grant peer review panels to help prevent the bulk of the funds going to right-wing research." Indeed, a revolution is not around the corner, and left realists have helped facilitate government-sponsored feminist studies of woman abuse and other social problems. And, as stated previously, left realist research contributes to making some people's lives safer. However, Henry (1999a) asserts that such work only serves to strengthen "capitalist exploitative reality." We contend that by not viewing the state as a site of struggle and by not conducting surveys of crime in socially and excluded communities, critical criminologists simultaneously minimize the seriousness of street crime, woman abuse, and other harms in poor and racially segregated communities and ignore the state's potential to help solve these and other problems that continue to plague "the truly disadvantaged" (Wilson 1987). Such an approach, as Currie (1992, 91) reminds us, is "mind-bogglingly wrong."

Left Realist Policies

North American left realists devote more attention to anticrime proposals than those based in the U.K. and elsewhere.[7] Thus far, the bulk of British left realist policies focus on criminal justice reforms, including democratic control of policing, "minimal policing,"[8] and "preemptive deterrence."[9] As one might expect, these initiatives are subject to sharp attacks from the left. For example, some progressives criticize British realists' failure to address the power of police subcultures and accuse them of accommodating the state's repressive crime control policies (Gilroy and Sim 1987; Henry 1999a). What, then, is to be done instead? After all, every advanced industrial society requires a combination of informal and formal processes of social control, and is it appropriate to completely ignore criminal justice reforms for fear that they will only serve to "reinforce the existing structure" (Henry 1999a, 141)? Victims of "fixing broken windows" know that major changes in policing are necessary, and if the current situation continues to be ignored by the left, policy makers will have even more freedom to create laws allowing the police to infringe on our rights. Consider that on January 24, 2005, the U.S. Supreme Court gave police broader search powers. Now, the police can use drug-sniffing dogs to check motorists even if officers have no reasonable grounds to suspect that they might be carrying drugs.

Still, Taylor, who contributed to the development of British left realism, is right to point out that:

> policies toward the reform of law or policing cannot be substitutes for the initial fundamental economic and social reconstruction. Demands for the democratization of policing, therefore, are not in themselves a part of an integrated program of socialist transformation, and they are not, and cannot be, substitutes for any such program. (1981, 184)

British left realists, and all left realists for that matter, concur with Taylor's argument. Since their principal goals are to fill a vacuum in New Left thinking about street crime and domestic violence, and to provide a criminology that offers progressive alternatives to the right-wing law and order agenda, it might not be fair to criticize British left realists for excluding strategies aimed at curbing economic and gender inequality. After all, knowledge is cumulative, and a new direction in critical criminology specifically designed to address selective inattention to crimes of the powerless cannot be expected to address every possible progressive solution in a relatively short period of time. Nevertheless, a discourse on targeting broader social forces is necessary because a silent response to the relationship between wider political economic forces and crime perpetuates a dominant tendency "to compartmentalize social problems along bureaucratic lines" (Currie 1985, 18).

For example, it is an important argument of North Americans that those who assume that the criminal justice system is solely responsible for dealing with crime and that other state agencies should manage the social, economic, or family problems that cause it do not consider how decisions on economic issues (e.g., factory closures, reductions in welfare benefits, etc.) may significantly influence the rate of predatory street crime and woman abuse in intimate relationships. Consequently, according to Currie:

> The failure to make these necessary connections between causes and consequences stifles the development of intelligent policies to prevent criminal violence, and burdens the criminal justice system with the impossible job of picking up the pieces after broader social policies have done their damage. (1985, 19)

North American realists are sensitive to these concerns. For example, to curb various types of interpersonal crimes in Canadian public housing, guided by solutions advanced by U.S. realists Currie (1985; 1993), Messerschmidt (1986), Michalowski (1983), and Wilson (1996), DeKeseredy et al. (2003) call for minimal policing and strategies such as:

- A higher minimum wage.
- Job rationing.
- Meaningful jobs.
- State-sponsored, affordable, and quality daycare.
- Housing subsidy and refurbishment programs.
- Improved public transportation.

What about the role of the media and harms spawned by gender inequality? More recently, the authors of this chapter have added "newsmaking criminology" to their progressive crime control agenda. This approach involves the "conscious efforts of criminologists and others to participate in the presentation of 'newsworthy' items about crime and justice" (Barak 1988, 565). For example, in a book on our Canadian public housing study (see DeKeseredy et al. 2003), we contend that if more people become aware of our research and similar work through media reports, more people may voice their discontent with the prevailing inequitable status quo by electing politicians committed to a more progressive way of dealing with the problems facing poor inner-city residents. At the very least, newsmaking criminology makes issues of central importance to critical criminologists very visible to the public in the same way that media coverage of a September 28, 2000, domestic violence audit in the U.K. raised considerable public awareness of violence in family/household settings (Stanko 2001).

Our own left realist agenda also includes using profeminist men's strategies aimed at curbing woman abuse. There are variations in the profeminist men's movement, but a general point of agreement is that men must take an active role in stopping woman abuse and eliminating other forms of patriarchal and social domination throughout society (DeKeseredy, Schwartz, and Alvi 2000). Further, profeminist men place the responsibility for woman abuse squarely on abusive men. A widely cited assertion is that "since it is men who are the offenders, it should be men—not women—who change their behavior" (Thorne-Finch 1992, 236). Below are some examples of short-term profeminist men's strategies incorporated into our left realist agenda:

- Protesting and boycotting strip clubs, bars with live sex shows, and "adult" stores that rent or sell pornography.
- Confronting men who make sexist jokes and who abuse their female partners.
- Supporting and participating in woman abuse awareness programs.
- Actively listening to women and reading literature on their issues, problems, and concerns (DeKeseredy, Alvi, Renzetti and Schwartz 2004; Funk 1993; Johnson 1997; Thorne-Finch 1992).

Contrary to what some critics claim, left realists do not neglect crimes of the powerful. In fact, they argue that suite crime may affect poor people in the same way as middle-class citizens, or it may affect them more (DeKeseredy and Schwartz 1999). Moreover, left realists assert that the more vulnerable a person is politically and economically, the more likely it is that a person will be victimized from all directions; by corporate and white-collar crime, street crime, unemployment and poverty, and a host of other social ills (Lea and Young 1984).

To curb corporate crime, realists call for policies such as the democratization of corporations (Messerschmidt 1986), the organization of citizen patrols based on democratic principles and representative of all members of the community to gather information and to study complaints of corporate crime (Michalowski 1983), and more formal mechanisms to ensure that regulatory laws are strictly enforced (Pearce and Tombs 1992). Yet, there is no question that left realists pay far more attention to street crime and woman abuse, and in light of what Friedrichs (2004) refers to as the Enron et al. cases that occurred between 2001 and 2004,[10] any attempt to increase left realist efforts to curb crimes of the powerful would be useful.

New Directions in Left Realism

Given that the U.S. is currently run by a federal government decidedly committed to cutting even more social services, further weakening environmental and occupational health and safety legislation, and widening the gap between the rich and poor over the next few years, the question of "What is to be done now?" is hardly a trivial one because these and other right-wing strategies are likely to help increase the rates of predatory crime and intimate violence (DeKeseredy and Schwartz 2005a). Left realism, as stated above, offers some progressive short-term answers to this question and hopefully, more critical criminologists will see the value of abandoning what Currie (1992) refers to as "progressive retreatism" and "progressive minimalism." Retreatism involves embracing parts of the conservative crime control model to win elections, while minimalism entails minimizing the seriousness of street crime, illicit drug use, and domestic violence. Unfortunately, fifteen years after Currie published a critique of these two approaches, "minimalism is still probably the dominant voice of American progressives" (1992, 91).

Will we see a resurgence of interest in left realism resembling the attention it received in the 1980s and early 1990s? Indeed, the time is right. Still, left realism needs to evolve, and we point to several new directions in theoretical, empirical and political work. For example, it is claimed that since left realism's theoretical framework draws primarily from strain and subcultural theories and that it is restricted to interpersonal relations between individuals, it can't adequately explain corporate crime (Henry 1999a; Pearce and Tombs 1992). However, some critical criminologists offer a novel challenge to the assertion. Consider Box (1983), who asserts that Merton's (1938) assumption about strain is more valid for corporate executives in capitalist societies than for lower-class individuals.[11] Central to Box's Mertonian analysis is the idea that corporate crime is a response to corporate anomie. Obviously, the primary goal of companies is profit, but they frequently lack legitimate opportunities to achieve it because they operate in an "uncertain and unpredictable environment" (Box 1983). According to Box, there are a number of factors that potentially preclude corporations from achieving their monetary goals. Some factors, such as employee unions, are internal to companies. Others are external to them and fall into two groups. Consumers with their complaints and governments with their laws represent one group. Companies' competitors, that is, other organizations producing the same or similar goods and services, form the second group (1983, 35–36).

Box argues that these and other environmental uncertainties cause some corporate executives to experience strain, which often results in the use of innovative illegitimate means to achieve their companies' goals. A simple, testable hypothesis can be inferred from this theory: when environmental uncertainties increase, so will the strain towards corporate crime and deviance. Or, more simply stated: when corporate profits go down and there is no simple, legitimate way to raise them back up, executives will feel more pressure to engage in illegal or unethical behavior to raise profits. Some studies support this hypothesis, much more research is needed to provide more conclusive support.

Perhaps Box's work will influence left realists to build on his theory, which could be improved by devoting more attention to broader political economic forces (DeKeseredy and Schwartz 1996). However, should any theory be expected to explain all types of criminal behavior? Jock Young (2004, 557) states that attempting to create an "inclusivist theory which explains all crime" is a "futile enterprise." This point is well taken, but certainly, many theories of particular behaviors are modified or integrated with parts of other theories to explain harms they were not originally intended to explain. One recent example is Godenzi, Schwartz and DeKeseredy's (2001) gendered social bond/male peer support theory of university woman abuse. Hirschi's (1969) social bond theory was not designed to explain woman abuse, but Godenzi et al. (2001) turned it upside down with an argument that attachment and involvement with conventional peers may in fact promulgate violence against women on college campuses when it is noted that conventional institutions are patriarchal and part of a rape culture.

Left realists also need to explain women's offending. Women, too, suffer from relative deprivation, belong to subcultures, and are exposed to the same mass media and cultural influences promoting capitalist and individualist materialist acquisition, all of which should give them the motivation needed to commit street crimes and to obtain desired objects (DeKeseredy and Schwartz 2005b). Yet, compared to men and boys, most females do not do this. Left realist theory is still weak on this case and could benefit by addressing the work of feminist scholars such as Chesney-Lind and Pasko (2004) and Miller (2001).

More can and will be said about how to advance left realist theory. Equally important are advances in empirical work. For example, self-report surveys are necessary to effectively test left realist hypotheses. More ethnographic work is also needed and there are many models to choose from, including Bourgois' (1995) study of crack dealers in New York City. His project focused on how broader structural changes influenced criminal street activity and gender relations. Note, too, that realists should build on Pearce's (1992) survey research of commercial crime in the London borough of Islington by conducting local corporate crime victimization surveys in North America. Basran et al.'s (1995) study of corporate violence against Punjabi farm-workers and their children shows that this can be done, despite Walklate's (1989, 88) claim that that corporate victimization surveys are highly problematic because "people on the whole fail to recognize the activities of business corporations as criminal." Arguments such as Walklate's are stated so often that they are considered by many to be truisms (Ellis and DeKeseredy 1996). Yet, no concrete evidence is presented to prove that the local victimization survey is an inadequate method of studying corporate crime.

Financial support is necessary for the purpose of administering local surveys and doing other types of empirical work aimed at progressive social change. Nevertheless, what Brickey (1989) argued close to twenty years ago still holds true today: a relatively small number of critical scholars ask state institutions to fund their research. Perhaps the rationale for not seeking state support is heavily informed by a variant of a school of thought that Edwards (1989) refers to as "feminist idealism." Proponents of this approach generally argue that, "the state and the law, the legal mechanism and the police are part of a patriarchal structure under which attempts at legal reform are only tinkerings within the overall system" (Edwards 1989, 15). There is substantial evidence to support this position (see, for example, Snider 1990). However, some state-sponsored research helps many battered women, ethnic victims of corporate crime, and other disenfranchised people receive better social support. Consider, too, that the authors of this chapter have received federal, state, and local funding for their research and are not required to compromise their beliefs. Thus, left realists should constantly ask state agencies to fund their work.

For victims of crimes of the powerless and the powerful, film maker Michael Moore's (2003, 205) question "So what do we do now?" is much more important than improving the left realist theoretical and empirical agenda. Here, we could provide a long list of answers, which are likely to remain only blueprints for action unless left realists and other critical criminologists mobilize a broad base of activism and influence many progressives to break out of their molds of progressive retreatism and progressive minimalism (DeKeseredy and Schwartz 1991b; Platt 1984). Further, in addition to continuing to do the policy work described previously, left realists based in different countries should establish stronger relations with each other.

Increased communication among an international body of left realists may strengthen their struggles against their respective countries' law and order polices.

Another point to consider is that if left realism is to emerge as a significant discourse in the U.S., it requires a greater exchange of ideas within the international criminological community. In the late 1980s and early 1990s, left realist panels were among the best attended at the American Society of Criminology meetings (DeKeseredy and Schwartz 1991b), and in 1989 Brian MacLean and John Lowman organized a well attended conference in Vancouver, British Columbia, that attracted left realists from Canada, the U.S., the U.K., and Australia.[12] It is time to organize similar panels and events. Further, it is time to develop alliances with progressive journalists, politicians, and community groups and to work closely with them to craft studies and to do grassroots work that challenges the patriarchal capitalist status quo. Above all, it is important to come to grips with an argument left realist Elliott Currie (1992, 93) made thirteen years ago that is still relevant today: "We are now a generation further down the road and we are, indeed, in worse trouble. So it is already past the time to put the half-forgotten realist agenda back in the center of the public debate."

Conclusion

While it is true that left realism may be "half-forgotten," it is still very much at the forefront of an unknown number of criminologists' minds. Many scholars continue to review (often inaccurately) this school of thought in undergraduate texts and in scholarly books and journals. Note, too, that left realism is still the subject of sharp attacks from both left- and right-wing criminologists. Obviously, then, left realism continues to be granted some importance by the international criminological community. The key problem addressed in this chapter is that much of what left realism has to offer theoretically, empirically, and politically is given short shrift for many reasons articulated in this chapter, and many we can only speculate about.

Also pointed out in this chapter is that left realism can make new scholarly and policy contributions. Regardless of what directions left realism takes, given the new rabid right-wing assault on women's rights, civil liberties, same-sex relationships, and other progressive elements of our society, it is absolutely necessary to advance new ways of thinking realistically about crime and social order from a progressive standpoint. Critique, of course, is necessary. However, useful alternatives to conservative polices, theories, and research should be provided because "critical discourse divorced from critical practice degenerates into mere literary criticism, the value of which is a *purely scholastic question*" (Currie, DeKeseredy, and MacLean 1990, 50; emphasis in original).

Notes

This is a revised version of a paper presented at the 2004 annual meeting of the American Society of Criminology, Nashville. We thank Meda Chesney-Lind, Joseph Donnermeyer, Stephen Muzzatti, Barbara Perry, and Ken Tunnell for their comments and criticisms.

1. For more detailed critiques of left realism, see DeKeseredy (1996; 2003), Henry (1999a), Matthews and Young (1992), Michalowski (1991), Ruggiero (1992), Schwartz and DeKeseredy (1991), Sim, Scraton and Gordon (1987), and Taylor (1992).
2. For example, see Barak (1998).
3. See, for example Lynch, Michalowski and Groves (2000).
4. As Schwartz and Hatty (2003, xii) correctly point out, even though left realism is "one of the most important critical criminologies in the English-speaking world," it has not "been deeply powerful in the United States." One of the reasons for this is that "one of the world's best-selling left realists, Elliott Currie, is an American who does not use this term to identify himself."
5. See, for example, DeKeseredy and Goff (1992), Pearce (1992), and Pearce and Tombs (1992).
6. For example, the research team used a broad definition of abuse, conducted preparatory research, asked questions sensitive to the experiences of the disenfranchised, and it obtained partnership funding. These are some of the key principles of local crime survey research advocated by left realists such as Brian MacLean (1992).
7. See DeKeseredy and Schwartz (1991b) for an in-depth comparison of British and U.S. left realist policies.
8. The principles of minimal policing are: maximum initiation of police action; minimum necessary coercion by the police; minimal police intervention; and maximum public access to the police (Kinsey et al. 1986).
9. This involves working in a neighborhood to try to prevent crime from happening, rather than coming in with a massive police presence after the fact.
10. Friedrichs (2004, 113–14) uses the term Enron et al. to refer to "specific cases involving the Enron corporation and some of its top personnel, but also to the linked case of the Anderson accounting firm, and a series of cases that surfaced in the wake of the Enron case."
11. This is because lower-class individuals are not exclusively committed to the cultural goals of success as Merton assumes (DeKeseredy, Ellis and Alvi 2005). They have a variety of goals, and so far as occupational achievement goes, their goals are realistic and limited. Hence, the disjunction between goals and means is not as great as Merton supposes (Box 1983).
12. This conference culminated in a collection of readings edited by Lowman and Maclean (1992).

References

Adler, F., G. O. Mueller, and W. S. Laufer. 2004. *Criminology.* 5th ed. Boston: McGraw Hill.

Alvi, S., M. D. Schwartz, W. S. DeKeseredy, and M. O. Maume. 2001. "Women's Fear of Crime in Canadian Public Housing." *Violence against Women* 7: 638–61.

Barak, G. 1988. "Newsmaking Criminology: Reflections on the Media, Intellectuals, and Crime." *Justice Quarterly* 5: 565–88.

———. 1998. *Integrating Criminologies.* Boston: Allyn & Bacon.

Basran, G. S., C. Gill, and B. D. MacLean. 1995. *Farmworkers and Their Children.* Vancouver: Collective Press.

Boehringer, G., D. Brown, B. Edgeworth, R. Hogg, and I. Ramsey. 1983. "Law and Order for Progressives: An Australian Response." *Crime and Social Justice* 25: 200–203.

Bourgois, P. 1995. *In Search of Respect: Selling Crack in El Barrio.* New York: Cambridge University Press.

Box, S. 1983. *Power, Crime and Mystification.* London: Tavistock.

Brickey, S. 1989. "Criminology as Social Control Science: State Influence in Criminological Research in Canada." *Journal of Human Justice* 1: 43–62.

Carlen, P. 1992. "Women, Crime, Feminism, and Realism." Pp. 203–220 in J. Lowman and B. D. MacLean, eds., *Realist Criminology: Crime Control and Policing in the 1990s.* Toronto: University of Toronto Press.

Chesney-Lind, M., and L. Pasko. 2004. *The Female Offender: Girls, Women, and Crime.* 2nd ed. Thousand Oaks, CA: Sage.

Cohen, A. K. 1955. *Delinquent Boys.* New York: Free Press.

Currie, E. 1985. *Confronting Crime: An American Challenge.* New York: Pantheon.

———. 1992. "Retreatism, Minimalism, Realism: Three Styles of Reasoning on Crime and Drugs in the United States." Pp. 88–97 in J. Lowman and B. D. MacLean, eds., *Realist Criminology: Crime Control and Policing in the 1990s.* Toronto: University of Toronto Press.

———. 1993. *Reckoning: Drugs, the Cities and the American Future.* New York: Hill and Wang.

Currie, D. H., W. S. DeKeseredy, and B. D. MacLean. 1990. "Reconstituting Social Order and Social Control: Police Accountability in Canada." *Journal of Human Justice* 2: 29–54.

DeKeseredy, W. S. 1988a. *Woman Abuse in Dating Relationships: The Role of Male Peer Support.* Toronto: Canadian Scholars' Press.

———. 1988b. "The Left Realist Approach to Law and Order." *Justice Quarterly* 5: 635–40.

———. 1996. "The Left Realist Perspective on Race, Class, and Gender." Pp. 49–72 in M. D. Schwartz and D. Milovanovic, eds., *Race, Gender, and Class in Criminology: The Intersection.* New York: Garland.

———. 2003. "Left Realism on Inner-city Violence." Pp. 29–42 in M. D. Schwartz and S. E. Hatty, eds., *Controversies in Critical Criminology.* Cincinnati: Anderson.

DeKeseredy, W. S., S. Alvi, C. M. Renzetti, and M. S. Schwartz. 2004. "Reducing Private Violence Against Women in Public Housing: Can Second Generation CPTED Make a Difference?" *The CPTED Journal* 3: 27–36.

DeKeseredy, W. S., S. Alvi, M. D. Schwartz, and B. Perry. 1999. "Violence against and the Harassment of Women in Canadian Public Housing." *Canadian Review of Sociology and Anthropology* 36: 499–516.

DeKeseredy, W. S., S. Alvi, M. D. Schwartz, and E. A. Tomaszewski. 2003. *Under Siege: Poverty and Crime in a Public Housing Community*. Lanham, MD: Lexington Books.

DeKeseredy, W. S., D. Ellis, and S. Alvi. 2005. *Deviance and Crime: Theory, Research and Policy*. Cincinnati: Anderson.

DeKeseredy, W. S., and C. Goff. 1992. "Corporate Violence against Canadian Women: Assessing Left-realist Research and Policy." *Journal of Human Justice* 4: 55–70.

DeKeseredy, W. S., and M. D. Schwartz. 1991a. "British Left Realism on the Abuse of Women: A Critical Appraisal." Pp. 154–71 in R. Quinney and H. Pepinsky, eds., *Criminology as Peacemaking*. Bloomington: Indiana University Press.

———. 1991b. "British and U.S. Left Realism: A Critical Comparison." *International Journal of Offender Therapy and Comparative Criminology* 35: 248–62.

———. 1993. "Male Peer Support and Woman Abuse: An Expansion of DeKeseredy's Model." *Sociological Spectrum* 13: 394–414.

———. 1996. *Contemporary Criminology*. Belmont, CA: Wadsworth.

———. 1998. *Woman Abuse on Campus: Results from the Canadian National Survey*. Thousand Oaks, CA: Sage.

———. 1999. "Rejoinder to Dr. Stuart Henry." Pp. 144–48 in J. R. Fuller and E. W. Hickey, eds., *Controversial Issues in Criminology*. Boston: Allyn & Bacon.

———. 2002. "Theorizing Public Housing Woman Abuse as a Function of Economic Exclusion and Male Peer Support." *Women's Health and Urban Life* 1: 26–45.

———. 2005a. "Left Realist Theory." In S. Henry and M. Lanier, eds., *The Essential Criminology Reader*. Boulder, CA: Westview Press.

———. 2005b. "Masculinities and Interpersonal Violence." Pp. 353–66 in M. S. Kimmel, J. Hearn, and R. W. Connell, eds., *Handbook of Studies on Men and Masculinities*. Thousand Oaks, CA: Sage.

DeKeseredy, W. S., M. D. Schwartz, and S. Alvi. 2000. "The Role of Profeminist Men in Dealing with Woman Abuse on the Canadian College Campus." *Violence against Women* 6: 918–35.

Dennis, N., ed. 1997. *Zero-tolerance Policing in a Free Society*. London: Institute of Economic Affairs.

Devine, J. A., and J. D. Wright. 1993. *The Greatest of Evils: Urban Poverty and the American Underclass*. New York: Aldine de Gruyter.

Edwards, S. 1989. *Policing Domestic Violence*. London: Sage.

Ellis, D., and W. S. DeKeseredy. 1996. *The Wrong Stuff: An Introduction to the Sociological Study of Deviance*. 2nd ed. Toronto: Allyn and Bacon.

Feeley, M., and J. Simon. 1992. "The New Penology: Notes on the Emerging Strategy of Corrections and Its Implications." *Criminology* 30: 449–74.

Friedrichs, D. O. 2004. "Enron et al.: Paradigmatic White Collar Crime Cases for the New Century." *Critical Criminology* 12: 113–32.

Funk, R. E. 1993. *Stopping Rape: A Challenge for Men*. Philadelphia: New Society Publishers.

Getlin, J. 2002, November 30. "N.Y. Officer Suspended for Refusing to Arrest Homeless." *The Columbus Dispatch*: A3.

Gibbons, D. 1994. *Talking about Crime and Criminals: Problems and Isues in Theory Development in Criminology*. Englewood Cliffs, NJ: Prentice Hall.

Gilroy, P., and J. Sim. 1987. "Law, Order and the State of the Left." Pp. 71–106 in P. Scraton, ed., *Law, Order and the Authoritarian State*. Philadelphia: Open University Press.

Godenzi, A., M. D. Schwartz, and W. S. DeKeseredy. 2001. "Toward a Gendered Social Bond/Male Peer Support Theory of University Woman Abuse." *Critical Criminology* 10: 1–16.

Henry, S. 1999a. "Is Left Realism a Useful Theory for Addressing the Problems of Crime?: No." Pp. 137–144 in J. R. Fuller and E. W. Hickey, eds., *Controversial Issues in Criminology*. Boston: Allyn & Bacon.

———. 1999b. "Rejoinder to Dr. Schwartz and Dr. DeKeseredy." Pp. 134–37 in J. R. Fuller and E. W. Hickey, eds., *Controversial Issues in Criminology*. Boston: Allyn & Bacon.

Hirschi, T. 1969. *Causes of Delinquency*. Berkeley, CA: University of California Press.

Ismaili, K. 2001, April. "The Social Costs of Urban Crime Reduction Initiatives: Some Lessons from New York City." Paper presented at the annual meeting of the Academy of Criminal Justice Sciences, Washington, DC.

Johnson, A. G. 1997. *The Gender Knot: Unraveling Our Patriarchal Legacy*. Philadelphia: Temple University Press.

Kelling, G., and C. Coles. 1997. *Fixing Broken Windows*. New York: Free Press.

Kinsey, R., J. Lea, and J. Young. 1986. *Losing the Fight against Crime*. Oxford, UK: Blackwell.

Lea, J., and J. Young. 1984. *What Is To Be Done about Law and Order?* New York: Penguin.

Lowman, J., and B. D. MacLean, eds. 1992. *Realist Criminology: Crime Control and Policing in the 1990s*. Toronto: University of Toronto Press.

Lynch, M. J., R. J. Michalowski, and W. B. Groves. 2000. *The New Primer in Radical Criminology: Critical Perspectives on Crime, Power and Identity*. 3rd ed. Monsey, NY: Criminal Justice Press.

MacLean, B. D. 1988. "The New Victimology: Political Praxis or Left Unrealism." Paper presented at the annual meeting of the Canadian Law and Society Association, Windsor, Ontario.

———. 1992. "A Program of Local Crime Research for Canada." Pp. 336–366 in J. Lowman and B. D. MacLean, eds., *Realist Criminology: Crime Control and Policing in the 1990s*. Toronto: University of Toronto Press.

Matthews, R., and J. Young. 1986. "Editors' Introduction: Confronting Crime." Pp. 1–3 in R. Matthews and J. Young, eds., *Confronting Crime*. London: Sage.

———, eds. 1992. *Issues in Realist Criminology*. London: Sage.

Merton, R. K. 1938. "Social Structure and Anomie." *American Sociological Review* 3: 672–82.

Messerschmidt, J. W. 1986. *Capitalism, Patriarchy, and Crime: Toward a Socialist Feminist Criminology*. Totowa, NJ: Rowman & Littlefield.

———. 1993. *Masculinities and Crime: Critique and Reconceptualization*. Lanham, MD: Rowman & Littlefield.

Michalowski, R. J. 1983. "Crime Control in the 1980s: A Progressive Agenda." *Crime and Social Justice* (Summer): 13–23.

———. 1991. "'Niggers, Welfare Scum and Homeless Assholes': The Problems of Idealism, Consciousness and Context in Left Realism." Pp. 31–38 in B. D. MacLean and D. Milovanovic, eds., *New Directions in Critical Criminology*. Vancouver: Collective Press.

Miller, J. 2001. *One of the Guys: Girls, Gangs, and Gender*. New York: Oxford University Press.

Moore, M. 2003. *Dude, Where's My Country?* New York: Warner Books.

O'Reilly-Fleming, T. 1996. "Left Realism as Theoretical Retreatism or Paradigm Shift: Toward Post-critical Criminology. Pp. 1–25 in T. O'Reilly-Fleming, ed., *Post-critical Criminology*. Scarborough, ON: Prentice Hall.

Pearce, F. 1992. "The Contribution of 'Left Realism' to the Study of Commercial Crime." Pp. 313–35 in J. Lowman and B. D. MacLean, eds., *Realist Criminology: Crime Control and Policing in the 1990s*. Toronto: University of Toronto Press.

Pearce, F., and S. Tombs. 1992. "Realism and Corporate Crime." Pp. 70–101 in R. Matthews and J. Young, eds., *Issues in Realist Criminology*. London: Sage.

Platt, T. 1984. "Criminology in the 1980s: Progressive Alternatives to Law and Order." *Crime and Social Justice* 21/22: 191–99.

Raphael, J. 2001. "Public Housing and Domestic Violence." *Violence against Women* 7: 699–706.

Rock, P. 1992. "Foreword: The Criminology That Came In from the Cold." Pp. ix–xii in J. Lowman and B. D. MacLean, eds., *Realist Criminology: Crime Control and Policing in the 1990s*. Toronto: University of Toronto Press.

Rose, H., and S. Rose. 1976. *The Political Economy of Science: Ideology of/in the Natural Sciences*. London: Macmillan Press.

Ruggiero, V. 1992. "Realist Criminology: A Critique." Pp. 123–140 in J. Young and R. Matthews, eds., *Rethinking Criminology: The Realist Debate*. London: Sage.

Sampson, R. J., and S. W. Raudenbush. 2001. *Disorder in Urban Neighborhoods: Does It Lead to Crime?* Washington, DC: U.S. Department of Justice.

Savelsberg, J. J., R. King, and L. Cleveland. 2002. "Politicized Scholarship: Science on Crime and the State." *Social Problems* 49: 327–48.

Schmalleger, F., and R. Volk. 2005. *Canadian Criminology Today: Theories and Applications*. 2nd ed. Toronto: Pearson Prentice Hall.

Schwartz, M. D., and W. S. DeKeseredy. 1991. "Left Realist Criminology: Strengths, Weaknesses and the Feminist Critique." *Crime, Law and Social Change* 15: 51–72.

———. 1997. *Sexual Assault on the College Campus: The Role of Male Peer Support*. Thousand Oaks, CA: Sage.

Schwartz, M. D., and S. E. Hatty. 2003. "Introduction." Pp. ix–xvii in M. D. Schwartz and S. E. Hatty, eds., *Controversies in Critical Criminology*. Cincinnati: Anderson.

Sernau, S. 2001. *Worlds Apart: Social Inequalities in a New Century*. Thousand Oaks, CA: Pine Forge Press.

Sim, J., Scraton, P., and Gordon, P. 1987. "Introduction: Crime, the State and Critical Analysis." Pp. 1–70 in P. Scraton, ed., *Law, Order and the Authoritarian State*. Philadelphia: Open University Press.

Snider, L. 1990. "The Potential of the Criminal Justice System to Promote Feminist Concerns." *Studies in Law, Politics and Society* 10: 141–69.

Stanko, E. A. 2001. "The Day to Count: Reflections on a Methodology to Raise Awareness about the Impact of Domestic Violence in the U.K." *Criminal Justice* 1: 215–26.

Statistics Canada. 1993. *Violence against Women Survey*. Ottawa: Statistics Canada.

Taylor, I. 1981. *Law and Order: Arguments for Socialism*. London: Macmillan Press.

———. 1992. "Left Realist Criminology and the Free Market Experiment in Britain." Pp. 95–122 in J. Young and R. Matthews, eds., *Rethinking Criminology: The Realist Debate*. London: Sage.

Thomas, J., and A. O'Maolchatha. 1989. "Reassessing the Critical Metaphor: An Opportunistic Revisionist View." *Justice Quarterly* 2: 143–72.

Thorne-Finch, R. 1992. *Ending the Silence: The Origins and Treatment of Male Violence against Women*. Toronto: University of Toronto Press.

Tjaden, P., and N. Thoennes. 1998. *Stalking in America: Findings from the National Violence against Women Survey*. Washington, DC: National Institute of Justice and Centers for Disease Control and Prevention, Department of Justice Publication.

Vaux, A. 1985. "Variations in Social Support associated with Gender, Ethnicity, and Age." *Journal of Social Issues* 41: 89–110.

Walklate, S. 1989. *Victimology: The Victim and the Criminal Justice Process*. London: Unwin Hyman.

Wilson, W. J. 1987. *The Truly Disadvantaged: The Inner-city, the Underclass and Public Policy*. Chicago: University of Chicago Press.

———. 1996. *When Work Disappears: The World of the New Urban Poor*. New York: Knopf.

Wright, R. A., and D. O. Friedrichs. 1998. "The Most Cited Scholars and Works in Critical Criminology." *Journal of Criminal Justice Education* 9: 211–32.

Yar, M., and S. Penna. 2004. "Between Positivism and Post-modernity?: Critical Reflections on Jock Young's *The Exclusive Society*." *British Journal of Criminology* 44: 533–49.

Young, J. 1991. "Asking Questions of Left Realism." Pp. 15–18 in B. D. MacLean and D. Milovanovic, eds., *New Directions in Critical Criminology*. Vancouver, BC: Collective Press.

———. 1992. "Ten Points of Realism." Pp. 24–68 in J. Young and R. Matthews, eds., *Rethinking Criminology: The Realist Debate*. London: Sage.

———. 1999. *The Exclusive Society*. London: Sage.

———. 2004. "Crime and the Dialectics of Inclusion/Exclusion: Some Comments on Yar and Penna." *British Journal of Criminology* 44: 550–61.

2

Transgressing Boundaries: Feminist Perspectives in Criminology

MaDonna R. Maidment

OVER THE PAST SEVERAL DECADES, feminist criminology has gathered considerable momentum and attracted unprecedented attention from scholars who have carved a niche for this subdiscipline within the wider context of mainstream criminology. Where once there existed only a handful of feminist scholars devoting serious attention to the topic of women and crime, mainly in the United States and Britain, the discrete contributions of feminists to the larger study of crime continues to draw global attention. Research in this area has been expansive, with its concentration on the criminalization and victimization of women, identifying gender discrimination within all aspects of the criminal justice system, positing theoretical perspectives, and identifying methodological tools for conducting feminist research with criminalized women. While these contributions have opened the debates and sparked discussions surrounding women's criminalization, there are still many questions and gaps that persist.

One persistent debate centres around the question of whether or not a singular "feminist criminology"[1] exists or whether what we are actually referring to are feminist perspective(s) within criminology or feminist criminology(ies). It is from this quandary over "feminist criminology as an oxymoron" that I frame my interrogations of feminist contributions within the broader field of criminology. A major objective of this chapter, then, is to contemplate the claim that a feminist criminology exists merely as a critique and/or adjunct to the already established body of "malestream" criminological knowledge (i.e., the "add women and stir" approach). Moreover, this essay addresses the following specific questions, as articulated by Carol Smart (1990, 83): What does feminism have to offer to criminology and, more importantly, what does criminology have to offer to feminism? This line of inquiry forces a shift in focus toward the broader fundamentals of feminist thought. It also forces a critical analysis of the traditionalist underpinnings of criminology as an androcentric discipline that fails to take gender[2] seriously by placing it at the periphery of inquiry and analysis. By deconstructing the "feminist criminology as oxymoron" claim, this chapter begins by exploring the trajectory of feminist criminology in an attempt to demarcate its central theoretical contribution to the larger discipline of criminology. In doing so, various strands of feminism (liberal, socialist, Marxist, radical, postmodern, and standpoint) are first discussed. In addressing fundamental theoretical questions surrounding feminist perspectives in criminology, it is also critical to look toward feminist epistemologies to gain insight into theory construction. Lively debates related to the deconstruction of knowledge production and legitimation persist within feminist criminology (e.g., Smart 1990; Morris and Gelsthorpe 1991; Cain 1990). These important debates are interwoven throughout this chapter.

Feminist Contributions to Criminology

Feminist contributions to criminology over the past four decades began with a critiquing of criminological theories for their failure to consider gender and for characterizing women in sexist ways. From here, feminist work in criminology began to problematize the term "women" as a monolithic category; to acknowledge that women's experiences are, in part, constructed by legal and criminological discourse; to deconstruct gender; and to reflect on the strengths and limitations of constructing feminist truths and knowledge (Daly and Maher 1998, 2). Many of these intellectual projects have remained on the feminist agenda alongside attempts to integrate race and class into an analysis of women's oppression.

Feminist scholars have stressed the importance of distinguishing biological sex from gender and of developing a comprehensive feminist theory distinct from a liberal, Marxist, or positivistic approach. This development was propelled by theoretical contributions on the margins (e.g., women of colour, lesbians) and postmodern theories which served as a catalyst for the emergence of a feminism which calls for greater inclusivity from different class, racial and ethnic backgrounds. It aims for the voices of individual women to be legitimated and seeks to accommodate the intersections of varied identities such as race, class, and gender, but also sexual identity, disability, nationality, age, and so forth. Postmodern discussions regarding the production and legitimation of knowledge have been integral to these debates by revealing the exclusivity of earlier feminist approaches. To work backwards then, an exploration of feminist theoretical contributions to "malestream" traditional criminology is proffered.

Feminist Critiques of "Malestream" Criminology

A common tenet of early feminist criminological research points to the gender-blindness of mainstream criminology. Like other social sciences, criminology is androcentric in its orientation to understanding the social world. The study of crime, then, is shaped by male experiences and continues to exalt men as the standard by which research and theory construction are premised. Women are seen as "Other" (Cain 1990), when they are taken into account at all. The "legacy of sexism" inherent in mainstream criminology can be traced to early biological explanations of female criminality. For example, Lombroso and Ferrero (1895) posited a theory of female delinquency based on the faulty construction of women offenders as "wicked" and lacking in virtue (DeKeseredy 2000). The work of positivist criminologists provided ample grist for later criticism by feminists who pointed to the severe methodological and theoretical flaws within their work. The essentialist rootings of biological derivations based on sex are denounced largely because of their failure to capture the wider social, cultural and economic forces that serve to construct gender realities.

Almost a half-century later, the positivistic approach to the study of female crime is revisited in the work of Otto Pollak (1950). Pollak introduces the "chivalry" thesis by arguing that women are better able to disguise their criminal involvement by their cunning and deceit. Therefore, female crime is "masked" by the greater leniency with which females are treated by chivalrous criminal justice personnel (DeKeseredy 2000, 73). Again, feminists have criticized the work of Pollak and others based on their failure to consider the wider structural conditions (e.g., patriarchy, poverty, family violence) that account for gender differences in crime. In addition to the sexist nature of classical studies, such approaches have been criticized for being classist, racist, and heterosexist as their focus has been on white, middle-class, and married women as the standard by which all other women are judged.

The works of Adler (1975) and Simon (1975) are widely regarded as the first feminist attempts to theorize about women's involvement with crime and the criminal justice system. The "liberation/emancipation" thesis suggests that the women's movement has brought about unintended negative consequences, including an increase in the female crime rate. For example, Adler (1975) proposed that women's violent crime rates would increase as a result of their liberation, while Simon (1975) argued that only property crimes would increase due to women's economic liberation. While parting ways in their approach to how feminism would be played out, both authors posit that the women's liberation movement contributed to an increased involvement by women in crime. Both authors rejected the biological assumptions that had been previously put forth to explain crime differences between the sexes. According to Adler (1975), as women's social roles expand to resemble those of men, so too does their criminal behaviour. Simon (1975), on the other hand, focuses more narrowly on the impact of women's increased participation in the paid labour force and proposes an "opportunity model" to explain women's increased involvement in property crimes.

Having been criticized heavily for their faulty assumptions about the influences of the women's movement on crime rates (e.g., increased economic and structural opportunities and that the feminist movement made women behave like men), Adler (1975) and Simon (1975) are partially credited with opening the arena for debate and the subsequent growth of research on women's criminalization. Their research sparked discussions of feminism(s) and spurred the development of other feminist criminological formulations. As Laster (1996, 193) points out:

> Criminology's failure literature forces us to confront the limitations of our own theories, methods and politics. Frequently, failure is the catalyst for the development of new (but not necessarily more successful) strategies for imagining crime and responses to it. . . . Successfully proving failure creates space for new ideas and people. Feminist criminology's successes have come, in part, from its ability to capitalise on the failures of main (male) stream criminological theory.

Developments in Feminist Criminology(ies)

Feminist criminology cannot advance an understanding of women's involvement in the criminal justice system without first probing the bases of feminist thought. Feminism itself, then, can be defined as "a set of theories about women's oppression and a set of strategies for social change" (Daly and Chesney-Lind 1988, 502). According to Danner (1991, 51), feminist theory "is a woman-centered description and explanation of human experience and the social world. It asserts that gender governs every aspect of personal and social life." While there are many variations of feminist theory, patriarchy is at the centre of each strand's explanation of women's oppression.

Daly and Chesney-Lind (1988, 504) characterize five elements of feminist thought that distinguish it from other types of social and political thought. They include the following guiding principles:

(1) Gender is a complex social, historical, and cultural product; it is related to but not simply derived from, biological sex difference and reproductive capacities;
(2) Gender and gender relations order social life and social institutions in fundamental ways;
(3) Gender relations and constructs of masculinity and femininity are not symmetrical but are based on an organizing principle of men's superiority and social and political-economic dominance over women;
(4) Systems of knowledge reflect men's views of the natural social world; the production of knowledge is gendered; and
(5) Women should be at the centre of intellectual inquiry, not peripheral, invisible, or appendages to men.

Each of these characteristics is discussed in more detail below.

First, that gender is not simply a product of biology but is much more complex is a cornerstone principle of feminist thought. On this point, feminists argue that there are crucial distinctions between sex and gender.[3] Gender is a socially constructed phenomena that shapes and influences all spheres of social, political and economic life. Based on this distinction, criminological theories that place biological sex differences between men and women as the axis of examination are flawed. Second, an understanding of gender relations in all spheres of society is paramount. Accordingly, criminological research that fails to account for the social hierarchy of gender relations cannot adequately theorize men's or women's involvement in crime. Third, patriarchy is a consistent unifying element of feminist theory. Sexual, economic, and political control by men over women in society must be a central organizing feature in criminological theory. Fourth, knowledge production is based on men's views of seeing the world. Feminists have critiqued the knowledge-making and legitimation process as androcentric and similarly critique theories that argue objectivity and scientific rigour. Subjectivities and personal experiences must feature prominently in research and subsequent theory construction. Finally, feminists maintain that women's experiences should be at the centre of our attempts to understand the social order. Likewise, criminology as a discipline must reorganize its hierarchical structure to account for gender.

Based on these central organizing principles, several feminist criminological theories have been formulated. Arguably, there are at least a dozen strands of feminist criminological theory.[4] I examine briefly the major claims and shortcomings of six of the most widely discussed perspectives including: liberal, Marxist, socialist, radical, postmodern, and standpoint. Each of these is discussed only briefly below as they have been sufficiently canvassed and critiqued elsewhere (see, e.g., Tong 1998; Danner 1991; Daly and Chesney-Lind 1988; Chesney-Lind and Faith 2001).

Liberal Feminism

Liberal feminism focuses primarily on the effects of the differential socialization of males and females, sex stereotyping of the workplace, and the legal and political disenfranchisement of women. Liberal feminism has traditionally sought to remedy these problems through advocating women's increased education, integration, and litigation (Chesney-Lind and Faith 2001). It takes a noncritical stance on gender and seeks to eradicate discrimination through institutional change. Liberal feminists do not attempt to resolve questions of gender-based differences but focus on overcoming equality before the law and inclusion of women through legal redress.

Within criminological discourse, liberal feminist theory has focused on discrimination and equity issues which exist within the criminal justice system. Influential work in this area has focused on issues of inequality, such as barriers to women's employment in policing, the law and the judiciary. A major criticism directed at liberal feminism is a failure to question or challenge the structural inequalities that exist between men and women in society, including discrepancies of work opportunities and pay, and child care responsibilities. The rationale behind liberal feminism is one of equal opportunity and individual choice. That is, women are deprived of the same opportunities as men and therefore denied access to the opportunity and choices available to men.

Liberal feminism has also been critiqued for ignoring women's traditional work as mothers, child care providers, and homemakers. They have ignored the private sphere in exchange for advocating the movement of women into the public domain of the paid labour market, which, in turn, has devalued women's participation in the private sphere. Another major limitation of the liberal perspective is the fact that men are taken as the standard by which women are judged. That is, "equality has often translated into treating girls and women as if they were boys or men" (Chesney-Lind and Faith 2001, 291). This "equality with a vengeance" has translated into tougher sentences for women and a concomitant prison-building marathon for criminalized women (Davis 2003; Sudbury 2005).

Marxist Feminism

Marxist feminism regards economic class relations as the primary source of women's oppression. Gender relations are regarded as secondary. The material basis, then, of women's marginalization and inequality lies in the fact that as a group women work outside the labour economy. Women's labour is in the home and is reproductive, not productive. Therefore, it is argued that women do not create surplus value in the economy. For Marxist feminists, the oppressor is capitalism, which exploits and benefits greatly from women's labour (Daly and Chesney-Lind 1988). This overreliance on economic class to the near exclusion of gender relations to explain women's oppression is hailed as the major shortcoming of Marxist feminism. Moreover, its failure to account for social relations of inequality (patriarchy) between men and women in the home is criticized.

Marxist feminists propose a number of strategies for transforming women's oppressed position within a capitalist society. These include: bringing women fully into economic production, socializing housework and child care, abolition of marriage and sexual relations founded on notions of private property, and eradication of working-class economic subordination (Daly and Chesney-Lind 1988). They believe that abolition of a class society will liberate women because it will free them from their economic dependency on men. Marxist feminists have also advanced an understanding of the value of women's work within the private sphere (especially child care) and argue in favour of economic market value being attached to women's work in the home.

Radical Feminism

Radical feminism reverses the balance of power by presenting gender relations as the primary source of women's inequality and class inequalities as secondary. Patriarchy is the driving force behind women's oppression and is reinforced through such institutions as marriage, child rearing, and sexual practices ranging from rape through to prostitution and sexual intercourse itself. Some radical feminists see the biological family as the centre of sex class struggle wherein women are at the mercy of their biology, making them dependent on males for physical survival (Daly and Chesney-Lind 1988).

Radical feminism has been central to our understanding of violence against women as a means of social control of women and not as isolated events. It regards the continuum of violence against women as a direct product of patriarchy. Strategies for change, then, rest on the overthrow of patriarchal relations, which would permit women's sexual autonomy and obliterate the "oppressive nature of sexual and familial relations for women with their link to relations in the public sphere" (Daly and Chesney-Lind 1988, 538).

The major criticism directed at radical feminism is its exclusivity. It is seen to appeal to a largely white, middle-class group of women. It is seen as excessively radical in its call for women-only organizations, agencies and relationships. Finally, it is criticized on the grounds that it dismisses male agency in its assumption that males are all agents of the patriarchy and as such are contributors to the oppression of women as a group.

Socialist Feminism

Interpreting the work of Marxist and radical feminism, socialist feminism "recognized that familial reproduction and the nuclear family are as important to the needs of capitalism as production in the workplace" (Chesney-Lind and Faith 2001, 293). Moreover, it recognized that patriarchy affects the ways by which men control women's productivity. Socialist feminists differ from their Marxist predecessors in that they view women's interests as inherent in, rather than subordinate to, the working-class struggles. They recognize the gender factor as well as the economic factor in the division of labour and the distribution of criminalization.

Socialist feminism, like Marxist feminism, stresses that crime occurs for both men and women in an economic context. For example, both theoretical perspectives would view the increase in women's incarceration as part of the larger "prison industrial complex"[5] that acts as a response to social problems (e.g., cuts to social welfare, criminalizing the mentally ill). The state, acting on behalf of corporate interests, has targeted a massive spending increase on women's prisons. In turn, expenditures on welfare and education have dropped dramatically to fund the prison endeavour. Resources that were once used to support low-income women and their children and to enhance education efforts have been exchanged in favour of an expanding prison industrial complex for women (Sudbury 2005).

Socialist feminists take account of the intersections of class and gender in their analyses. They understand that class and gender intersect to shape the experiences of men and women in capitalist societies. However, it has also been rightly argued that socialist feminism has not gone far enough in integrating racial inequalities into their analyses. Patriarchy cannot be separated from capitalism just as racism is integrally connected to oppression.[6] Another major criticism of socialist feminist theory is that it fails to account for agency, that is, it demonstrates an overreliance on structural explanations (class-based inequality, patriarchal subordination of women, racial/ethnic inequalities) to account for gender inequality.

Postmodern Feminism

Postmodern feminism is a

> collection of myriad strands of postmodernist thought that critique and deconstruct "modernity" . . . [that is, the] intellectual tradition that, while stressing democracy, equality, and rationality, also accommodated both the development of capitalism and the resistance of working people to exploitation by the owners of production. . . . Postmodernists emphasize culture and the production of knowledge, rather than structure. . . . It is those that have power who are authorized to know and whose knowledge is afforded privilege. In other words, knowledge is not necessarily an expression of truth and it is never neutral. (Chesney-Lind and Faith 2001, 296)

Chesney-Lind and Faith (2001) point out the usefulness of postmodern thought to criminology, in general, and feminist criminology, in particular. They cite several examples including the role of the media in creating "truths" about female involvement in crime and hence the generation of "moral panics."[7] Postmodern feminism links the knowledge/power nexus and helps to deconstruct the androcentric and class-based origins of "knowledge" and "truth." Women are excluded from the knowledge/power arena, as evidenced in various institutions including the state, media, and church. Similarly, Carol Smart (1990, 82) pinpoints knowledge deconstruction as a core feature of feminist postmodernism. It is:

> the rejection of the one reality which arises from the "falsely universalizing perspective of the master." It refers to subjugated knowledges, which tell different stories and have different specificities. Thus the aim of feminism ceases to be the establishment of feminist truth and becomes the deconstruction of truth and analysis of the power effects which claims to truth entail. It is this recognition that knowledge is a part of power that underlines the claims made by feminist postmodernists.

Considered a major limitation of postmodern theory is its "disciplinary reliance on relatively obscure, theoretical jargon, and the absence of a clear way for deconstruction to deal with pressing social problems, such as the nation's increasing prison rate, [which] has led some scholars to talk about gender, race and class" (Chesney-Lind and Faith 2001, 297).

Standpoint Feminism

Standpoint feminism relies on the notion that previous feminist attempts to integrate the varied interactions of race, class, and gender have been deficient. It is argued that "the field has particularly focused attention on the fact that the predominantly white and middle-class women's movement had, in its focus on gender alone, essentially ignored the diversity of women's experiences, lives, and communities" (Chesney-Lind and Faith 2001, 297). Smart (1990, 80), in her analysis of standpoint feminism, states,

> The epistemological basis of this form of feminist knowledge is experience. Feminist experience is achieved through a struggle against oppression; it is, therefore, argued to be more complete and less distorted than the perspective of the ruling group of men. A feminist standpoint then is not just the experience of women, but of women reflexively engaged in struggle (intellectual and political).

One of the major criticisms of standpoint feminism is that it has tended not to problematize masculinity. Many feminists recognize the importance of questioning what it is about masculinity that singularly makes it the most predictable variable of criminal involvement. Hegemonic masculinity also remains "defined as different and separate from, in opposition and superior to, femininity" (Danner and Carmody 2001). Countering the criticism that standpoint feminism excludes masculinity studies, Smart (1990, 81) states,

> It is precisely because standpoint feminism in this area has risen from a grassroots concern to protect women and to reveal the victimization of women, it has not been sympathetic to the study of masculinity(ies). Indeed, it would argue that we have heard enough from that quarter and that any attempts by feminists to turn their attention away from women is to neglect the very real problems that women face.

However, given the feminist urging to deconstruct gender, it is important to take account of this shortcoming while at the same time heeding the warning of not falling into the androcentric trap of taking men's experiences as the starting point of analysis and subsequently the standard by which women's experiences are evaluated.

The above discussions elucidate the claim that there is no monolithic feminist criminology. Rather, there exist a multitude of viewpoints about women's subordination and subsequent criminalization. As Boritch (1997, 78) points out, "Many feminists now take the position that to adopt any single definition of feminism, or approach to gender and crime, would limit the development of feminist perspectives in criminology." While some feminists have moved more toward an examination of social control issues that propel women into crime (e.g., Daly and Maher 1998; Miller 1998), others argue that we need to move away from the traditional confines of criminology altogether (e.g., Cain 1990; Smart 1990), as it restricts an examination of central questions about women and fails to liberate them from their oppression. Recognizing the contradictory assumptions inherent to feminist criminology, it is to the investigation of a "transgressive criminology" that I now turn.

Towards a Transgressive Criminology

As Maureen Cain (1990) points out, feminist criminology started out with the understandable concern that women were being treated differently from men in the criminal justice system. Attempts to remedy or address this concern led to a doctrine of equal treatment. However, it has been rightly argued that equal treatment studies are also androcentric because males are again the yardstick by which women's actions are measured. Cain (1990) therefore contends that it is not possible to make theoretical sense of the results of research analysis posed solely in equal treatment terms and further argues that such an approach is a nonstarter. On this point, Cain (1990, 2) states,

> The implied policy of such an approach [equal treatment] boils down to a "non-policy." The possibility exists that even if boys/men are treated badly by the system then women/girls are brought up to a level playing field. It does nothing to address the fundamental inadequacies of such a system.

Cain (1990) sees feminist criminology as routinely marginalized, as it fails to problematize gender and argues that the questions posed should be questions about the social construction of gender. This approach would conceivably include the deconstruction of masculinities as well as femininities. A major defining characteristic of transgressive criminology is that it starts from outside criminological discourse. Cain (1990, 10) argues that feminist criminology "must explore the total lives of women, and there are no tools in existing criminological theory with which to do this." Furthermore, she contends,

> It simply has not proved possible to make adequate sense of what is going on in these areas of concern by starting from inside criminological discourse. Only by starting from outside, with the social construction of gender, or with women's experiences of their total lives, or with the structure of the domestic space, can we begin to make sense of what is going on. (Cain 1990, 10)

In keeping with a transgressive doctrine, one of the major contributions of feminism to criminology has been its focus on the deconstruction of knowledge. This includes the notion that there are no grand theories, rather, there exist multiple truths extrapolated from the lives/experiences of women. This focus on knowledge deconstruction/legitimation has become a key area of investigation for feminist thought and subsequent political action. Feminist perspectives in criminology are very much about "ways of knowing"—the way questions are framed and the research results interpreted remain tied to masculinist perspectives. Feminist ways of knowing therefore need to be more fully explored.

Feminist Epistemologies

Smart (1990, 70) argues that the "core enterprise of criminology is problematic, that feminists' attempts to alter criminology have only succeeded in revitalizing a problematic enterprise, and that, as feminist theory is increasingly engaging with and generating postmodern ideas, the relevance of criminology to feminist thought diminishes." She regards criminology as something of a siding for feminist thought, with feminist criminologists risking something of a marginalized existence—marginal to criminology and to feminism (Smart 1990, 71). This challenges the modernist assumption that once we have the theory (master narrative) which will explain all forms of social behaviour, we will also know what to do and that the "rightness" of this doing will be verifiable and transparent (Smart 1990, 72).

A large body of feminist empiricist literature rejects claims to objectivity, grand theory, and the deconstruction of knowledge (see, e.g., Keller 1996; Smith 1987; Haraway 1996; Hartsock 1998). Feminist empiricism criticizes the claims to objectivity made by mainstream social science. It points out that what has passed for science is in fact the world perceived from the perspective of men, what looks like objectivity is really sexism, and the kinds of questions social science has traditionally asked have systematically excluded women and the interests of women. Feminist empiricism, therefore, claims that a truly objective science would take account of both genders. To simply direct research at women without problematizing traditional assumptions about methodology and epistemology can result in making women an addendum to the study of men.

It is important to recognize that knowledge in the everyday world is socially constructed and that the political, economic, social, and cultural contexts of knowledge generation, acquisition, and transmission have to be taken into account. Whose knowledge comes to be accepted as the "truth," who has a voice in the creation of knowledge, and what the intervening factors are that play into the legitimation process of knowledge, such as the "relations of ruling,"[8] are important tenets of feminist methodology. In this regard, issues surrounding who decides what becomes acceptable as knowledge in a particular spatial, temporal, and cultural context are paramount.

Before knowledge gets to be accepted in the everyday world it has to undergo a "legitimation process" which results in an "official" decision being made as to an explanation's legitimacy or lack thereof. If the decision makers perceive some knowledge to challenge the status quo, an approving assessment of this threatening type of knowledge might be withheld as a consequence, and the finding will be denounced as (legitimate) knowledge. Consequently, this leads to the marginalization of knowledge, and many creators of subsequently marginalized knowledge have come from oppressed groups, such as women and nonwhite, including Aboriginal, people. Conversely, much legitimized knowledge has come from members of the dominant group(s)—primarily white, heterosexual and male—who had (have) some affiliation with the ruling class.

Feminist writings on the value-laden and androcentric bases of scientific knowledge have pioneered the deconstruction of knowledge claims and have argued for the inclusion of feminist ways of knowing in the experimental design of (social) scientific research. Keller (1996) discusses the relationship between knowledge and power and notes that both are intermeshed. More and more, feminists critiques of the objectivity and legitimation of science have entered the criminological discourse (e.g. Naffine 1996; Smart 1990; Scraton 1990). One attempt to value knowledge at the margins that lacks "official knowledge status" (i.e., legitimation) has been offered by proponents of standpoint perspectives (Haraway 1996; Collins 1991, Smith 1987). Smith (1987, 108) illustrates the connection between power and the legitimation of knowledge and the exclusionary nature of these processes as follows:

> A standpoint in the everyday world is a fundamental grounding of modes of knowing developed in a ruling apparatus. The ruling apparatus is that familiar complex of management, government administration, professions, and intelligentsia, as well as the textually mediated discourses that coordinate and interpenetrate it.

A standpoint perspective is based on the assumption that one's positionality is crucial in gaining knowledge and understanding. In other words, one's position in the social hierarchy potentially broadens or limits one's understanding of others. Members of the dominant group will have viewpoints that are partial in contrast to those from subordinated groups, who have greater potential to have fuller knowledge. Smith (1987) emphasizes that the only way we can know a socially constructed world is to know it from within. But since our knowledge and perceptions about reality are shaped by our own unique experiences and how we interpret them, there is little or no possibility for value-free and objective knowledge. Similarly, nobody's knowledge should be worth more or less than somebody else's.

Feminist postmodernism, therefore, accepts multiple voices and experiences as valid and asserts that there is no single truth, rather there are multiple truths. This perspective points to the importance of listening to marginalized voices and the experiences of people whose interests are generally not represented by mainstream perspectives and those having a stake in maintaining the status quo. According to Fraser and Nicholson (1994, 34–35), feminist postmodern theory seeks to "replace unitary notions of woman and feminine gender identity with plural and complexly constructed conceptions of social identity, treating gender as one relative strand among others, attending also to class, race, ethnicity, age, and sexual orientation."

Feminist Methodologies as "Ways of Knowing"

Epistemological contributions that attempt to deconstruct and expose the value-laden assumptions of scientific knowledge have also sparked feminist writings in the area of research methodologies. Issues grappling with power relations inherent during the research process have been an integral part of the discussions and debates. On this point, Ristock and Pennell (1996, 68) argue that "feminist discussions of research have yet to describe fully the complexity of power and struggles with subjectivity in research."

One such feminist methodological tradition for uncovering subjectivities in research is the attempt for the researcher to locate themselves within the context of their research and to share much of this standpoint with their readers. This practice of positionality is often achieved by locating or situating themselves in the context of their research. In understanding the relationship between researcher and researched, whereby the biographies of the researched are often times revealed, it is important to situate the experiences of the researcher in relation to the study. However, as Ristock and Pennell (1996, 67) caution:

> What we want to avoid is feeling satisfied that we have adequately located ourselves when we have merely listed the social and identity groups to which we belong. Research as empowerment strives to explore the contingent and variable sense of self that postmodernists refer to as subjectivity as a way of analyzing the power relationships in research.

Another epistemological tradition invoked by feminist researchers to garner a more full understanding of women's experiences is achieved through the process of reflexivity. Reflexivity, as defined by Mauthner and Doucet (1998, 121) means:

> reflecting upon and understanding our own personal, political, and intellectual autobiographies as researchers and making explicit where we are located in relation to our research respondents. Reflexivity also means acknowledging the critical role we play in creating, interpreting and theorizing research data. Reflexivity during the data collection process requires constant and intensive scrutiny of what we know and how we come to know as researchers. This involves a process of actively constructing interpretations of field experiences and then interpreting how those experiences came about.

Hertz (1997) discusses the importance of reflexivity in the generation of knowledge and argues that since researchers are active participants in the data collection process, it is imperative that we know and understand the positionality of the researcher (e.g., gender, race, and class) before interpreting the data. Hertz (1997, viii) further notes:

> Through personal accounting, researchers must become more aware of how their own positions and interests are imposed at all stages of the research process—from the questions they ask to those they ignore, from who they study to who they ignore, from problem formulation to analysis, representation, and writing—in order to produce less distorted accounts of the social world.

DeVault (1996) identifies as another major goal of feminist methodology the attempt to extrapolate the voices of marginalized women. The goal is to shift the focus of standard practice from research concerned with men's agendas in order to bring in the locations and perspectives of all women. Throughout the research process, it is imperative that we listen to the voices of our respondents and not selectively hear or document what fits neatly with our own subjective orientations. Failing to listen to the voices of our respondents runs the risk of recreating knowledge that suits our own personal, theoretical, or political agendas.

Feminist methodologies and epistemologies, therefore, are inextricably linked to subsequent theory construction. Before we can theorize from data, we must acknowledge the knowledge construction/legitimation processes that guide our research. We need to recognize the subjectivities of the researcher and take account of the power that is institutionalized in a masculinist form throughout all aspects of the criminal justice system. As Scraton (1990, 15) points out, "if academic discourse and its patriarchal context is to be challenged it needs to be considered within a broader framework of how ideas gain currency, become transmitted and eventually become institutionalized or consolidated as knowledge." It is from this vantage that feminism offers its greatest potential to transform the criminological discourse.

Future Directions: Feminism at the Centre of Inquiry

At this point, a return to the questions raised at the beginning of this chapter is needed: What does feminism offer to criminology? What does criminology offer to feminism? On the first count, the offerings of feminism seem clear. Feminist epistemological contributions to the deconstruction of knowledge/truth claims, identifying subjectivities of the researcher and the researched, and placing gender at the centre of inquiry holds promise for transforming the criminological enterprise and moving closer to a theoretical understanding of crime and/or conformity. Naffine (1996, 4) elaborates on these feminists contributions to the criminological discourse by pointing out:

> Feminists have carried out the more conventional (but necessary) empirical work of documenting sex bias within the criminal justice system. Feminists have questioned the scientific methods deployed by criminologists, as well as their highly orthodox approach to the nature of knowledge. Feminists have engaged with criminological theory, across the range, questioning its ability to provide general explanations of human behaviour. Feminists have provided an abundance of data about crime from the viewpoint of women (to counter the more usual viewpoint of men), and feminists have also helped to develop new epistemologies that question the very sense of writing from the perspective of a woman (or, for that matter, from the perspective of a man).

On the other hand, the contributions of criminology to feminism are somewhat less apparent. Mainstream criminology continues to be developed and presented largely as the study of men. It has failed to problematize gender, despite the fact that overwhelmingly men are both the perpetrators and victims of crime. In view of the remarkable sex bias in crime, "it is surprising that gender has not become the central preoccupation of the criminologist, rather than an afterthought. . . . The costs to criminology of its failure to deal with feminist scholarship are perhaps more severe than they would be in any other discipline. The reason is that the most consistent and prominent fact about crime is the sex of the offender" (Naffine 1996, 5–6).

It is precisely on this last point that I regard criminology as having a great deal to offer to feminism by studying what it is about the construction of masculinities[9] that propels men into crime. Put another way the question becomes, what is it about the construction of femininities that makes women law-abiding? An inquiry into why women typically obey the law would surely advance a criminological and feminist understanding of gender. However, as Naffine (1996, 8) points out, "the idea that an exploration of the lives of women might provide the [criminological] discipline with powerful insights into human behaviour has not been considered. . . . [It would] allow women a degree of separateness and subjectivity that has not been accorded them by the discipline."

While recognizing the ongoing debates about the future of feminist criminology, it is perhaps unproductive to point fingers at who brings more or less to the respective discourses. However, feminism holds a huge potential for transforming criminology through its epistemological rootings. The basic tenets of feminist thought have the potential for invigorating the theoretical and methodological landscape of criminology. It also has the potential to pioneer work in the area of racial/ethnic, sexual identity, and class intersections in crime through an epistemological focus on knowledge deconstruction and researcher subjectivities. Following this line of inquiry, several important questions may be raised: What would criminology look like if women were at the centre of inquiry? How can feminist methodologies "transgress and transform" mainstream criminological traditions? How would criminology transform and progress if gender deconstruction of both women and men were forefront? Gender needs to be a central focus of inquiry in criminology. As a result:

> A deeper understanding which studying women and crime [would] bring to criminology ought to result in a paradigm shift. Gender, and hence the explanations of gender-related patterns, should become central. That has clearly not happened. Instead, there is now a vast store of material on women offenders, women and crime and women and penology which is, no doubt, taken seriously and widely used for its impact on women. But the importance of gender for criminality is only perceived in terms of victimology. . . . A central question therefore remains about gender: how can it be built into criminology to play the central part in explanation and analysis it must? (Heidensohn 1987, 24)

To return to the "transgression of boundaries" found in the title of this chapter, I would espouse a "broader vision" to the pioneering work of feminist criminologists. In examining the myriad factors that propel people into crime (men) and, likewise, the social control mechanisms in place that restrict criminal involvement (women), we need to move beyond the boundaries of criminology and look toward the broader social, economic, political, and cultural institutions that contribute to the construction of gender roles. We need to critique the androcentric knowledge-making in criminological theories that exclude women and then argue objectivity and scientific rigour. As Morris and Gelsthorpe (1991, 19–20) point out,

> [This must be] a journey for both men and women as women do not have a monopoly on understanding feminist perspectives. . . . [Furthermore] to promote separatism [between feminism and criminology] would be self-defeating . . . because it would mean the perpetuation of traditional methodologies and conventional knowledge boundaries, and it is these which feminist perspectives seek to challenge.

Notes

1. Although a core focus of this chapter is to critically assess the existence of a monolithic "feminist criminology," I employ the term to describe the varied contributions of feminist theories/methodologies in criminology and thus use "feminist perspectives" and "feminist criminology(ies)" interchangeably.
2. Criminology has also been criticized for its failure to examine pivotal intersections of race and ethnicity, class, and gender.
3. Sex differences are biological differences, including differences in reproductive organs, body size, and hormones. Gender differences, on the other hand, are those that are ascribed by society and relate to expected social roles. Gender differences are rooted in inequality and therefore social change is seen as necessary to achieve equality.
4. For example, structured action theory (Messerschmidt 1986); libertarian and cultural feminism; multicultural and global feminism; multicultural/multiracial theory (Chesney-Lind and Faith 2001); psychoanalytic (Tong 1998); existentialist (Tong 1998).
5. This refers to corporate profit-making as the motive behind the prison industry boom (cf. Davis 2003).
6. It is recognized that socialist feminism still focuses largely on gender and class and does not adequately address race as a contributing factor to women's oppression.
7. This term was coined by Cohen (1980) and refers to "a situation in which a condition, episode, person, or a group of persons come to be defined as a threat to society" (DeKeseredy 2000, 38).
8. Smith (1987, 107–9) argues that women's lives have been outside or subordinate to the relations of ruling. However, she argues, it is not only women that are excluded. The ruling apparatus is "an organization of class and as such implicates dominant classes. It also excludes the many voices of women and men of colour, native peoples, and homosexual women and men. From different standpoints different aspects of the ruling apparatus and of class come into view."
9. A plethora of research on masculinities and crime has been advanced over the past decade (see, e.g., DeKeseredy and Schwartz 2005; Barak 2003; Schwartz and Hatty 2003; Hatty 2000; Messerschmidt 2000; Bowker 1998; Connell 1995).

References

Adler, F. 1975. *Sisters in Crime: The Rise of the New Female Criminal.* New York: McGraw-Hill.

Barak, G. 2003. *Violence and Nonviolence: Pathways to Understanding.* Thousand Oaks, CA: Sage.

Boritch, H. 1997. *Fallen Women: Female Crime and Criminal Justice in Canada.* Toronto: Nelson.

Bowker, L. 1998. *Masculinities and Violence.* Thousand Oaks, CA: Sage.

Cain, M. 1990. "Towards Transgression: New Directions in Feminist Criminology." *International Journal of the Sociology of Law* 18: 1–18.

Chesney-Lind, M., and K. Faith. 2001. "What about Feminism? Engendering Theory-making in Criminology." Pp. 287–302 in R. Paternoster and R. Bauchnan, eds., *Exploring Criminals and Crime.* Los Angeles, CA: Roxbury.

Cohen, S. 1980. *Folk Devils and Moral Panics.* London: Oxford University Press.

Collins, P. H. 1991. *Black Feminist Thought: Knowledge, Consciousness, and the Politics of Empowerment.* London: Routledge.

Connell, R. W. 1995. *Masculinities.* Sydney, Australia: Allen & Unwin.

Daly, K., and M. Chesney-Lind. 1988. "Feminism and Criminology." *Justice Quarterly* 5, no. 4: 497–538.

Daly, K., and L. Maher, eds. 1998. *Criminology at the Crossroads: Feminist Readings in Crime and Justice.* Oxford University Press.

Danner, M. 1991. "Socialist Feminism: A Brief Introduction." Pp. 51–54 in B. MacLean and D. Milovanovic, eds., *New Directions in Critical Criminology.* Vancouver: Collective Press.

Danner, M., and D. C. Carmody. 2001. "Missing Gender in Cases of Infamous School Violence: Investigating Research and Media Explanations." *Justice Quarterly* 18, no. 1: 87–114.

Davis, A. 2003. *Are Prisons Obsolete*? New York: Seven Stories Press.

DeKeseredy, W. 2000. *Women, Crime, and the Canadian Criminal Justice System.* Cincinnati: Anderson Publishing.

DeKeseredy, W., and M. Schwartz. 2005. "Masculinities and Interpersonal Violence." Pp. 353–56 in M. Kimmel, R. Connell, and J. Hearn, eds., *The Handbook of Studies on Men and Masculinities.* Thousand Oaks, CA: Sage.

DeVault, M. 1996. "Talking Back to Sociology: Distinctive Contributions of Feminist Methodology." *Annual Review of Sociology* 22: 29–50.

Fraser, N., and L. Nicholson. 1994. *Feminism/Postmodernism.* London: Routledge.

Haraway, D. 1996. "Situated Knowledges: The Science Question in Feminism and the Privilege of Partial Perspective." *Feminism and Science*: 249–63.

Hartsock, N. 1998. *The Feminist Standpoint Revisited, and Other Essays.* Boulder, CO: Westview.

Hatty, S. 2000. *Masculinities, Violence, and Culture.* Thousand Oaks, CA: Sage.

Heidensohn, F. 1987. "Women and Crime: Questions for Criminology." Pp. 16–27 in P. Carlen and A. Worrall, eds., *Gender, Crime and Justice.* Philadelphia: Open University Press.

Hertz, R. 1997. *Reflexivity and Voice.* Thousand Oaks, CA: Sage.

Keller, E. 1996. "Feminism and Science." In E. Keller and H. Longino, eds., *Feminism and Science*. New York: Oxford.

Laster, K. 1996. "Feminist Criminology: Coping with Success." *Current Issues in Criminal Justice* 8, no. 1: 192–200.

Lombroso, C., and W. Ferrero. 1895. *The Female Offender*. New York: Philosophical Library.

Mauthner, N., and A. Doucet. 1998. "Reflections on a Voice-centered Relational Method: Analysing Maternal and Domestic Voices." Pp. 119–44 in J. Ribbens and R. Edwards, eds., *Feminist Dilemmas in Qualitative Research: Public Knowledge and Private Lives*. London: Sage.

Messerschmidt, J. 1986. *Capitalism, Patriarchy, and Crime: Toward a Socialist Feminist Criminology*. Totowa, NJ: Rowman & Littlefield.

———. 2000. *Nine Lives: Adolescent Masculinities, the Body, and Violence*. Boulder: Westview.

Miller, S., ed. 1998. *Crime Control and Women: Feminist Implications of Criminal Justice Policy*. Sage: Thousand Oaks.

Morris, A., and L. Gelsthorpe. 1991. "Feminist Perspectives in Criminology: Transforming and Transgressing." *Women and Criminal Justice* 2, no. 2: 3–26.

Naffine, N. 1996. *Feminism and Criminology*. Philadelphia: Temple University Press.

Pollak, O. 1950. *The Criminality of Women*. New York: Barnes.

Ristock, J., and J. Pennell. 1996. *Community Research as Empowerment: Feminist Links, Postmodern Interruptions*. Oxford University Press.

Schwartz, M., and S. Hatty. 2003. *Controversies in Critical Criminology*. Cincinnati: Anderson Publishing.

Scraton, P. 1990. "Scientific Knowledge or Masculine Discourses? Challenging Patriarchy in Criminology." Pp. 10–25 in A. Morris and L. Gelsthorpe, eds., *Feminist Perspectives in Criminology*. Milton Keynes: Open University Press.

Simon, R. 1975. *Women and Crime*. Lexington, MA: Lexington Books.

Smart, C. 1990. "Feminist Approaches to Criminology, or Postmodern Woman Meets Atavistic Man." In A. Morris and L. Gelsthorpe, eds., *Feminist Perspectives in Criminology*. Milton, Keynes: Open University Press.

Smith, D. 1987. *The Everyday World as Problematic: A Feminist Sociology*. Milton Keynes: Open University Press.

Sudbury, J. 2005. *Global Lockdown: Race, Gender and the Prison-industrial Complex*. London and New York: Routledge.

Tong, R. 1998. *Feminist Thought: A More Comprehensive Introduction*. Boulder: Westview Press.

3

Cultural Criminology: A Decade and Counting of Criminological Chaos

Stephen L. Muzzatti

Cultural criminology is a relatively recent development in sociology and criminology. Barely a decade old, this orientation, rooted largely in the work of Ferrell (1994; 1995) and Ferrell and Sanders (1995), seeks to explore the complex interplay of crime, crime control, the media and popular culture in late modernity. Perhaps more than any other of the critical orientations, cultural criminology recognises the intersections of cultural and criminal processes in the new century and the ways in which they interweave along a multiplicity of intersecting axes; pain and pleasure, production and consumption, accommodation and resistance, privacy and public display, messages and audiences, approved and fugitive meanings, intertextuality and reification. Drawing upon critical and interactionist criminological traditions, as well as postmodern sociological theory, media studies, American and British cultural studies and varied qualitative methodologies, cultural criminology seeks to establish a homology between eclectic subjects and diverse criminological ontologies and epistemologies (Ferrell et al. 2004). As such it offers not only a toolbox with which to deconstruct and demystify the mediated realities of crime and control, but also the acumen to put forth alternative, more socially just readings.

At the first level of approximation cultural criminology is a response to Cohen's challenge to criminologists to adopt a structurally and politically informed version of Labelling Theory (Cohen 1988). It was born of a coalescence of collective frustration at the unimaginative and soul-crushing, not to mention highly problematic, character of much of mainstream (i.e., "administrative") criminology.

While critiques of the constraining and dehumanising character of conventional criminology have existed in one form or another since at least the 1970s (see Quinney 1970; Cohen 1972; Cohen and Young 1973; Taylor et al. 1973; Fishman 1978; Hall et al. 1978; Tifft and Sullivan 1980), cultural criminology is, to borrow a professional cycling metaphor from Ferrell and his colleagues (2004), a *casinista* amid *domestiques.*

History and Genealogy

Crime, deviance and control are ever shifting and contested terrains. They are inextricably linked to issues of governance, social control, order maintenance and moral regulation and are played out not only on street corners, boardrooms and court houses, but also in the media. While crime, delinquency and deviant behaviour do exist, they do not, as an increasing number of scholars contend, exist outside of the sociopolitical and cultural contexts in which they are presented, (re)presented and reified. And it is through this hyper-real process of creation, display, carnival and mediation that behaviours, individuals and communities come to be exalted, celebrated, castigated, demonised and controlled by co-optation, stigmatisation or sanction. Cultural criminology focuses upon image, style, meaning, and representation in the complex interplay of crime and its control. Specifically, it examines the stylised frameworks and experiential dynamics of youth tribes, "deviant" subcultures, the symbolic criminalisation of popular culture artefacts, practices and actors; and the mediated construction of crime and crime control issues. As such, it draws heavily upon the long history of interactionist and critical sociologies and criminologies, such as Labelling Theory, critical constructionism and content/media analysis.

Roots in Labelling Theory

It makes sense that an examination of crime and deviance should include an analysis of the processes and strategies by which certain forms of behaviour and certain individuals, groups and communities come to be defined as deviant and/or criminal and are therefore subjected to any number of informal and formal mechanisms of social control and moral regulation. As Pfohl (1985) astutely points out, sociologists, psychologists and other behavioural scientists have used an interactionist orientation to describe the social interaction between women and men, teenagers and adults, parents and children, and so forth. Economists have used it to account for fluctuations in the stock market. Anthropologists and historians have used it to describe the exchanges between white European settlers and explorers and the indigenous populations throughout the Americas, Africa, Asia, and so forth. Hence, its application to crime/deviance was a logical extension.

The work of historian and anarchist Frank Tannenbaum (1938) is cited by many as the precursor to modern labelling theory and hence the first step on the circuitous route towards a critical cultural criminology. Tannenbaum contributed several significant concepts to our understanding of the interactional process of crime, deviance and control. Tannenbaum, who was interested not only in juvenile delinquency, but also in the formation of delinquent subcultures, examined youths engaged in a variety of youth subcultural activities, most notably, shoplifting, smoking and drinking, to illustrate "the dramatisation of evil," "tagging" and "deviance actualisation."

Tannenbaum suggests that deviant/delinquent behaviour was not an inherent quality of the act—but rather a result of a conflict between a small group (the "delinquent" youths) and a larger group (the "community" on the whole). He writes, "The first dramatisation of the 'evil' which separated the child out of his group for specialised treatment plays a greater role in making the criminal than any other experience" (1938, 19). Hence here we can see the first clear indication of what was later to become a hallmark of Labelling Theory: the reaction, not the action as the true source of deviance. Tannenbaum describes "tagging" as "the process of making the criminal, therefore, a process of tagging, defining, identifying, segregating, describing, emphasising making, conscious and self conscious: it becomes a way of stimulating, suggesting, emphasising and evoking the very traits that are complained of" (1938, 19). As such, he contends that it is this label, tag or more contemporarily, signing, that is applied to a youth caught in the act that is the true source of the "delinquency."

It was Tannenbaum's assertion that the delinquent/deviant behaviour of the boys that he studied and the subsequent development of the youth gangs was a result of the interplay between the actions and responses of a variety of actors that is possibly the most significant of his contributions to the development of cultural criminology. Terming it "deviance actualisation," he theorised that neighbourhood youth and agents of social control, most notably parents, storekeepers and truant and police officers, interacted in different ways (i.e., provided varying degrees and types of affirmation or stigmatisation), which in turn worked to constitute the "deviant individual" and the "delinquent gang." The "gang" specifically was a product resulted from the neighbourhood play groups' collective stigmatisation at the hands of adults for activities such as skipping school, hanging out on roof tops and generally "horsing around" (1938, 17). In short, there is a conflict over the signing of an activity. Activities defined by youths as leisure and recreation are identified by adults as "trouble-making."

Edwin Lemert, whose work first appeared in the early 1950s, represented a powerful epistemic challenge to the extant normative theories of conventional criminology, specifically in the form of the concepts of primary and secondary deviance. Not unlike the tethers binding much of conventional criminology today, the dominant criminology of Lemert's time took deviance and crime for granted. It failed to consider how some behaviours and some people come to be defined as deviant in the first place, and furthermore to recognise the impact on the person(s) being labelled and processed as deviant. On the contrary, Lemert (1951; 1967) theorised that transgressive behaviours do not become "deviance" (i.e., subject for public discourse and official action) until some audience identifies and proclaims them as such. He argues that behaviours "are not significant until they are organised . . . and become the social criteria for assigning status" (1951, 75). As such, it was Lemert's contention that the interactional dynamics of disapproval, and the consequences thereof, should be the business of criminologists.

Howard Becker's (1963; 1964) early contributions to Labelling Theory paid close attention to fundamental questions such as: "Who applies a label?," "Under what conditions are labels successfully applied?," and "What are the consequences of the application of deviant label for those being so designated?" Becker's work also paid close attention to "non-deviants." He and other labelling theorists were particularly interested in the way in which audience members react to the deviant behaviour of others, for it is here, and not in simple rule breaking behaviour, that the true catalyst of deviance is to be found. As such, the Labelling perspective can tell us as much, if not more, about "non-deviants" as it can deviants.

Crime and the Media

Possibly the single most relevant contribution of Becker to the development of cultural criminology was his analysis of rule creation/creators and enforcement/enforcers. Informed by the Labelling work of his American colleagues, Stan Cohen's concept of moral panic proved to be a significant next step toward the development of cultural criminology. Published in 1972, Cohen's book *Folk Devils and Moral Panics* was an outgrowth of research conducted while he was a doctoral student at the University of London between 1964 and 1967 and the first place that the concept was fully developed. He defines a moral panic as occurring when:

> A condition, episode, person or group of persons emerges to become defined as a threat to societal values and interests; its nature is presented in a stylized and stereotypical fashion by the mass media; the moral barricades are manned by editors, bishops politicians and other right-thinking people; socially accredited experts pronounce their diagnoses and solutions; ways of coping are evolved or (more often) resorted to; the condition then disappears, submerges or deteriorates and becomes more visible. Sometimes the object of the panic is quite novel and at other times it is something that has been in existence long enough, but suddenly appears in the limelight. Sometimes the panic passes over and is forgotten, except in folklore and collective memory; at other times it has more serious and long lasting repercussions and might produce such changes as those in legal and social policy or even in the way the society conceives itself. (Cohen 1972, 9)

Simply put, a moral panic is an exaggeration or distortion of some perceived deviant behaviour or criminal activity. According to Cohen this includes grossly exaggerating the seriousness of the events according to criteria such as the numbers of people taking part, the number involved in violence and the amount and effects of violence and/or damage (1972, 31). Cohen's work focused on the reactions of the media, agents of social control and the general public to relatively minor clashes between youth subcultures (the mods and the rockers) in England, and, as the above excerpt illustrates, the ways in which these reactions influenced the formation and enforcement of law and social policy as well as societal conceptions of the youth culture–delinquency nexus. While many subsequent scholars have similarly applied the concept to youth subcultures (punks, skinheads, goths, ravers, etc.) others have gone beyond the original focus to apply it to more generalised and adult manifestations of deviance and crime (soccer hooligans, motorcycle gangs, immigrants [both illegal and legal], welfare mothers, Satanists, paedophiles, squeegee merchants, serial killers, etc.). While some thirty years old, with antecedents perhaps even a generation older, the concept of moral panic continued to grow in importance in the 1990s and into the twenty-first century, spurring among others the emergence and growth of cultural criminology.

As indicated in the previous section, the concept of moral panic has antecedents that can be traced back a full generation prior to the publication of Cohen's book. He drew upon several earlier developments from the interactionist understanding of deviance. In addition to the aforementioned work of Tannenbaum, Lemert and Becker, Cohen was also informed by Sutherland's examination of sexual psychopath laws (1950) and Gusfield's work on prohibition and the temperance movement (1963).

Cohen theorised that the emergence of a moral panic is not spontaneous, but rather is a result of a complex interplay of behaviours and responses involving several actors. For a moral panic to take hold, there need to be in place six sets of actors. These include: 1) folk devils, 2) rule enforcers, 3) the media, 4) politicians, 5) the public and 6) action groups.

Folk devils are the individuals responsible for the deviant or criminal behaviour. Unlike "normal" deviants or criminals, these folks are "unambiguously unfavourable symbols" (1972, 41); the embodiment of evil. While it is often members of youth subcultures (zoot-suiters, hippies, skinheads, gamers, etc.) that are designated folk devils, the label is not solely restricted to them. As the work of many scholars (Goode and Ben-Yehuda 1994; Kidd-Hewitt and Osborne 1995; Kappeler et al. 2000; Visano 1998; Berry 1999) illustrates, folk devils are highly stylised images of despised and marginalised masses of people (immigrants, people of colour, the working class, gays and lesbians, etc.). In short, folk devils are demonised groups that are all that "we" (i.e., good clean living, law-abiding folks) are not.

As those responsible for the enforcement of norms, codes of conduct and law, rule enforcers are a vital part of the moral panic. These groups/organisations, particularly the police, prosecutors and the judiciary, are expected to detect, apprehend and punish the folk devils. These agents often present the social situation as one that teeters on the brink of chaos; if it were not for them, deviance/crime and all that it entails would abound. They present themselves, often quite melodramatically, as the "thin blue line" which separates "order and civilisation" from "mayhem and anarchy." Depending upon the strength of the discourse, it often includes calls for increased numbers of rule enforcers, and more extensive authority (i.e., greater power) for them.

The media is likely the single most influential actor in the orchestration and promulgation of a moral panic. Media coverage of certain kinds of deviant/criminal behaviour, particularly those involving perpetrators of the aforementioned type is usually distorted. It serves to inflate the seriousness of the incidents, making them appear more heinous and frequent than they truly are. Public anxiety is whipped up through the use of journalistic and linguistic devices. "Special cover story," "in-depth exposé" or "investigative report" style coverage employs dramatic photos, video and sound bites along with highly moralistic editorialising. In such instances terms/phrases such as "plague," "scourge," "hordes" and "orgy of violence" serve the function of making the occurrences appear more serious and rampant than they are. In such instances alienated and frustrated youth become "teen super-predators," small cohorts of young people—"rampaging mobs," minor property damage—"wholesale destruction" and scuffles—"riots."

Politicians are also vital actors in a moral panic. As individuals who live and die in the court of public opinion, is extremely important that politicians present themselves as purveyors of the moral high ground. As such, they often align themselves with the press and the rule enforcers in a struggle against the evils perpetrated by the folk devils. Self-righteousness and the politics of rage (Berry 1999) characterise the response of politicians in dealing with crime. Even the most "liberal" politicians usually take a moralistic, no-nonsense, "war on crime" stance, advocating punitive, even reactionary strategies to deal with this new threat. Common calls include special hearings or subcommittees to deal with the problem, zero-tolerance policies, increased police powers, tougher laws and harsher sentences.

Action groups are a natural step in the progression of a moral panic. Theses groups of moral entrepreneurs (Becker 1963; Becker 1964) are comprised of prototype crusading reformers. They hold an absolute ethic. These individuals define the problem (e.g., pregnant drug users, aggressive panhandlers, migrant farm labourers, etc.) as an absolute evil and hence believe that their mission to combat it is holy. While not always the case, these moral entrepreneurs are often affiliated the political and/or religious right, as the historical examples of successful crusades against gambling, alcohol, prostitution and other vices clearly illustrate (see: Sutherland 1950; Becker 1963; 1964; Gusfield 1963; 1981). It is important to note that unlike the humorous, though inaccurate caricatures by political satirists, the moral entrepreneurs are not meddling busybodies. They truly believe that their cause is just, and pursue it with fervent self-righteousness. They feel that if others follow their lead and crusade to eliminate the "evil," the quality of everyone's lives will be improved.

The final and some would argue ultimately the most important actor in a moral panic is the general public. The success of the media, politicians, rule enforcers and moral entrepreneurs in generating and sustaining a moral panic is ultimately contingent upon how successfully they enrage the public and marshal support against the folk devils. The vox populi is enlisted as a front-line agent in the crusade against the designated evil. Members of the public express contempt for the folk devils and support for the rule enforcers, hungrily consume the media coverage and wait with bated breath for the latest pronouncements from politicians and action groups on how the problem is to be solved.

Characteristics

How is a moral panic distinguished from normal levels of societal concern over deviant/criminal behaviour? Goode and Ben-Yehuda (1994, 33–41) define five characteristics that indicate that a moral panic has taken hold. These are: 1) heightened concern, 2) hostility, 3) consensus, 4) disproportionality and 5) volatility.

While there is always social concern about crime, heightened concern refers to an increase in the level of public consternation about a particular group, their behaviour and its impact. This, as Goode and Ben-Yehuda point out, can be quantified (public opinion polls showing increased fear, greater media coverage of the problem, etc.). Hostility refers to a greater level of intolerance for the behaviour and contempt for those responsible for it. Consensus, as the name implies, pertains to an increased level of public agreement on the behaviours as harmful and the situation as something in need of greater scrutiny, police attention and ultimately, a solution. Disproportionality is likely the most telling of the characteristics. It refers to a collective overreaction to the problem—to its frequency, scope, severity, and finally its volatility. Moral panics, while always having historical and structural antecedents, do "appear" quickly and to the casual observer often "without warning." It is interesting to note that while they often dissipate just as quickly, they usually leave in their wake a litany of repressive social control strategies and mechanisms (Goode and Ben-Yehuda 1994, 33–41).

Through the Media Looking Glass: Criminology of News-Breaking

The suggestion that media organisations do not simply report the news, but instead determine what "is news" is not a new concept. Cohen's *Folk Devils*, and his coedited collection with Jock Young (1973), were the first in a long line of studies conducted both in the U.K. and in North America which critically examined the media's role in constructing the reality of crime and deviance, and the interconnectedness of mediated realities of crime and crime control. As such, these pieces were early precursors of the cultural criminological canon that *images* of crime and control are now as "real" as crime and criminal justice itself (Ferrell et al. 2004). The exploitative and sensationalistic media coverage of crime that we are today accustomed to is not so much designed to "inform" as to "entertain" and "sell" (both advertising space, as well as a value system). As Cohen and Young (1973) point out, crime stories about drugs, sex and street violence, particularly those involving youths, immigrants or other socially disenfranchised groups, always make for successful copy and hence disproportionately comprise the negotiated accomplishment, "crime news." The discourse, which increasingly mirrors that of the police and other hegemonic agenda setters within the criminal justice system, privileges conventional criminology through the "expert analysis" of academic authorities and state techno-bureaucrats and is, as Hall and his colleagues state, "the end product of a complex process which begins with a systematic sorting and selecting of events and topics according to a socially constructed set of categories" (1978, 53). Media coverage of crime is not about the reality of crime; rather it constitutes crime as a reality through narrative contextualisation. Drawing upon this rich history, cultural criminology is particularly attentive to the ways in which the media's images shape the perceptions of the public and reflect and recreate capitalist economic relations. The media-generated images of crime are "what society tells itself about crime" (Barak 1994a, 9). As exemplified by coverage of the O.J. Simpson case, and evidenced throughout the 1990s and into the twenty-first century, crime news acts as a buffer of social reality—omitting, suppressing, homogenising and converting the message into crime—infotainment (Barak 1994a, 271). Public perceptions about "the crime threat" are shaped by underlying elements of social organisation, particularly the production and distribution of cultural services like news.

Youth Culture

Cultural criminology also draws upon the rich legacy of studies on youth subcultures. While some of this influence was drawn from American authors on American subjects (see particularly Cohen 1955; Irwin 1973; 1977) most came from British scholars, primarily those from the Birmingham School during the late 1970s and early 1980s (Willis 1977; 1978; Hebdige 1979; Brake 1980). The work of these authors alerted criminologists to the subtle, situated dynamics of deviant and criminal subcultures, and to the importance of symbolism and style in shaping meaning and identity. So too a cultural studies informed orientation draws much needed attention to the complex web of influence patterns among youth, popular culture, the media and agents of moral regulation and social control.

Methods: Embracing an Ongoing Criminology of the Moment[1]

Cultural criminology offers revamped terms of engagement with the spheres of crime and deviance through edgy countercurrent methodologies that directly confront the convenient fictions which privilege quantitative analysis. The use of content and discourse analysis as well as field ethnography as primary research strategies gives cultural criminology an edgy, counterflow which prioritises the aesthetic and emotive over the detached sterility of numerical alchemy.

Cultural criminology is possibly best known for it rich, multilayered ethnographies. The driving ethos behind much of that ethnographic research is *criminological verstehen* (Ferrell and Hamm 1994; Ferrell and Sanders 1995; Ferrell 1998). Informed by Weber's case for an "interpretive understanding" and "sympathetic participation," *criminological verstehen* signifies not only the researcher's commitment to naturalism, but more specifically her/his appreciation and empathic understanding of crime's situated meanings, symbolism, and emotions (Ferrell 1998, 72). Unlike abstract empiricism, such an approach provides tremendous insight into the cultures of crime and its control by challenging the researcher-subject dichotomy reified by much mainstream criminology. This novel approach demystifies much of the common-nonsense about crime and control that the methodological shackles of empiricism fail to recognise. The edgy methodologies of cultural criminology inherently function to dismantle hierarchies of knowledge and undermine a methodological framework which is as obsolete as it is oppressive. Indeed, as Ferrell (2004, 300) contends, the immersion of the cultural criminologist in the everyday/night worlds of marginalised and despised groups is driven by the need to sabotage the machinery of boredom and dehumanisation that defines mainstream criminology.

Perhaps less well known, though no less illuminating than these ethnographies are works by cultural criminologists that have employed content and discourse analysis. While many of these studies utilise traditional content analysis techniques[2] to measure crime's mediated presentation, others use more unconventional methods informed by grounded-labelling, critical constructionism, cultural studies and postmodernism's nuanced sensibilities to rigorously deconstruct the mediated reality of crime. A wide range of media texts examined have included local, national and international news reports, independent and Hollywood films, magazines, prime-time TV crime dramas, popular music and websites, covering a vast array of deviant, criminal and control enterprises from graffiti artists and roadside memorials to phone sex and the "war on terrorism."

Major Studies

In the twenty-first century the cultural industries produce a seemingly endless flow of crime images and crime texts, and disparate groups engage in ongoing struggles over meaning and ownership of these discourses. Hence considering the glut of raw material in the crime and culture pool, not to mention the speed with which it is replenished, it is not surprising that cultural criminologists have produced a range of substantive scholarship in a relative short span of time.

Some of the earliest and most celebrated pieces of cultural criminology focused on the connections among music, youth culture and crime. In the early 1990s Mark Hamm's research on neo-Nazi skinheads (1993; 1995) blended ethnographic methods with a detailed analysis of hate-core and related musical genres[3] to unpack the subculture's symbolism and reveal its homology. Similarly, Ferrell and Hamm (1994), along with many other cultural criminologists, worked, often quite publicly, to refute claims by moral entrepreneurs, police and politicians that Body Count's songs "Cop Killer" and "Smoked Pork" were "a step-by-step guide on how to ambush and murder the police,"[4] and rap and hip hop more generally as the music of murder and gang violence. As new genres emerged as the foci of control strategies, so too did cultural criminologists' challenge to the interrelated moral entrepreneurship work of interest groups, politicians, criminal justice organisations and the media (Hollywood 1997; Killingbeck 2001; Muzzatti 2004).

Likewise, Ferrell's (1993; 1996) much celebrated study of hip hop graffiti artists in Denver is as much an analysis of moral panic and mediated anti-crime campaigns as it is an ethnographic account of the delights of deviance he experienced with the scene's writers and clowns. Equipped with krylon and alcohol Ferrell spent nights wandering, talking and painting while at the same time producing a complex narrative documenting the interplay between cultural innovation and institutional intolerance; a case study in fugitive art, recreation, resistance, marginality and the politics of crime and culture—framed by anarchist sensibilities.

Similarly, Miller's (1995) interviews with probation officers in Los Angeles reveal much about the reciprocal influence patterns and meaning loops embedded within relationships of control, resistance, display and masculinity. Her work aptly addresses the myriad ways in which gang style exists as the medium of meaning for both gang members and the probation officers to whom they must report.

Other pieces of cultural criminology devoted to an exploration of subcultural style, such as Lyng and Bracey's (1995) document the dynamic interplay between subcultural resistance and corporate marketing strategies. Tracing the development of "one percenter" style from an acutely class-conscious form of cultural resistance to a marketable commodity over thirty years, Lyng and Bracey reveal much about lifestyle fetishism, the media and the transpraxis of fugitive style.[5]

Other studies have focused on how "mass culture" or "common culture" is recast as crime. Cultural criminologists have recognised that the criminalisation of everyday life is a cultural enterprise of the powerful and must be investigated as such (Ferrell and Sanders 1995, 7). Presdee's (2000) analysis of carnival desire and the sensualness of wickedness sheds much light on how our everyday responses to late modernity come to be defined as criminal. Analogising mediated crime to the board game Monopoly, Presdee examines the way in which crime, like monopoly capitalism, is dehistoricised, whitewashed, and transmogrified into mass-marketed pleasure. Citing a range of examples from internet bondage sites and arson to racing stolen cars and raving, Presdee explores the contradictions and irrationality of a commodity oriented society from which criminalised culture emanates.

Critiques

Cultural criminology has borne many slings and arrows, more so than almost any other of the critical criminologies in the last few years, save perhaps some of the feminist orientations. This, however, should not be surprising, for an orientation which so openly and defiantly proclaims its distance from the epistemological canon should really expect no less. However, what is somewhat surprising is the lack of scholarly ingenuity and creativity on the part of most of the critics. Most of the critiques levelled against cultural criminology are at least a generation old—many in fact are the same as (or at least very similar to) those directed at earlier critical criminologies. While to say that they should never have been salvaged from the academic scrap heap may be somewhat unfair, to suggest that they carry great merit or heuristic value would be unduly kind. Some of these critiques point to alleged methodological shortcomings, though most focus on epistemological matters and substantive content.

Worth Counting

Much of cultural criminology's alleged methodological flaws are the same as those said to afflict qualitative research methodologies in general. Among cultural criminology's most frequently cited of foibles are its idiosyncratic approach and the blatant violation of the "scientific method," particularly the failure of researchers to remain neutral and detached. Unlike many positivists, and even some traditional ethnographers, cultural criminologists do not embrace the academically convenient (and anachronistic) fallacy of scientific objectivity (Polsky 1970; Adler and Adler 1998; Kane 2004). Instead, celebrating a plurality of traditions, most embrace the outsiders' methodologies as useful tools for exploring difference and for offering resistance to dominant paradigms precisely because they do not rely upon hegemonic tools of order specified by state funding agencies, criminal justice organisations and indeed the prevailing conventions of "mainstream journal-article sociology" (Ferrell and Hamm 1998, 5). Cultural criminology's qualitative approaches facilitate the exploration of human experience in a rich and multifaceted manner. Ethnographic studies in particular present informed testimony from the heart of experience; tangible, authentic accounts from the intersections of the cultural and the criminal. Rather than a hindrance to the method, immersion and investment in the enterprise is evidence of liberation. Indeed it can be argued that criticisms of the cultural criminology's methods are in fact means of reasserting orthodoxy and resisting change. Such criticisms function to preserve the very types of dominant viewpoints that cultural criminology questions (Muzzatti and Samarco 2006).

Intellectual Politics

As in the case of its methodologies, cultural criminology has come in for a good deal of criticism for its intellectual politics—or lack thereof—depending on the critic. Cultural criminology has been critiqued by proponents of mainstream criminology as well as some critical criminologists. At the first level of approximation cultural criminology is frequently criticised for prioritising the aesthetic. While it's true that cultural criminology is particularly attendant to the style, argot, imagery and symbolic displays of crime and its control, this type of engagement does not inherently constitute a "decorative criminology" of voyeurism or self-indulgence (Ferrell et al. 2004, 7). To be certain, cultural criminology's engagement with high profile crime and criminalisation campaigns is not a criminology of "nuts, sluts and perverts" and "the exotic, the erotic and the neurotic" (Liazos 1972; Adler and Adler 2003). These critiques incorrectly equate style with a lack of substance. Because the mediated reality of crime is fundamentally a political endeavour cultural criminology's engagement with these actors, texts and processes can be seen as a retaliatory strike in the culture wars. Cultural criminology offers an avenue for intellectual resistance and self-defence against conventional constructions of crime and prescriptions for control. Far from being "apolitical," it is a politically attuned strategy capable of revealing the subtle and insidious ways in which control is exercised and inequality reproduced.

Limitations and New Directions

The past few years have seen tremendous growth in the scope and quantity of cultural criminology pieces. For example, chapters devoted to cultural criminology have begun to appear in criminological theory texts, deviance collections, and anthologies such as this one. Similarly, sessions on cultural criminology are becoming regular (and popular) fixtures at major sociology and criminology conferences. So too, the publication of edited collections such as *Cultural Criminology Unleashed*, the launch of new journals such as *Crime, Media, Culture*, and special editions of established journals such as *Theoretical Criminology* devoted to the works of cultural criminology all attest to this growing orientation.

Despite its growth and increased influence, some criminologists, even some critical criminologists are leery that the edifice of cultural criminology may be a house of cards—an emerging paradigm built upon (the admittedly thorough and creative) examination of rather trivial matters; Marilyn Manson (or some other profane "artist of the week"), tattoo artists, comic books, avant garde photography, crime-reality shows and petty vandalism. Even if one were to ignore the value judgement which informs such a critique (i.e., that there are some serious crimes that warrant scholarly attention, and others that are not as worthy of scrutiny) and leave it unproblematised, directing such an attack against cultural criminology is somewhat unwarranted. While it is true that a portion of the scholarship in this area has been devoted to the study of youth, popular and subcultural formations, a sizable and growing segment is attendant to criminology of corporations, the state and globalisation. Recently, cultural criminologists have produced studies on genocide (Morrison 2004), corporate crime (Ferrell 2003) and terrorism (Jenkins 2003; Hamm 2004; Rothe and Muzzatti 2004). Cultural criminology's continued growth and development is in part contingent upon continued engagement with the intersecting spheres of dominant criminological paradigms, mediated realities and public understandings of crime and justice, and its ability to broaden both the subject matter, as well as the mode of inquiry.

Notes

1. In his piece on the criminology of boredom Ferrell (2004) writes that illicit fieldwork facilitates the embrace of the moment.
2. More so than traditional media analysis, which while useful can easily fall victim to "forces of quantification" which pervade mainstream criminology, such as Qualrus.
3. RaHoWa, Sudden Impact, the 4 Skins, No Remorse, and Vengeance are among the more frequently cited examples. See Hamm 1993 and Hamm 1995.
4. See Dennis R. Martin's "The Music of Murder," *ACJS Today* (November/December 1993).
5. In light of the explosion of interest in motorcycling and the creation/lionisation

of heavy metal icons such as Jesse James and the Tuttles, this piece is perhaps more relevant today than when it was written more than a decade ago.

References

Adler, P. A., and P. Adler. 1998. "Moving Backward." Pp. xii–xvi in J. Ferrell and M. S. Hamm, eds., *Ethnography at the Edge: Crime, Deviance, and Field Research.* Boston: Northeastern University Press.

———, eds. 2003. *Constructions of Deviance: Social Power, Context, and Interaction.* 4th ed. Belmont, CA: Thomson/Wadsworth.

Barak, G., ed. 1994a. *Media, Process, and the Social Construction of Crime.* New York: Garland Publishing.

———. 1994b. "Newsmaking Criminology: Reflections on the Media, Intellectuals, and Crime." Pp. 237–64 in G. Barak, ed., *Media, Process, and the Social Construction of Crime.* New York: Garland Publishing.

Becker, H. S., ed. 1963. *The Other Side: Perspectives on Deviance.* Chicago: University of Chicago Press.

———. 1964. *Outsiders: Studies in the Sociology of Deviance.* New York: The Free Press.

Ben-Yehuda, N. 1990. *The Politics of Morality and Deviance: Moral Panics, Drug Abuse, Deviant Science and Reverse Stigmatization.* Albany: State University of New York Press.

Berry, B. 1999. *Social Rage: Emotion and Cultural Conflict.* New York: Garland Publishing, Inc.

Best, J., ed. 1989. *Images of Issues.* New York: Aldine de Gruyter.

Brake, M. 1980. *The Sociology of Youth Culture and Youth Subculture.* London: Routledge and Kegan Paul.

Chermak, S. 1994. "Crime in the News Media: A Refined Understanding of How Crime Becomes News." Pp. 95–129 in G. Barak, ed., *Media, Process, and the Social Construction of Crime.* New York: Garland Publishing.

Cohen, A. K. 1955. *Delinquent Boys: The Culture of the Gang.* New York: The Free Press.

Cohen, S., ed. 1971. *Images of Deviance.* Harmondsworth: Penguin Books.

———. 1972. *Folk Devils and Moral Panics: The Creation of the Mods and Rockers.* Oxford: Basil Blackwell.

———. 1988. *Against Criminology.* New Bruswick, NJ: Transaction.

Cohen, S., and L. Taylor. 1978. *Escape Attempts: The Theory and Practice of Resistance to Everyday Life.* New York, NY: Penguin Books.

Cohen, S., and J. Young, eds. 1973. *The Manufacture of News.* Beverley Hills: Sage Publications.

DiCristina, B. 1995. *Method in Criminology: A Philosophical Primer.* New York: Harrow and Heston Publishers.

Donovan, P. 2002. "Crime Legends in a New Medium: Fact, Fiction and Loss of Authority." *Theoretical Criminology* 6, no. 2: 189–215.

Douglas, J. D., ed. 1970. *Observations of Deviance.* New York: Random House.

Downes, D., and P. Rock. 1998. *Understanding Deviance: A Guide to the Sociology of Crime and Rule Breaking*. 3rd ed. New York: Oxford University Press.

Doyle, A. 2003. *Arresting Images: Crime and Policing in Front of the Television Camera*. University of Toronto Press.

Fenwick, M. 2004. "New Directions in Cultural Criminology." *Theoretical Criminology* 8, no. 3: 377–86.

Ferrell, J. 1993. *Crimes of Style: Urban Graffiti and the Politics of Criminality*. New York: Garland.

———. 1994. "Confronting the Agenda of Authority: Critical Criminology, Anarchism and Urban Graffiti." Pp. 161–78 in G. Barak, ed., *Varieties of Criminology*. New York: Praeger.

———. 1995. "Culture, Crime and Cultural Criminology." *Journal of Criminal Justice and Popular Culture* 3, no. 2: 25–42.

———. 1996. *Crimes of Style: Urban Graffiti and the Politics of Criminality*. Boston: Northeastern University Press.

———. 1997. "Criminological Verstehen: Inside the Immediacy of Crime." *Justice Quarterly* 14, no. 1: 2–23.

———. 1998. "Criminalizing Popular Culture." Pp. 71–84 in F. Bailey and D. Hale, eds., *Popular Culture, Crime and Justice*. Belmont, CA: West/Wadsworth Publishing Co.

———, ed. 1998. *Ethnography at the Edge: Crime, Deviance, and Field Research*. Boston: Northeastern University Press.

———. 1999. "Anarchist Criminology and Social Justice." Pp. 93–108 in B. Arrigo, ed., *Social Justice—Criminal Justice: The Maturation of Critical Theory in Law, Crime and Deviance*. Belmont, CA: Wadsworth Publishing Co.

———. 2000. "Dancing Apart: Youth, Criminal Justice, and Juvenile Justice." Pp. 171–82 in the Criminal Justice Collective of Northern Arizona University, *Investigating Difference: Human and Cultural Relations in Criminal Justice*. Needham Heights, MA: Allyn and Bacon.

———. 2003. "Speed Kills." *Critical Criminology* 11, no. 3: 185–98.

———. 2004. "Boredom, Crime and Criminology." *Theoretical Criminology* 8, no. 3: 287–302.

Ferrell, J., and M. S. Hamm. 1994, May/June. "Rap, Cops and Crime: Clarifying the "Cop Killer" Controversy." *ACJS Today*: 1, 2, 29.

Ferrell, J., K. Hayward, W. Morrison, and M. Presdee, eds. 2004. *Cultural Criminology Unleashed*. London: Glasshouse Press.

Ferrell, J., and C. Sanders, eds. 1995. *Cultural Criminology*. Boston: Northeastern University Press.

Ferrell, J., and N. Websdale. 1999. *Making Trouble: Cultural Constructions of Crime, Deviance and Control*. New York: Aldine de Gruyter.

Fishman, M. 1978. "Crime Waves as Ideology." *Social Problems* 25: 531–43.

Fishman, M., and G. Cavender, eds. 1998. *Entertaining Crime: Television Reality Programs*. New York: Aldine de Gruyter.

Goode, E. 1994. *Drugs in American Society*. 4th ed. New York: McGraw Hill.

Goode, E., and N. Ben-Yehuda. 1994. *Moral Panics: The Social Construction of Deviance*. Oxford: Basil Blackwell.

Gray, H. 1989. "Popular Music as a Social Problem: A Social History of the Claims against Popular Music." In J. Best, ed., *Images of Issues.* New York: Aldine de Gruyter.

Groves, W. B., and G. Newman. 1990. "Criminology and Epistemology: The Case for a Creative Criminology." Pp. 91–112 in D. M. Gottfredson and R. V. Clark, eds., *Policy and Theory in Criminal Justice: Contributions in Honour of Leslie T. Wilkins.* Brookfield: Avebury.

Gusfield, J. R. 1963. *Symbolic Crusade: Status Politics and the American Temperance Movement.* Urbana: University of Illinois Press.

———. 1981. *The Culture of Public Problems: Drinking-driving and the Symbolic Order.* University of Chicago Press.

Hall, S., C. Critcher, T. Jefferson, J. Clarke, and B. Roberts. 1978. *Policing the Crisis: Mugging, the State and Law and Order.* London: Macmillan.

Hamm, M. S. 1993. *American Skinheads: The Criminology and Control of Hate Crime.* Westport, CT: Praeger.

———. 1995. "Hammer of the Gods Revisited: Neo-Nazi Skinheads, Domestic Terrorism and the Rise of the New Protest." Pp. 190–212 in J. Ferrell and C. Sanders, eds., *Cultural Criminology.* Boston: Northeastern University Press.

———. 2004. "Apocalyptic Violence: The Seduction of Terrorist Subcultures." *Theoretical Criminology*, 8, no. 3 (August): 323–39.

Hayward, K. J., and J. Young. 2004. "Cultural Criminology: Some Notes on the Script." *Theoretical Criminology* 8, no. 3: 259–73.

Hebdige, D. 1979. *Subculture: The Meaning of Style.* London: Routledge

Henry, S. 1994. "Newsmaking Criminology as Replacement Discourse." Pp. 287–318 in G. Barak, ed., *Media, Process, and the Social Construction of Crime.* New York: Garland Publishing.

Hollywood, B. 1997. "Dancing in the Dark: Ecstasy, the Dance Culture and Moral Panic." *Critical Criminology* 8, no. 1: 62–77.

Irwin, J. 1973. "Surfing: The Natural History of the Urban Scene." *Urban Life and Culture* 2, no. 2: 131–60.

———. 1977. *Scenes.* Beverly Hills: Sage Publications.

Jenkins, P. 1994. *Using Murder: The Social Construction of Serial Homicide.* New York: Aldine de Gruyter.

———. 2003. *Images of Terror: What We Can and Can't Know about Terrorism.* New York: Aldine de Gruyter.

Kane, S. C. 2004. "The Unconventional Methods of Cultural Criminology." *Theoretical Criminology* 8, no. 3: 303–21.

Kappeler, V., M. Blumberg, and G. W. Potter. 2000. *The Mythology of Crime and Criminal Justice.* 3rd ed. Prospect Heights: Waveland Press.

Kidd-Hewitt, D. 1995. "Crime and the Media: A Criminological Perspective." In D. Kidd-Hewitt and R. Osborne, eds., *Crime and the Media: The Post-modern Spectacle.* East Haven, CT: Pluto Press.

Kidd-Hewitt, D., and R. Osborne, eds. 1995. *Crime and the Media: The Post-modern Spectacle.* East Haven, CT: Pluto Press.

Killingbeck, D. 2001. "The Role of Television News in the Construction of School Violence as a "Moral Panic." *Journal of Criminal Justice and Popular Culture* 8, no. 3: 186–202.

Lemert, E. 1951. *Social Pathology: A Systematic Approach to the Theory of Sociopathic Behavior.* New York: The McGraw Hill Book Company.
———. 1967. *Human Deviance, Social Problems and Social Control.* 2nd ed. Englewood Cliffs, NJ: Prentice Hall.
Liazos, A. 1972. "The Poverty of the Sociology of Deviance: Nuts, Sluts and Perverts." *Social Problems* 20: 103–20.
Lyng, S. 1998. "Dangerous Methods: Risk Taking and the Research Process." Pp. 221–51 in J. Ferrell and M. S. Hamm, eds., *Ethnography at the Edge: Crime, Deviance, and Field Research.* Boston: Northeastern University Press.
———. 2004. "Crime, Edgework and Corporeal Transaction." *Theoretical Criminology* 8, no. 3: 359–75.
Lyng, S., and M. L. Bracey. 1995. "Squaring the One Percent: Biker Style and the Selling of Cultural Resistance." Pp. 235–76 in J. Ferrell and C. Sanders, *Cultural Criminology.* Boston: Northeastern University Press.
Manning, P. K. 1998. "Media Loops." Pp. 25–39 in F. Bailey and D. Hale, eds., *Popular Culture, Crime and Justice.* Belmont, CA: West/Wadsworth Publishing Co.
McRobbie, A. 1995. "Folk Devils Fight Back." Pp. 249–58 in S. Caffrey and G. Mundy, eds., *The Sociology of Crime and Deviance: Selected Issues.* Avon, UK: Bath Press.
Miller, J. A. 1995. "Struggles over the Symbolic: Gang Style and the Meanings of Social Control." Pp. 213–34 in J. Ferrell and C. Sanders, eds., *Cultural Criminology.* Boston: Northeastern University Press.
Morrison, W. 2004. "Reflections with Memories: Everyday Photography Capturing Genocide." *Theoretical Criminology* 8, no. 3: 341–58.
Muzzatti, S. L. 1996. "The Urban Speed Gang: An Exploration of Motorcycle-youth Culture." Pp. 354–70 in N. Herman, ed., *Deviance: A Symbolic Interactionist Approach.* New York: General Hall Publishers.
———. 2002. "Anarchy against the Discipline." Pp. 9–13 in M. Schwartz and M. O. Maume, eds., *Teaching the Sociology of Deviance.* 5th ed. Washington, DC: American Sociological Association.
———. 2004. "Criminalising Marginality and Resistance: Marilyn Manson, Columbine and Cultural Criminology." Pp. 143–53 in J. Ferrell et al., eds., *Cultural Criminology Unleashed.* London: Cavendish/Glasshouse.
Muzzatti, S. L., and V. Samarco, eds. 2006. *Reflections from the Wrong Side of the Tracks: Class, Identity, and the Working Class Experience.* Lanham, MD: Rowman and Littlefield Publishers Inc.
Pfohl, S. J. 1985. *Images of Deviance and Social Control: Sociological Perspectives.* New York: McGraw Hill.
Polsky, N. 1970. "The Hustler." Pp. 218–36 in J. D. Douglas, ed., *Observations of Deviance.* New York: Random House.
Potter, G. W., and V. Kappeler. 1998. *Constructing Crime: Perspectives on Making News and Social Problems.* Prospect Heights: Waveland Press.
Presdee, M. 2000. *Cultural Criminolology and the Carnival of Crime.* London: Routledge.
———. 2004. "Cultural Criminology: The Long and Winding Road." *Theoretical Criminology* 8, no. 3: 275–85.

Presdee, M., and G. Carter. 2000. "From Carnival to the Carnival of Crime." Pp. 31–56 in M. Presdee, ed., *Cultural Criminolology and the Carnival of Crime*. London: Routledge.

Quinney, R. 1970. *The Social Reality of Crime*. Toronto: Little, Brown and Company Canada Ltd.

Rock, P. 1973. "News as Eternal Recurrence." Pp. 73–80 in S. Cohen and J. Young, eds., *The Manufacture of News*. Beverley Hills: Sage Publications.

Ross, J. I. 1998. "The Role of the Media in the Creation of Public Police Violence." Pp. 100–110 in F. Bailey and D. Hale, eds., *Popular Culture, Crime and Justice*. Belmont, CA: Wadsworth Publishing Company.

Rothe, D., and S. L. Muzzatti. 2004. "Enemies Everywhere: Terrorism, Moral Panic and U.S. Civil Society." *Critical Criminology* 12, no. 3: 327–50.

Sasson, T. 1995. *Crime Talk: How Citizens Construct a Social Problem*. New York: Aldine de Gruyter.

Schiller, H. I. 1989. *Culture Inc.: The Corporate Takeover of Public Expression*. New York: Oxford University Press.

Surette, R. 1998. *Media, Crime, and Criminal Justice: Images and Realities*. 2nd ed. Belmont, CA: Wadsworth Publishing Company.

Sutherland. 1950. "The Sexual Psychopath Laws." *Journal of Criminal Law and Criminology* 40 (January–February): 543–54.

Tannenbuam, F. 1938. *Crime and the Community*. New York: Ginn.

Taylor, I., P. Walton, and J. Young. 1973. *The New Criminology: For a Social Theory of Deviance*. London: Routledge and Kegan Paul.

Tifft, L., and D. Sullivan. 1980. *The Struggle to Be Human: Crime, Criminology and Anarchism*. Orkney, UK: Cienfuegos Press.

Visano, L. A. 1998. *Crime and Culture: Refining the Traditions*. Toronto: Canadian Scholars' Press, Inc.

Walton, P. 1998. "Big Science: Dystopia and Utopia—Establishment and New Criminology Revisited." Pp. 1–13 in P. Walton and J. Young, eds., *The New Criminology Revisited*. New York: St. Martin's Press.

Welch, M., J. Sassi, and A. McDonough. 2002. "Advances in Critical Cultural Criminology: An Analysis of Reactions to Avant-garde Flag Art." *Critical Criminology* 11, no. 1: 1–20.

Williams, J. 1994. "Comics: A Tool of Subversion?" *Journal of Criminal Justice and Popular Culture* 2, no. 6: 129–46.

Willis, P., ed. 1978. *Profane Culture*. London: Routledge and Kegan Paul.

———. 1977. *Learning to Labor: How Working Class Kids Get Working Class Jobs*. New York: Columbia University Press.

Young, J. 1971. "The Role of the Police as Amplifiers of Deviance: Negotiators of Drug Control as Seen in Notting Hill." Pp. 27–61 in S. Cohen, ed., *Images of Deviance*. Harmondsworth: Penguin Books.

4

Emotionality, Rationality, and Restorative Justice

Kimberly J. Cook and Chris Powell

Emotions and Restorative Justice

In this chapter, we begin by analysing observations of diversionary conferences in Australia. While there, Cook observed twelve conferences and interviewed sixteen coordinators/administrators in Tasmania, Queensland, South Australia, the Australian Capital Territory (ACT), Victoria, and the Northern Territory. Daly (2001) summarises the variety of conference schemes in Australia, and while those distinctions are interesting, the focus here is on Cook's observations of restorative justice programs, especially emotional dynamics and bureaucratic pressures affecting diversionary conferences. The final part of this chapter involves a broader discussion of the relationships between restorative justice and more traditional justice practices in regard to emotionalism, rationalism, and social interest.

Restorative justice is a "new paradigm" for thinking about crime and its aftermath (Zehr 1990). Advocates argue that, rather than processing cases through courts, offenders' and victims'[1] needs and interests are better served in a system that encourages their emotional presence, personal "accountability" and collective views on how to repair the acknowledged damage. Rather than emphasising punitive responses to the harms done, a restorative approach intends to concentrate on the apparently damaged relationships. Recognizing that punitive responses often compound the harms, advocates for restorative justice argue that offenders are less likely to reoffend when given the opportunity to make amends for their actions. Advocates claim, therefore, that if crime is about harm then justice should be about healing (Braithwaite 2002).

Courts present an imposing and intimidating setting for the resolution of the harms caused by crime. The ritual space of adjudication in courtrooms takes place within a ritualized language of "rights and responsibilities" as well as "rules and procedures," where various people play ritualized roles such as "judge" and "prosecutor," and so forth. In this sense, the physical location of "justice" is formal, where the emotional injuries arising from crime are often dismissed as irrelevant (Christie 1977) in favour of rationally evaluating the evidence brought to bear on the particular case at hand. Christie (1977) argues that people whose conflicts proceed through courts ultimately lose "ownership" of those conflicts (and outcomes) to lawyers, judges and other decision-makers within the system. What occurs, then, is that the "irrelevant" (perhaps emotional) issues are dismissed as not central to the legal dispute and thus have no place in the rationalized discourse of "justice." The formalized rituals of justice in courts can be disorienting experiences for many participants, who are required to negotiate their problems within an unfamiliar conceptual framework by relying on professionally trained advocates who navigate this foreign land. On the contrary, in theory and to some extent in reality, restorative justice programs generally take place in a less formal setting, where there is reduced (some may say relatively little) emphasis on the procedural rules to be observed by participants, and more emphasis on exploring and resolving the emotional and material injuries of crime (Braithwaite 2002; Ahmed, Harris, Braithwaite, and Braithwaite 2001). Depending on the format used and the facilitator's idiosyncracies, the scripted model (O'Connell, Wachtel and Wachtel 1999) can provide an opportunity for the emotional and material injuries of crime to be at the forefront of concern during a conference.

There are various mechanisms for accomplishing restorative outcomes when crimes are committed. It is beyond the scope of this chapter to summarize all mechanisms, but a few comments are in order. While this approach has been used to varying degrees in Australian jurisdictions and elsewhere, it mainly focuses on conventional crimes committed by young people, as does the research. In particular, when juveniles are criminally processed in Australia (depending on the jurisdiction), it is quite likely that they will be afforded the opportunity to "make amends" by attending a diversionary conference. Relying heavily on the scripted model, the conference typically includes the "offender[s]," the "victim[s]" and their respective supporters, a police officer and/or juvenile case worker, and perhaps community representatives. The conference is normally opened by a facilitator who summarizes the details of the offense, then asks the young person to talk about the event and its consequences. When this happens the young person is generally, though not always, contrite. By recalling the events, and reporting on what the young person believes to be the consequences of these actions, he or she is able to declare himself/herself aware of and accountable to the situation.

The facilitator then asks the victim for his or her perspective, the impact of the offense and how life has been since that event. Depending on the nature of the offense, the victim sometimes becomes quite emotional. Here, victims might cry, plead, and express their continuing fears, embarrassment, and shame associated with being victimized. One example from observed conferences is:

> [T]he victim said that she was shocked and scared when she came home that night from a night evening out to dinner with her daughters to see her new car so damaged. She's a single mother raising three daughters on her own and waited many years to buy a new car. Even though this car is eight years old, it's new to her and she was very proud of it. She could not believe that someone would be so malicious. She was also very scared by the symbolism of the swastika on the pavement. What did it mean? Who was it aimed at? Who would do such a thing to her? She immediately called the police, and then went to the neighbours to find out if they'd seen anything. No one slept well that night due to their fears. When she learned about [the offender's] actions, it was unbelievable to her that he would walk so far [10 kilometres] for vengeance. The damaged car is embarrassing to drive around. She's not proud of the car like she had been.

In this case, clearly, the emotional reaction to the image of the swastika spray-painted on her driveway gave rise to her fear. Yet, emotions are socially constructed (Jaggar 1989), as this instance clearly illustrates. As in many cases of victimization, the injured person conveys an emotion-frame around the experience that invokes socially constructed meanings. Emotions are not just involuntary or irrational responses; they are often companion with our rational knowledge of the world and willful choices made in response to a particular circumstance. Hochschild (1979) uses an example of a bride miserable on her wedding day because her close friends were unable to attend the wedding. The incongruity results from the cultural expectation that the wedding day should be "the happiest day of her life," but the desire to share it with her close friends results in her unhappiness. The rational actor here is understandably unhappy about her friends' absence. In the instances of diversionary conferences, emotional expressions are similarly bound by rational culturally constructed meanings of the crime experience and its attempted resolution, as in this woman's understandable distress at the symbol of hate and other damage done to her property. Culturally constructed rationality, then, provides "scripts" for the expression of emotions.

After hearing from the victim, the facilitator generally asks the young person if he or she has any response to share directly, face to face, with the victim. This is a first opening for the young person to apologize, or express his or her own feelings about the impacts of the offense. The apology, when offered, is usually not heard until the end of the conference. The following is an example of this dynamic; the situation involves two school aged boys having a fight on school property. The aggressor has been charged with a crime and has opted to participate in the conference.

> He reports that he was punished at home, his mum made him hang out laundry and clean his room, and he's been grounded. The facilitator encourages him to think of an apology, but without directly suggesting it. His mother directly suggests he might want to apologize, and the facilitator asks him what he thinks would be the result of an apology. "If I say sorry then he won't have to be scared anymore."

Next, the offenders' and victims' supporters are asked to discuss their experiences of the offense, and eventually the participants develop an agreement as to how the offender can 'fix' the damage caused by his or her actions. Agreements usually involve an apology, community service, monetary compensation, and other forms of restitution to the victims, or in the case of drink-driving experiments to the "community of potential victims." In some situations the "victims" were satisfied with an apology from the offender and nothing more was expected.

It is important to note that prior to the conference the offender has admitted his or her involvement in the offense, and that is not open to question. Restorative justice is not concerned with establishing guilt or innocence, blame or fault, but rather it attempts to provide a forum for healing the injuries that were created as a result of the offense. During these diversionary conferences it is quite common for people to weep, to laugh, to express anger, to forgive, and to show renewed affection for each other. Expressions such as these involve emotional risks, where the participants trust that their feelings will be respectfully received and heard, thus leading to acceptance, understanding, and ultimately healing when it goes well. These gestures of healing and/or cleansing are an important source of the "magic" for the restorative justice approach that courts have neglected. The most commonly documented and discussed emotion associated with the diversionary conferences approach is "shame" (see Braithwaite 2001 for a current review of these findings, and Ahmed et al. 2001 for the latest revisions in shaming theory). These are complex theories and findings, which cannot be fully summarized in this chapter. We are concerned about examining the panoply of emotions, beyond offenders' sense of shame, as they emerge and are negotiated in conferences.

Several concepts are important for restorative justice theory and practice. First, and perhaps most prominent is the issue of "accountability" (Roche 2003; Cook 2006). For advocates and participants, accountability consists of the offender recognizing the damage caused by his or her actions, without necessarily being subject to punitive sanctions. If offending is dehumanizing, then accountability is recognizing such dehumanization and reversing it. By discussing the harms, injuries and other consequences, the victim and offender can regain perspective on each other as people who are connected through a series of events. These events, however damaging, can be repaired when accountability involves a holistic view of the injuries endured by the offender's actions.

Second, is the framing of an "apology." For people to make amends for the harm they caused, they often separate themselves from that action by sincerely apologizing for it. As an act of "grace" an apology is a process whereby the offender communicates to those present that the offense is not the most salient part of her or his identity (Braithwaite and Mugford 1994). It provides the offender a chance to distinguish himself or herself from the offense, and reclaim moral personhood in front of those who have sustained the harms. This, then, also provides an opportunity for the victims to re-connect with the offender on a personal level.

Third, is the dynamic of "voice." The typical court process limits people in how they can voice their perspectives on events that affect their lives. The very strict parameters surrounding the rules of evidence and procedure in criminal trials systematically marginalizes voices of those people most deeply injured by the offenses. With restorative justice, the voices of the offenders, victims, and community are structured into the process and outcomes. It is critical to the success of restorative justice programs that multiple voices be heard. The polyphonic dialogue (Hydle 2001) requires that the voices of the victims, offenders, their respective supporters and the community members present bear equal weight and value in deciding the outcomes and resolutions. This should not imply, however, that each participant is morally defended, as is often the case with mediation programs. Braithwaite and Braithwaite argue that an important advance for diversionary conferences, over mediation, is that the facilitators and participants should not be morally neutral (Ahmed et al. 2001, 58–69).

Masters and Smith (1998) suggest that restorative justice programs such as those in Australia actively represent "feminine" justice, whereas traditional court-based processes are "masculine" or "rational" justice. Drawing from Gilligan (1982) and Heidensohn (1986), Masters and Smith advocate for an expansion of restorative justice programs in order to honor the emotional experiences of crime. For Masters and Smith, restorative justice is "relational justice" more likely to produce satisfying outcomes to the participants. "In theory and practice, reintegrative shaming is contextual, immediate and relational, rather than universalist, remote, and abstract" (Masters and Smith 1998, 14). In fact, they declare boldly that "viewed in this light, reintegrative shaming is perhaps the first feminist criminological theory" (20). There are feminist criminologists who would certainly dispute the point, however (i.e., Daly 2002). Nonetheless, diversionary conferences provide a venue for people to share their feelings and repair the emotional and material damage done. The dynamics of these emotional processes are a main theme of this chapter. We explore this issue employing feminist and sociological theory of emotions, and our own observations of diversionary conferences in Australia.

Susan Drummond (1997) argues that restorative justice programs provide a "just and loving gaze" (cited in Ahmed et al. 2001, 58). Braithwaite and Braithwaite believe that restorative justice conferencing is far more 'benevolent' than traditional court proceedings. This is true across all cultural and ethnic communities, from complex modern Western societies such as Australia, and complex Eastern societies such as Japan, to remote indigenous communities in Canada and throughout the world (Ahmed et al. 2001). They argue that the "genius of restorative circles is their collective emotional dynamics" (59). Because conferences are opportunities for participants to stake a moral claim about the wrongdoing, the process can reinforce the morality of right and wrong, moral and immoral, just and unjust actions, within and across multiple cultural contexts. This sometimes requires a relatively passionate strategy for communicating to the "offender" who has agreed to participate in the conference. Thus, "they are not about defusing emotion but about creating ritual spaces into which emotion can be infused, where right and wrong can be discussed by concerned and affected citizens" (Ahmed et al. 2001, 69).

Emotion work and feeling rules dictate the ritual space for discussions of moral behavior (Hochschild 1979; 1983). Hochschild writes that people obey certain cultural rules for their interactions that are *appropriate to the situation* (1979, 552). These feeling rules are socially constructed, evaluated for their propriety, and supported (or rejected) depending on the social circumstances. A feeling rule "delineates a zone within which one has permission to be free of worry, guilt, or shame with regard to the situated feeling" (Hochschild 1979, 565). When a conference facilitator opens the proceedings he or she provides what Hochschild refers to as the "framing rules" that articulate the appropriate conduct for the proceedings and also illuminates some foundational expectations for the group. Indeed, the process of preparing for the conference is one of articulating such framing rules. These framing rules convey a particular ideological value system upon which a degree of consensus must be granted. For example, a diversionary conference for a young person who had shoplifted candy (A$3.41) on Easter weekend, during when the framing rules declared the behaviour a *crime* (supported by statute, of course), the young person tried to reframe the situation for himself and others to understand, declaring that he did it because he was "heaps hungry" since he didn't follow his mother's advice to eat lunch before venturing out. The ideological value system that was reinforced in this particular conference was that of corporate interest and private profit. Interestingly, in this case, the seemingly *rational* choice of the corporation to send two representatives to the conference costing hundreds of dollars in wages, is questioned by the fact that the stolen merchandise was not actually lost to the store, but confiscated and returned to the store shelves unopened.

An important feeling rule in the process of diversionary conferences, of course, is the ritual of apologizing. It is, as Hochschild points out, "an exchange of display acts" (1979, 568). When an offender[2] offers such an apology in a conference that statement is "I exchange my apology to you for your understanding, acceptance, and/or forgiveness." By expressing contrition and seeking emotional understanding the offender must take on board for himself or herself the definition of the situation as expressed by the victim and her or his supporters. For example, the shoplifting offender in the previous example heard the following from the loss prevention specialist and store manager:

> She asks [offender] to realize that a large company like [hers] is just as affected by shoplifting as a small company in the following ways: sales are affected, profits are reduced, staff members are paid less, shareholders don't make as much, and the price of goods increases. The police officer present at the conference asks for the statistics specific to their store. The store manager says that in a six month period they lose between A$80,000 and $100,000 mostly because of shoplifting. The police officer says that everyone is affected because they're paying higher prices for items they buy at that store, and that much money would pay the wages for at least four people. [Offender] looks around the room to see who's looking at him, he's open-faced, listening and agreeing. The loss prevention specialist goes on to tell him that stores "have to install security systems and without theft these wouldn't be necessary and goods wouldn't be so expensive." Eventually the offender says, "I'm sorry I stole from your store and I won't do it again," in an unsure tone of voice. The store manager says that from her perspective, based on what she's seen in the conference and that his attitude is a lot better than before, "That apology would be enough." The offender is visibly pleased, relieved, and proud of himself (he sits a little taller) for being here and doing the right thing. Everyone points out that his attitude of cooperation makes a huge difference in how they see him now.

The feeling rules were understood by all participants in this conference, the framing of the process was unchallenged, and the "exchange display" was readily accepted. Of course, this conference illuminates the ideological framework of respect for corporate interests and the economic *need* to prevent shoplifting. Thus the broader socioeconomic interests are conflated with the specific offender and victim interests. The specific emotional object lesson here combines *shoplifting is wrong* because corporate interests prevail.

When these feeling rules are contested by participants, however, the emotional dynamics are fragile. Participants enter the diversionary conferences having been instructed in the typical process and therefore the feeling rules are outlined: victims feel "injured," offenders feel responsible and (hopefully) contrite, supporters feel concerned on behalf of their respective parties, and facilitators feel empowered to broker a resolution. In one conference, the young offender was a teenaged boy being charged with assault on a four-year-old neighbour. The four-year-old (Daniel) was present, along with his older brother and father. The *assault* was an unfortunate consequence of a conflict between the offender and the victim's older brother, which everyone present recognized as an *accident.*

> The facilitator asks Daniel, "How did you feel when Johnny hurt you?" to which Daniel replied "I was scared." His father articulates for him that he was scared, and shaking because he doesn't like police and the ambulance crew scared him, too. The confusion of the situation was scary for four-year-old Daniel, as it was for his father because he arrived to see the ambulance there and he didn't know who was hurt or how badly. He was not angry, however, because he knew that Johnny didn't mean to hurt Daniel. The facilitator points out that Daniel's father is very forgiving and how rare that is.

In this case, the young offender offered an apology immediately upon entering the room and then again during the conference. Each time, the father of the injured boy graciously accepted the apology and his concern was to ensure that the two families could become good neighbours again.

On the other hand, there are times when the victim's injury extends well-beyond that inflicted by the offender. The following example was the result of two high school aged boys (Jeremy and Thomas) engaged in a difficult relationship during their summer holidays. The conflict had been going on for some weeks, when one (Jeremy) eventually exploded and threatened to do violence to him directly and to "fuck" the other's mother. In this situation, the victims were asked how it affected them:

> Thomas was very afraid that Jeremy would follow through on the threats to burn down his family's house and rape his mother. At this point in the confer-

> ence, Thomas's mother indicates that she has been raped before and that her son knows it, and he's very concerned about her well-being and never wants to see her hurting, so this particular threat was especially scary. Plus, she said, "I have cancer and he's very worried about me anyway." At this point, Jeremy started to sob and it appeared that he was unfamiliar with these aspects of Thomas's life. The facilitator then asks Jeremy how he felt about the way his behaviour impacted the others, he said he felt bad about that, and realizes he made a stupid mistake when he threatened them.

It is clear that these broader contextual concerns would likely not have been revealed in an ordinary court proceeding. An adept and emotionally aware facilitator can allow these details to come to light while not disrupting the aim of the conference.

In another instance, however, the young person came to the conference after having been kicked out of his home, being intensely angry with his family, especially his mother. The young person, Clive, was charged with vandalism to the school where he had gone to escort two girls home from a party. When his mother is asked how her son's actions affected her, she claims the status of victim:

> Clive's mother is next asked what she thinks would be a good agreement for Clive, and she yells, "I feel like I'm a victim in this, BIG TIME, and that simply paying for the broken window is not enough for him. I work in a school and I know how they scrounge for money, I'd like to see him do some community service work at the school." Clive explodes at his mother at this point and says, "No way! You shut up, just keep quiet, just let me pay for it, I won't do community service." He is very angry at his mother and deeply resents her input in this matter: "It's not up to her to make these choices for me!"

At this point, the community representative, Terry, stepped in to smooth out the situation between Clive and his mother. He successfully defuses the situation by explaining the process to Clive that these are just suggestions and he, Clive, can refuse to do them if he wishes. Later in this conference, it is revealed that Clive's mother had recently suffered a minor stroke and was frail in her health and that Clive's lifelong problem with ADD has been a difficult burden for her. Clive rejects that label, however, and declares, "ADD is just a label, it's just an excuse," to which the facilitator replied, "Clive, you're just not getting it, are you?" A recalcitrant offender, such as Clive, is a frustration to the diversionary conference process. Clive admitted breaking the window, and was willing to "pay for it" but he was not willing to accept the "ADD label" or the insistence that he perform community service. In the end, this conference resulted in a signed agreement. But, Clive tore out of the room in tears, and later it was discovered that his copy of the agreement was ripped up and discarded on the floor outside the conference room.

Supporters of victims may engage with the broader social narratives of injury and harm endured by the victim in an attempt to display their concern. In the case of the boy who'd walked 10 kilometres on a hot summer day to spray paint a classmate's private property with a swastika as previously mentioned, a male neighbour attended to support the woman whose property was damaged.

> Stephen, the neighbour and friend, says that he knows how the victim feels. After all, she's a single mother raising three daughters on her own. "Four women in the same house experiencing this, it must have felt pretty defenceless."

He took this as an opportunity to demonstrate his good-neighbour masculinity and said in the conference that, as a man, he felt especially responsible to help them out in times of need because they were "on their own."

Ultimately, then, the feeling rules typically employed revolve around conventional (and implicitly conservative) social understandings of *good order* and *morality*. Advocates of restorative justice would postulate that providing opportunities for the articulation of feeling rules enables broader and deeper understanding of a specific situation to emerge. They might further argue that this exemplifies the differences between the purely clinical and cold world of formal legalism compared with the humanist and much warmer world of restorative justice. However, the fact remains that feeling rules are inevitably harnessed to common sense and hence fundamentally conservative versions of morality. Restorative justice bolsters rather than challenges the interests which lie behind this *morality*.

Rationality and Rationalization of Restorative Justice[3]

Restorative justice programs are becoming increasingly rationalized under the rubric of progressive reform. The family group conferences that began in New Zealand in the late 1980s were proclaimed to be an adaptation of Maori customary practice (Maxwell and Morris 1993). With a revised version spreading to Australia in the early 1990s, increased formalism emerged (Daly 2002) in terms of research programs just as ReIntegrative Shaming Experiments (RISE) (Sherman and Strang 1997) and South Australian Juvenile Justice (SAJJ) (Daly 2001) as well as in official practice and passage of state statutes.

In important ways, rationalized restorative justice is quite different from the theoretical conceptualizations developed by scholars and early activists. First, while restorative justice allows for the expression of remorse, regret, and apologies, the reality is that offenders are informed that these expressions are an anticipated element of the process, thereby tilling the soil for apologies that may be utilitarian rather than sincerely expressive. Second, while the theory predicts that once *shamed* the participants would be successfully reintegrated (Ahmed et al. 2001) in the community, a significant number of young people return to conferencing as a result of continuing law violations. Third, shaming theory is intended to be limited to shaming the offender, while in reality parents of the young person often express feelings of themselves being shamed (Prichard 2002). Fourth, in theory, reintegrative shaming is supposed to break down the obstacles between participants, it sometimes (and probably unintentionally) builds higher barriers. Regrettably, emotion becomes a rationally elicited product wheeled out to suit stage-managed circumstances.

Finally, while restorative justice may fit the outlines suggested by Nils Christie (1977) in theory, in practice it is becoming an approach that "steals" the events from the participants, as it becomes increasingly bureaucratized. Some of the restorative justice conferences observed involved *community representatives* who were intended to represent the community interest in the outcome of the conference. Community representatives were added to the conference process during the drink-driving experiments in Canberra in the early 1990s (Mugford, personal communication, 2001). The intent was to provide a voice for the potential victims of those intoxicated drivers arrested but who had not yet injured anyone. Community representatives volunteer to attend conferences and participate in developing agreements, even though they themselves are not directly impacted by the events being discussed. Facilitators, on the other hand, are not supposed to represent any one person in particular, but rather have the role of being moral agents encouraging shame and accountability of the offender while also serving victims' needs. Police officers, when they are not facilitators, are present to represent the state, which the young offender would have to confront in court should the diversionary conference fail. Therefore, community representatives, police officers, and facilitators take "ownership" of a portion of the problems from the direct participants. For example, as seen in the shoplifting case, it is routine in South Australia to inform the offender of the statutory trajectory of the law:

> The police officer says to the offender, "We work really hard here to keep people out of court, and since you've had the informal and formal cautions and now the family conference, and another family conference before this, next time

> it's off to court. There you'll have a conviction and a criminal record following you around for the rest of your life. Do you know what that might mean for your future?" The offender listens and he knows the *right* answer: "I won't get jobs and I won't be able to travel so freely." This is a very structural moment in the conference. The police officer is reading the law to the offender, in uniform, and with the authority of the state behind him. This highlights the inequality between these two people, and it highlights that the police are advocates for the victim's interests, in this case, the corporate interest of a large discount store. The offender's mother stays quiet and looks at the floor. The police officer says, "I don't want to see you again; I don't want to see your name come across my desk, because next time I won't be able to do anything else but send this to court. We're all here to help you, we just need to say it's up to you at this point."

In this case, it was clear this young person was *appropriately deferential* to the process and to the participants, thereby resulting in a relatively clear-cut outcome for him. Typical outcome agreements involve an apology, monetary compensation when appropriate, community service, and/or other gestures of remorse (in the ACT, for example, offenders may be encouraged to donate blood, which is a residual of the drink-driving experiments). The offender agrees, the victim approves, but the events, outcomes, and process are "owned" by the state, as illustrated when the facilitator (or police officer) is required to authorize it, and when failure to satisfy the agreement results in the case being referred to court regardless of the victim's desire or extenuating circumstances. Facilitators work very hard to get the "right" outcomes in conferences, and sometimes are personally distraught when the outcomes do not include what the facilitators believe to be fair and just resolutions. In another situation reported elsewhere (Cook and Powell 2003), it was clear that the young person, Roy, had a *phoney choice* (Cohen 1985) in terms of the outcomes and his participation. No agreement was possible for Roy because the facilitator had already established what she deemed the *appropriate* outcome for Roy, which was to be sent away to a residential facility that would treat him for his petrol sniffing problem. In her frustration with the extremely difficult situation, the facilitator ended the conference when it became obvious there was an impasse.

The new *experts* in restorative justice programs are the new owners of the conflict when their careers depend on successful outcomes. Facilitators in some jurisdictions also feel institutionalized pressures to *keep the numbers up*. While chatting over lunch with two facilitators in South Australia,

> we got into a discussion about "managerialism" where each facilitator is now required to complete at least sixteen conferences per month, and to dispose of cases within eight weeks. They said that's fair and reasonable in most situations,

> yet it doesn't take into consideration problems that occur through no fault of their own, but make their "numbers" look bad. For instance, if they spend the necessary amount of time to arrange a conference and the offender fails to show up, even after the facilitator has driven 50 kilometres to hold the conference, that's lost time and no conference is recorded. Their numbers suffer. They reported that there is increased pressure to keep the numbers going in order to satisfy the bureaucrats. This is a frustration in the office that is not easily resolved. Also, other material resources are shrinking such as access to vehicles. When much of their work requires them to be on the road, and seven staff sharing three cars, there are limits as to what they can accomplish. In the midst of the "numbers pressure" this adds a level of frustration on an already demanding job.

This overly rationalized approach violates the spirit of a pure restorative justice philosophy. Braithwaite and Mugford (1994) argue that when people keep reoffending, communities must relentlessly provide opportunities for successful reintegration ceremonies. To do otherwise, to outline the statutory trajectory of "three strikes and you're in court," risks alienating young people and diminishing the potential success of restorative justice. From Cook's field notes:

> What I saw repeatedly was that the young person was informed of this linear progression as if it were "etched in stone" by the police officer attending the conference. This is dishonest, though, and young people can sniff out an inconsistency faster than we can type it. Young people know that they have more than one chance to go through family conferencing, and to say there's only one chance violates that young person's right to the truth. What might be better to say to the young person is, "Look, we're going to keep coming back here as long as you keep getting into trouble, we're going to keep giving you chances to fix the problems that you've caused and we're going to keep trying to prevent you from having a conviction on your record. We're here because we care about you and we're not going to give up trying to help you. If you don't want to come back and go through this again, then try not to make mistakes again. We want you to learn from this problem as best you can, and we're trying to help you learn from it."

Analysis and Discussion: McDonaldized and Commoditized Emotions in a Rationalized Setting

In the broader social circumstance of diversionary conferences in Australia, given the increasing need for administrative oversight, conferences themselves run the risk of becoming "judicial happy meals." Citing Mestrovic, Williams writes that "McDonaldized emotions (i.e., bite-sized, pre-packaged, rationally manufactured emotions): a 'happy meal' consumed by the masses . . . is a system designed to avoid 'emotional disorder,' prevent 'loose ends' in emotional exchange, civilize 'wild' arenas of emotional life, and in general to order emotions so that the social world 'hums as smoothly as a well-maintained machine'" (1998, 755). Thus, diversionary conferences can be seen as "ways of escape," which have been rationalized through scripted models and administrative demands to meet quotas. Williams writes that "the McDonaldization of emotions, in short, has been an attempt to make the 'Enlightenment project, therapy, civilisation, and communities all seem predictably "nice" and to create Disneyesque, artificial realms of the authentic'" (1998, 755). Perhaps restorative justice is in danger of becoming another example of assembly line justice, albeit cheaper and engaging the bewigged Ronald McDonald rather than blind Lady Justice.

Students were debating the feasibility of restorative justice programs in a recent class at the University of Southern Maine. One student, Christine Olsen, identified herself as "optimistic" and said that restorative justice is like a field where a flower has been planted; perhaps in ten years that field will be full of beautiful flowers, she hoped. Her point is that the beauty and magic of restorative justice will not emerge overnight, but given time and effective cultivation, the long-range benefits are worth striving for. Another student, David Johnson, was somewhat more skeptical. He pondered that the field of flowers will only be able to grow so long as the planners do not come along, plow the field and pave it for a parking lot. While David appreciated the theory and philosphy of restorative justice programs ("I wish they were around when I was coming through the system!"), he also believes that once the state agents get into the business of rationalizing and orchestrating the programs, their effectiveness, and magic, will erode.

Simply structuring multiple voices into the process will not be enough to break down the institutional obstacles people face in the criminal justice system. The "polyphonic dialogue" of restorative justice (Hydle 2001), might liberate society from the very restrictive legal "monologue" that is the cornerstone of the conventional criminal processing system (Belknap 2001). This polyphonic dialogue is as much an internal dialogue within individuals (at least for these authors) as it is between participants in the restorative justice programs. As observers we must be ever vigilant of the multiple voices in our own hearts and heads, as well as those among the participants in the restorative justice process of "culture in the making" (Hydle 2001, 11).

Restorative justice initiatives aim to deal emotionally with emotional situations, and aim to deal practically with the practical realities of these situations, but do so within a complex bureaucratic setting. As such, they are regulated by a rationalist state that frames restorative justice programs within politically resonant discourses (Braithwaite and Mugford 1994) of rights, responsibilities and system efficiencies. The professionals who do restorative justice work are operating within an employment atmosphere that values their emotional sensitivity while at the same time encourages (and demands) their productivity by establishing a pseudo-quota system where they have to process a specific number of *cases* per month. The "emotional assembly line" that appears to be emerging in some jurisdictions (South Australia, in particular, where this was observed to be most pronounced), is producing emotional outcomes within a rationalized context. These are Fordist economic pressures of cost-efficiency and productivity within a post-Keynesian *kindness* and *ethic of care* framework.

Conclusion

We will draw to a conclusion by recommending that one should adopt a sound dose of skepticism when confronted with the apparent differences between restorative justice and more conventional processes of justice. Undoubtedly, advocates of restorative justice[4] have placed stress on the differences in terms described previously. In response, traditionalists have warned against adopting restorative justice's different procedures. Emotions, they would suggest, are invariably more liable to get out of hand. It is essential that the system should contain and control emotions by guaranteeing a standpoint of aloofness and detachment—indeed of *rationality*. Emotionality panders to victims' and offenders' presumed needs where what should be of more importance is the broader social interest.

First, let's state briefly that as so often we are faced with "straw people" despite the denial of a legitimate place for emotions in the conventional formal system, in fact, emotion plays a significant part in those proceedings. Indeed, the emergence of victim-impact statements specifically represents a recognition of the emotional, though one suspects that for true traditionalists these take a step too far in the direction of "touch-feely-ness." More fundamentally, though, surely at least part of what the ritualistic dimension of court procedures is about is concerned with stirring emotions. The ceremonial element can serve to conjure up a variety of different emotional responses ranging from a more *negative* awesome power of the state, to a more *positive* social consensus on values and morals. Furthermore, formal courts on occasions provide a forum for expression of *high emotion*—people regularly break down, get angry, and even laugh, in conventional courts. Hence, we should on no account assume the formal context to be a haven (however one evaluates it) of pure rationality.

We began by indicating that advocates of restorative justice justify their initiatives by primary reference to offender and victim needs and interests.

The argument was that needs fulfillment demanded an emotional dimension. However, a traditionalist might ask, "In which ways might it be possible to link the needs of any specific victim or offender with a broader social interest?" In conventional terms it seems there is a major problem here emanating from a quite different kind of emphasis. Do we sometimes have to *do justice* by failing to accommodate the needs of individuals? Can justice emerge from a negotiated settlement between needy parties, or rather is it essential for that old iron fist of rationality to oversee the process in the interests of nonparticipants? So, simple questions emerge from the traditional camp: Is restorative justice inevitably neglectful of the broader social interest in favour only of participants' interests? Does it illegitimately assume that the social interest is naturally maximized if individual needs are met or reconciled?

What may or may not pass for social interest, of course, lies at the heart, both of this discussion and of any attempt to analyze the strengths and weaknesses of two ostensibly different systems. Undoubtedly justice is seen as the desirable outcome of the "social interest being maintained." We have seen, however, that restorative justice and traditionalism regards that interest differently, one perhaps more concretely, the other more abstractly. Yet in another sense, restorative justice advocates and traditionalists actually agree on the social interest—that it is to be accomplished by restoration. The argument thus becomes reduced to merely addressing the question of the most effective means. Rarely do restorative justice advocates doubt the good faith of their ideological opponents, though they may well indicate, and of course do, that in pragmatic terms traditionalists have got it all woefully wrong. Both see the point of the criminal law to be about making broad social statements laying down markers as to the various gradations and parameters of acceptable behavior. While one would not anticipate traditionalists promoting anything other than conservative principles, we might expect something a little different (in substance as well as style) from those advocates of restorative justice who appeal to progressivism. The word "restorative" really says it all. In addition, the social interest is to be accomplished by the restoration of the status quo and any radical analyst should recognize that social interest in practice translates to the interests of the powerful and the established. Ultimately, perhaps restorative justice engages emotionality in practice to promote a specific version of rationality, one rooted in common sense and essentially conservative assumptions.

Notes

This chapter was originally presented at the Norwegian Ministry of Justice and Police; Oslo, Norway. The authors would like to thank Ida Hydle for her supportive conversations and organizational work in arranging this presentation. These ideas also provided the basis for a seminar we presented for the Kristiansand Conflict Council,

Kristiansand, Norway. We would like to thank all participants for their insights, and especially Liv Moreland for her generous hospitality, and Nils Christie for his warm hospitality. The research presented was conducted while Cook was a Fulbright Senior Scholar at the Australian National University in Canberra, ACT. Cook expresses gratitude to John Braithwaite, her benefactor while in Australia, and to Stephen and Jane Mugford for their warm support, friendship, and love. We also thank Walter DeKeseredy and Barbara Perry for all their efforts in editing this volume and their enthusiastic support for our work.

1. The phrases "offender and victim" are used with reluctance in this paper. We are mindful of the complex identities people construct for themselves throughout their lives, yet in the proceedings available with restorative justice programs and the rituals of emotional reparations, people come to conferences with these roles already ascribed or acquired. Furthermore, the scripted model of conferencing implicitly and explicitly require participants to accept these labels. When participants reascribe their roles during the conference ("I'm a victim here, too!" says the offender), the emotional dynamics of the process become more contested.

2. Conferences prioritize this aspect of the young person's identity as the most salient characteristic for the "exchange display" at hand. This prioritizing also applies to "victims" whose other characteristics and self-identities are wide-ranging. By applying these identities, of course, the participants are able to draw on culturally constructed discourses of fear, defiance, contrition, and retribution to bolster their claims.

3. We do not mean to imply a binary opposition between emotionality and rationality. It is, however, analytically helpful to prioritize one over the other in distinct sections of this chapter.

4. Including the first author of this paper, who is a certified facilitator and active in her local community's restorative justice program.

References

Ahmed, E., N. Harris, J. Braithwaite, and V. Braithwaite. 2001. *Shame Management through Reintegration*. New York: Cambridge University Press.

Belknap, J. 2001. *Invisible Woman*. New York: Routledge.

Braithwaite, J. 1999. "Restorative Justice: Assessing Optimistic and Pessimistic Accounts." Pp. 1–127 in M. Tonry, ed., *Crime and Justice: A Review of the Research*, vol. 25. Chicago: University of Chicago Press.

———. 2002. *Restorative Justice and Responsive Regulation*. New York: Oxford University Press.

Braithwaite, J., and K. Daly. 1994. "Masculinities, Violence, and Communitarian Control." Pp. 189–213 in T. Newburn and E. Stanko, eds., *Just Boys Doing Business*. New York: Routledge.

Braithwaite, J., and S. Mugford. 1994. "Conditions of Successful Reintegration Ceremonies: Dealing with Juvenile Offenders." *British Journal of Criminology* 34: 139–71.

Christie, N. 1977. "Conflicts as Property." *British Journal of Criminology* 17, no. 1: 1–15.

Cohen, S. 1985. *Visions of Social Control.* London: Polity Press.

Cook, K. J. 2006. "Doing Difference and Accountability in Restorative Justice Conferences." *Theoretical Criminology* 10, no. 1: 107–24.

Cook, K. J., and C. Powell. 2003. "Unfinished Business: Aboriginal Reconciliation and Restorative Justice in Australia." *Contemporary Justice Review* 6: 279–91.

Daly, K. 2001. "Restorative Justice in Australia and New Zealand: Variations, Research Findings, and Prospects." Pp. 59–84 in A. Morris and G. Maxwell, eds., *Restoring Justice for Juveniles: Conferencing, Mediation and Circles.* Oxford: Hart Publishing.

———. 2002. "Restorative Justice: The Real Story." *Punishment and Society* 4: 55–79.

Drummond, S. 1997. *Incorporating the Familiar: An Investigation into Legal Sensibilities in Nunavik.* Montreal: McGill-Queen's University Press.

Gilligan, C. 1982. *In a Different Voice: Psychological Theory and Women's Development.* Cambridge, MA: Harvard University Press.

Heidensohn, F. 1986. "Models of Justice: Portia or Persephone?" *International Journal of the Sociology of Law* 14: 287–96.

Hochschild, A. 1979. "Emotion Work, Feeling Rules, and Social Structure." *American Journal of Sociology* 85: 551–75.

———. 1983. *The Managed Heart: Commercialization of Human Feeling.* Berkeley: University of California Press.

Hydle, I. 2001. "Anthropological Reflections on Restoring Justice in Norway." Paper presented at the American Society of Criminology, Atlanta, GA.

Jaggar, A. 1989. "Love and Knowledge: Emotion in Feminist Epistemology." Pp. 145–71 in A. Jaggar and S. Bordo, eds., *Gender/Body/Knowledge: Feminist Reconstructions of Being and Knowing.* New Brunswick, NJ: Rutgers University Press.

Masters, G., and D. Smith. 1998. "Portia and Persephone Revisited: Thinking about Feelings in Criminal Justice." *Theoretical Criminology* 2: 5–27.

Maxwell, G., and A. Morris. 1993. *Families, Victims, and Culture: Youth Justice in New Zealand.* Wellington, New Zealand: Victoria University of Wellington, Social Policy Agency and Institute of Criminology.

O'Connell, T., B. Wachtel, and T. Wachtel. 1999. "Conferencing Handbook: The New Real Justice Training Manual." Pipersville, PA: The Pipers Press.

Powell, C. 2000. "Under the Influence: Of Drink Drivers and Communitarian Criminology!" *Journal of Postmodern Criminology.* Retrieved May 24, 2002, from <www.tryoung.com/journal-pomocrim/vol-8-shaming/powell.html>.

Prichard, J. 2002. "Parent-child Dynamics in Community Conferences—Some Questions for Reintegrative Shaming, Practice, and Restorative Justice." *Australian and New Zealand Journal of Criminology* 35, no. 3: 330–46.

Roche, D. 2003. *Accountability in Restorative Justice.* New York: Oxford University Press.

Sherman, L., and H. Strang. 1997. *The Right Kind of Shame for Crime Prevention.* Australian Institute of Criminology, Reintegrative Shaming Experiments (RISE),-Working Paper No. 1. Canberra: Australian National University, Law Program.

Williams, S. 1998. "Modernity and the Emotions: Corporeal Reflections on the (Ir)rational." *Sociology* 32: 747–69.

Zehr, H. 1990. *Changing Lenses: A New Focus for Crime and Justice.* Scottsdale, PA: Herald Press.

5

The New Penology in a Critical Context

Michelle Brown

Introducing the New Penology

> It is actuarial. It is concerned with techniques for identifying, classifying and managing groups assorted by levels of dangerousness. It takes crime for granted. It accepts deviance as normal. It is skeptical that liberal interventionist crime control strategies do or can make a difference. Thus its aim is not to intervene in individuals' lives for the purpose of ascertaining responsibility, making the guilty "pay for their crime" or changing them. Rather it seeks to regulate groups as part of a strategy of managing danger. (Feeley and Simon 1998, 375)

THE NEW PENOLOGY, as articulated above by its main theorists, Malcolm Feeley and Jonathan Simon, represents perhaps most fundamentally the understanding shared across much of criminology that "a different kind of historical change is unfolding in our contemporary penal practices" (Simon 1998, 452). In the closing moments of the twentieth century, the United States, for the first time in its history, imprisoned more people than anyone in the world with a total prison/jail population of over 2 million people.[1] This unprecedented transformation takes place at the precise moment when penal scholars begin to invoke terms like "penological crisis," "incarceration binge," "prison-industrial complex," and a "new penology" (Garland 1990; 1996; 2001; Colvin 1992; Feeley and Simon 1992; Christie 1994; Davis 1998; Irwin and Austin 2001; Schlosser 1998; Mauer 1999). Although the rate of incarceration has since slowed, it nevertheless continues to increase, and no other society has ever imprisoned this many of its citizens for the purpose of crime control. This trajectory also marks the kind of penal expansion that has taken place across various forms of punishment. However, crime rates in the U.S. have been decreasing for over a decade, while penal expansion continues. Historically, there is no significant correlation between crime rates and incarceration rates—penology's single most important contribution to our understanding of punishment. Prisons or any other mode of punishment have never been proven to reduce crime. In fact, offenders are more likely to commit a crime after release from prison than previous to incarceration. For these reasons, criminologists have been forced to consider the latent functions of punishment, those less apparent reasons and motives for the production of punishment that form the core of its social theory (Durkheim 1947; 1973; Rusche and Kirchheimer 1939; Elias 1939; Foucault 1977). This is the tradition from which critical criminology and the new penology emerges.

The conditions described above, however simplified or reductive, map the essential contours of penology and organize the field's central problematic: If the prison's function cannot be found in perhaps its most rational and logical justifications, including crime reduction, public safety, and rehabilitation, why, then, does the institution persist and why has it expanded exponentially in the past three decades of American social life? How has this transformation reconfigured the implementation of justice, notions of individual and collective identity, and the nature of governance? Explanations for these problems have been explored in a number of recent as well as classic accounts of punishment—with points of clarification emerging in the study of politics, economy, and social forces—such as race and class as well as the changing configurations of justice, crime control, everyday life, and intellectual history.[2] These accounts and debates remain centered upon a working through of the ironies of punishment.

Critical criminologists and penologists often center their work at the site of powerful contradictions such as the manner in which law or punishment tends not only to preserve the status quo or powerful interests, which may in and of themselves be criminogenic, but also may produce and exacerbate these relationships in a manner which goes unchecked. This kind of ambiguity is found in the scale of the contemporary penal system's expansion against the failures structuring its foundations, a phenomenon which poses a challenging theoretical problem for those who attempt to explain contemporary punishment. The new penology represents an account which seeks to add insight to the dimensions of that problem as well as highlight the potentially permanent effects these patterns in punishment may have upon the configuration of social life.

Malcolm Feeley and Jonathan Simon provide a provisional map of the new penology in their influential 1992 *Criminology* article and then subject their thesis to substantial revisions in later work (Feeley and Simon 1992). Their assertions continue to serve as a critical point of reaction within the field of criminology. For these authors, the predominant transformation in contemporary punishment is theorized to be centered upon a "change in conception—discourse, objectives, and techniques—in the penal process . . . shifts that have multiple and independent origins and are not reducible to any one reigning idea" (1992, 449). This change in conception centers upon three core assertions, which they describe as follows:

1. The emergence of new discourses: In particular, the language of probability and risk increasingly replaces earlier discourses of clinical diagnosis and retributive judgment.
2. The formation of new objectives for the system: The objectives we have in mind are not simply new to the system (some of them have old antecedents) but are in some sense newly "system." We are especially interested in the increasing primacy given to the efficient control of internal system processes in place of the traditional objectives of rehabilitation and crime control. Goals like reducing "recidivism" have always been internally shaped in important ways . . . , but in the contemporary setting the sense that any external social referent is intended at all is becoming attenuated.
3. The deployment of new techniques: These techniques target offenders as an aggregate in place of traditional techniques for individualizing or creating equity. (Feeley and Simon 1992, 450)

The emergent discourse, objectives, and techniques of the new penology express a fundamental reorganization in contemporary understandings of crime and punishment, identified in such patterns and practices of surveillance and regulation as preventive detention, profiling, intensive supervision programs, the buy-busts and drug testing practices at the heart of the drug war, the targeting of subpopulations through policies centered upon selective incapacitation (habitual, career, and "three strikes" offenders), emergent statistical and software packages which track crime, and the increase in imprisonment alongside of the rise in prominence of policy and crime experts. The primary contours of this reorganization, as marked by Jonathan Simon, include a shift from the individual to the aggregate, from normalization to management, and from social norms to systems. This perspective will privilege utilitarianism over moral reasoning, quantitative methods over qualitative analysis, and the notion of criminal justice as a series of operations and systems over individual-focused justice.

The Systems Approach: Historicizing the Rise of the New Penology

The shift in focus from individual-based understandings of crime and punishment to aggregate group behaviors and distributions marks a useful starting point in understanding the broader configuration of the new penology. A discourse of the aggregate often privileges particular kinds of approaches, such as the kind widely circulated in the late 1960s in the aftermath of the President's Commission on Law Enforcement and Administration of Justice, a systems analysis approach in which crime is envisioned as an actuarial problem centered upon assessments of risk. The President's Commission marked the first national research commission on crime since Hoover's administration and led to legislation which culminated in the Office of Law Enforcement Assistance, the Law Enforcement Assistance Administration's precedent. The creation of a federal grants program through OLEA crystallized the federal government's pivotal role in the administration of American criminal justice, one which would bring about long lasting effects in its implementation and its study (most early criminal justice programs would derive from this funding). Feeley and Simon have labeled the consequent Omnibus Crime Control and Safe Streets Act of 1968, which officially created LEAA, as the "master plan for the national war on crime" (1992, 450). When Alfred Blumstein was called in from the Department of Defense to coordinate the 1967 President's Commission on Law Enforcement and the Administration of Justice, he brought with him the feverish excitement surrounding the widespread application of systems analysis in military operations, economic systems, and government. Systems analysis, it was assumed, would provide the meticulous retrieval and effective utilization of long-needed aggregate data concerning the movement of offenders through criminal justice agencies. Moving well beyond the simple application of systems analysis, systematization was viewed as a way of streamlining the pursuit of justice.

The federal crime control initiatives and funding that were to result from this research in the newly politicized context for crime control would ultimately transform the identity of criminal justice administration from perceptions as a collection of autonomous social institutions into an American "system" of justice. What had been a fairly individualized series of social agencies was suddenly and irrevocably labeled a criminal justice system, whose goals and objectives were to reflect the necessary interrelationship of agencies within this structural framework. This "systems" approach would have a two-pronged effect within the organization of criminal justice, one emphasizing new models of efficiency, premised in flow charts, technology, and science, another grounded in the newly politicized context of the post–Civil Rights United States and a law-and-order movement. These two legacies each play a fundamental role in the emergence of the discourse of the new penology, the first mapping its fundamental contours through science and technology and the second a site for its critique in the omission of popular perspectives on punishment.

The Politicization of Science

The new penology, perhaps best understood as a convergence of a variety of schools of thought, including economic sociology, actuarial studies, a governmentality literature and the sociology of punishment and of risk, in many ways represents an emergent penological narrative which maps fundamental transformations in Western penal policy, particularly in the context of vast penal change in the United States. The essential elements of this "new" penology, centered in correctional managerialism, actuarial justice, and the privileging of custody, emerge in the context of the common penal predicaments of late modernity—the inability of the state to provide effective crime control, a heightened perception of rising crime rates against the apparent futility of punishment, a hardening of popular attitudes toward criminals, and the emergence of a vast prison-industrial complex in the midst of law-and-order politics. Thus, the new penology's introduction as a theoretical frame occurs amidst major sea changes not simply in the study and practice of punishment but in the organization of sovereignty and governance itself. Its focus is thus grounded in historical contingency and very much bound up with what it means to pursue punishment as a science. This historical context plays a primary role in the development of critical criminology as well.

The defining feature of critical criminology could be argued in many ways to be the absence of a single unitary theory but rather a conglomeration of theories gathered around a fundamental sociopolitical stance on what it means to do the science of crime. This position takes as its focus fundamental omissions and absences in traditional or mainstream criminology: the exclusion of women and minorities, the reproduction of racial and gendered categories, the entrenchment of inequality and poverty, in short the ideological dimensions of science, including its often invisible identity politics. For critical criminologists, their mandate has always centered upon the manner in which powerful interests and stakes were left unchallenged in a discipline whose questions, theory, and objectives always and inevitably risked collusion with the powerful interests of the state.

Thus, within critical criminology, we witness science deployed to deconstruct science, to expose the ideological implications of "neutrality" and "objectivity" in its manifestations of power, as well as the wielding of science to point to the inequalities in the applications of crime policy and the study of criminology. One year after the publication of Robert Martinson's "What Works?," the landmark penal study which served as the death knell for rehabilitation and argued in its concluding moments that "With few and isolated exceptions, the rehabilitative efforts that have been reported so far have had no appreciable effect on recidivism" (1974, 25), Ian Taylor, Paul Walton and Jock Young introduce critical criminology in a manner which foregrounds the ideological and political underpinnings of science. They mark this process of politicization as one which had and would redefine crime and social control in the Western world. Their discussion reflected a growing interest and fascination with the boundaries of appropriate and inappropriate, deviant and "normal," criminal and law-abiding behavior and the manner in which "at-risk" classifications of populations would come to be "more ambiguous and extensive," dimensions which would prove to be the hallmarks of a new penology (Taylor et al. 1975, 2). The era remains a time when these kinds of discussions centered upon sites of punishment, with the problematic state of American prisons surfacing in Senate hearings, news magazines, television reporting, popular culture, and correctional practice *as* sites of crisis. In the aftermath of this wave of critical attention, the displacement and "failure" of rehabilitation has widely been considered to be a legitimating factor in the rise of "law and order" politics and the use of incapacitation, with its corresponding emergent discourses and practices centered upon custody and surveillance.

The social map envisioned by Taylor et al. speaks to the manner in which the scope and application of the law had expanded through both an intensification (a specific focus on problematic groups and "dangerous" classes) as well as an extensionality (through a crime control focus which widened the net of social regulation in a manner that directly impacted a number of groups who had not historically been considered deviant) of social control within everyday life. The new penology is introduced in the aftermath of this historical precedent as an integral part of an emergent turn in the study of punishment dedicated to the reopening of significant penal debates centered upon the following, now fairly common predicaments. These include the challenging of all major philosophies of imprisonment (and punishment) in the past few decades; a general acceptance, in the absence of philosophy, on the part of the public and politicians of the inherently repressive, custodial trajectory of penal institutions; an awareness and growing sophistication in the application of the deeply politicized character of modern punishment (most apparent in changes in sentencing structure and the prison's end-of-the-century expansion in the U.S.); the expansion and deepening of a normalizing disciplinary social structure; the rise of volatile, particularly retributive social understandings of imprisonment; the redistribution of the offender and the "dangerous classes" through society based upon actuarial notions of risk and clearly racial demographics; as well as an increased perception of high crime, fear, and insecurity as essential properties of modern life.

For critical criminologists, the emergence of the new penology also indicates the manner in which such a transformation would have, as Taylor et al. (1975) foresaw, "profound consequences in the teaching, the application, the legitimacy and the meaning of traditional criminology" (2), warning of the consequent specialization and fragmentation of a field, one in which criminologists would be charged "with a moral responsibility they could often more easily avoid—the evaluation of the legal norms (and underlying morality) of a society that criminalizes activities developing out of the contradiction in its political economy" (Taylor et al. 1975, 2). In other words, there would be choices to make and those choices would reflect the trajectory of a discipline. They would remind us: There are social constructions and there are social facts, lived and experienced in real terms and with real consequences. As Bruno Latour argues, our "objects" of study are inevitably revealed to be always "simultaneously real, like nature, narrated, like discourse, and collective, like society" (1993). Out of these terms derive the two primary directives of early critical criminology:

1) the adequacy of the various theoretical offerings in critical criminology is to be assessed in practice—that is, in terms of their utility in demasking the moral and ideological veneer of an unequal society, and in terms of its ability to enliven the critical debate about the modes of change, and the post-capitalist alternatives, contemplated by those committed to a radical alternative (whether the agencies be intellectuals, workers or prisoners) and
2) a commitment to "the project of posing fundamental and consistent challenges to the everyday political assumptions, practices and implications of one of the most influential and State-dominated branches of applied social 'science'—the 'science' of criminology" (Taylor et al. 1975, 4–5).

This is one of the crucial intersections between critical criminology and the new penology, as the actuarial-based practices which Feeley and Simon position at the heart of contemporary penal practice are grounded in a reconfiguration of science and society in a manner that is distinctly disengaged from this fundamental set of critical challenges.

Actuarialism and Governmentality

The emphasis within the new penology upon actuarialism marks a compelling site for the excavation of one of critical criminology's key traditions, Marxist criminology and the notion of the dangerous class (Bonger 1916), but with a substantive twist. As Jonathan Simon writes, the actuarial emphasis of the new penology would invoke the dangerous class, but rather than apply this classification to bodies and individuals perceived as being in need of normalization and discipline, this classification would apply to the social distribution of groups, who would ultimately be afterthoughts in the production of justice:

> The disciplines were used in the nineteenth century to undermine the political potential of the urban "swarms" through technologies of surveillance, isolation, and normalization. Actuarial practices are used today to further diminish the potential for resistance by changing the representations through which we come into ourselves as collective subjects. Rather than concentrating power on particular "dangerous" subjects, actuarial technology changes the social context to make it immune to those subjects (who thus no longer need to be confined and controlled). Barricades are useless against a power that operates in the abstract space of statistical tables. (Simon 1988, 798)

The new penology thus marks a move away from one of critical criminology's more dominant frames in understanding punishment, a disciplinary model. Disciplinary modes of punishment are organized around an intense focusing upon the individual down to the most minute of details and habits. This kind of disciplinary focus, as exemplified by Foucault, is built around surveillance and the normalization of the offender, inmate, delinquent, worker, student, embodied in the closing of the gap between a norm and its deviation, the transformation of the individual self (soul over body). The new penology, which privileges an actuarial model, is no longer concerned with closing this gap between individuals and society but rather seeks an accommodation of such variations through the management and mapping of distributions of populations. As Jonathan Simon (1988) argues, in part, "the movement from normalization (closing the gap between distribution and norm) to accommodation (responding to variations in distributions) increases the efficiency of power because changing people is difficult and expensive" (714). In contemporary social and political contexts, "it is cheaper to know and plan around people's failings than to normalize them" (Simon 1988, 714).

Jock Young offers a similar perspective into this phenomenon in his exclusionary society thesis when he argues that contemporary social configurations reflect a bulimic social system built around both inclusion and exclusion, where, for instance, "the problem of the ghetto was not so much the process of its being simply excluded, but rather one where it was all too strongly included in the culture but then systematically excluded from its realization" (1999, 469). He centers this discussion around the blurred boundaries and shared value systems of both the poor and society at large, where the insistence upon classic binaries (such as community/disorganization, drug free/drug use, stable family/single mothers) represent unstable, artificial categories, unreflective of social realities, situated in uncertain contexts, but leading to patterns of exclusion:

> I want to suggest that it is the bulimic nature of late modern societies which helps to explain the nature and tenor of the discontent at the bottom of the social structure. It is rooted quite simply in the contradiction between ideas which legitimate the system and the reality of the structure which constitutes it. But the tensions between ideals and reality exist only because of the general and manifest awareness of them. Both the punitive anger of the righteous and the burning resentment of the excluded occur because the demarcation lines are transfixed, because the same contradictions of reward and ontology exist throughout society, because the souls of those inside and those outside the "contented minority" are far from dissimilar, sharing the same desires and passions, and suffering the same frustrations, because there is no security of place or certainty of being and because differences are not essences but mere intonations of the minor scales of diversity. (Young 1999, 477)

Similarly, the actuarial emphasis of the new penology, although reliant upon binary classifications, no longer seeks to normalize populations, but rather to regulate them and their differences through segregation across abstract spaces, groupings, and social distributions, which can ironically culminate in even deeper exclusionary divisions, including a "functional" or permanent underclass. This phenomenon is noted in the governmentality literature as governing from or at a distance.

Governmentality with its implied rationalities centers upon knowledges and practices that operate across and are shared between individuals, institutions, and the state. Within the framework of the new penology, punishment and its discourses, objectives, and techniques come to operate broadly across the social body as a form of governance. Within this new mode of governance, crime control efforts on the part of the state are defined by an abrogation of responsibilities to other kinds of social institutions that are already and historically undersourced and undertrained—thus governing from a distance or governing the least. This mode of governance will direct its classifications at an assessment of where risk is most likely to be best managed. Under the new penology, risk, in the form of "dangerous" populations, is most effectively managed, not through normalization, but spatialization marked by a well-mapped exclusion and isolation through mechanisms of classification rather than the more disciplinary mode of segregation through social control institutions. This pattern is most visible when social control is organized in a manner which extends beyond justice agencies into families, communities, schools, churches, and so forth. Studies have exemplified how an actuarial, risk-based discourse achieves some degree of articulation and practice increasingly across and within the criminal justice system in such traditional sites of criminal justice practice as bail decision-making (Kellough and Wortley 2002), probation (Bayens et al. 1998), parole (Lynch 1998), legal shifts in sentencing, such as three-strikes laws (Greenberg 2002; Shichor 1997), and juvenile justice (Kempf-Leonard and Peterson 2000). However, actuarial risk-based discourse has been most interesting when mapped more broadly in society in such instances as the management of sexuality and sexual deviance (Simon 1998; Petrunik 2002; Edwards and Hensley 2001), the coordination of community crime control "weed and seed" programs (Miller 2001), the construction of appropriate kinds of family roles (Silverstein 2001), public health policy (Marquart et al. 1999; Vaughn and Smith 1999), and, finally, the prevention or promotion of death (Carlen 2001). For instance, increasing attention and debate has centered upon the mapping of sex offenders in communities through social policy and legislation as groups who remain intractably in need of management, grounded in a fundamental public pessimism about the possibility of individual reformation or change. In the clinical and justice discourses surrounding that management, the vocabulary of the actuarialism through risk management models is strongly apparent.

For these reasons, the defining contours of the new penology are built around notions of governmentality and actuarialism, practices that

> are so familiar and banal that it is difficult to notice them at all, let alone see them as central components of a new regime of social ordering linked to myriad exercises of social control and power, e.g., hiring, admitting, campaigning, selling, sentencing, and educating. Yet these practices are generating fundamental changes in our political culture. (Simon 1988, 771)

These practices are argued to derive from actuarial techniques that "play a central role in a proliferating set of social practices. They are at the same time a regime of truth, a way of exercising power, and a method of ordering social life" (Simon 1988, 772). Actuarialist models emerge as complex mixtures of styles of thought, discourse, and vocabulary as well as sets of practices, strategies, and technologies. Grounded in efficiency, they value a certain technicism where system stream-lining on the basis of cost-benefit analysis and risk assessments are foregrounded. They are driven by an economy of management centered upon the distribution of aggregate numbers of individuals across the justice system and an extension of these patterns of control across the everyday life of offenders and system professionals—"a fundamental respatialization of control mechanisms, from the enclosed spaces of carceral institutions to the dispersed territory of 'the community'" (Rose 2002, 212).

Their primary tools are prediction instruments, classification schemes, distribution grids, and technology, all of which are conducive to the production of emergent, wider networks of control.

These features reflect the manner in which actuarial understandings of the world are perceived as having the potential to fundamentally transform social life, playing pivotal roles in the organization of power and, in the case of the new penology, punishment. In this systems-based focus, justice itself is reconfigured, and as David Garland argues, "new performance indicators tend to measure 'outputs' rather than 'outcomes,' what the organization does, rather than what, if anything, it achieves" (Garland 1996, 458). In this regard, the new penology marks a larger shift in the history of social control, one grounded in an implicit sense of futility, a strategy devoid of philosophical underpinnings or any attention to individuals or issues related to the ethics, morality, or necessity of humanity in punishment. Its power is in the implication of a particular form of logic that facilitates other kinds of penal aims (incapacitation, retribution, deterrence), although obliquely. Similarly, this logic is easily transposed into agencies and processes across the system and beyond. (After all, its origins are to be found in a capitalist free-market context in which liability must be harnessed and rendered predictable).

As Nikolas Rose argues, there is an undeniable sense of duty and precaution implied in this logic: "The option of acting in the present in order to manage the future rapidly mutates into something like an obligation" (2002, 214). Centered upon the prevalence of uncertainty in the discretionary patterns of justice, the new penology offers a formula for control and the semblance of predictability in terrain which has systematically denied and subverted efforts at reform and control. The center of the new penology is consequently and, not surprisingly, a paradox:

> Across its various forms and calculative techniques, one feature stands out: risk thinking seeks to bring the future into the present and make it calculable. We could say that it tries to discipline uncertainty, in the sense of making uncertainty the topic of a branch of learning and instruction. It acts as well to discipline it in a second sense, by bringing uncertainty under control, making it orderly and docile. Risk thinking tames chance, fate, and uncertainty by a paradoxical move. (Rose 2002, 214)

Its attention to risk assessment through testing instruments and statistics serves as well to automatize and conceal a host of decision-making processes which are occurring within the justice system through practitioners, experts, and legal frames. It marks consequently a convergence with private arrangements and market aims, orchestrated by state and public agencies but practiced by citizens themselves: again, governance at a distance. Thus, the promise of the new penology is founded in the fundamental dissatisfaction that informs those who work in the field of crime control:

> The appeal of actuarialism for criminal justice personnel is probably a reaction to feelings of frustration and pessimism that arise from working in an overcrowded, and oft publicly criticized system. The actuarial objective does not offer an answer to this perceived hopelessness. Instead, it takes for granted that no answer exists, and offers the placating alternative of at least managing this hopelessness in a less burdensome and more efficient fashion. In this respect, actuarial justice offers beleaguered personnel at least a chance to succeed, although only through a redefinition of goals. It is especially troubling that these changes to the criminal justice system are occurring without the benefit of adequate public discourse or scholarly investigation. (Kempf-Leonard and Peterson 2000, 68)

In the end, justice actors, experts, subjects, and citizens all find themselves caught up in the tensions that define the new penology. However, Feeley and Simon argue that the nature of the aggregate that actuarial practices exemplify constitutes a new kind of social collectivity, "one defined neither by internal bonds, nor external experiences, but by locations on a statistical distribution" (Simon 1988, 789). These classification schemes produce particular kinds of identities and individualities, but, as Simon argues, these techniques lack a distinctive sense of subjectivity and group identity itself is treated as "singularly sterile in [its] capacity for political empowerment" (Simon 1988, 789). Thus, "actuarial techniques can be used to identify people who are more or less likely to be high-rate offenders, but these variables are not integrated into a conception of the underlying subject" (Simon 1988, 791). Thus, "actuarial classification, with its de-centered subject, seems to eliminate, in advance, the possibility of identity, of critical self-consciousness and of intersubjectivity. Rather than making people up, actuarial practices unmake them" (Simon 1988, 792). In that sense, the new penology is a symptom of a larger crisis within governance and thus apparent in punishment, one which seeks to regulate rather than explain or change contemporary social problems. In doing so, meanings of the social and the self are argued to be fundamentally transformed.

The Critiques

In Simon and Feeley's (1994) own words, their "thesis has sparked vigorous debate" (148). Many have critiqued the "new-ness" of the new penology and instead perceive it as a repackaging to some extent of preexisting theoretical frames. For instance, the new penology resembles many of the dimensions of

Herbert Packer's (1968) crime control model or David Rothman's (1980) history of social control through the lenses of conscience and convenience. Penal strategies have consistently been framed through the lenses of "danger" across eugenics movements, the shift toward disciplinary models and the historical emergence of the "dangerous class." There is, as well, the criticism that the new penology represents simply an invocation of old penological and criminological themes with its emphasis upon classical Marxist terms like the "dangerous classes." David Garland specifically claims that the "break" envisioned in the theorizing of the new penology as an emergent paradigm is rather a continuation of the past, bearing primary markers of classical social theory and the key frames of modernity (Garland 1990; 1995). Feeley and Simon have stood steadfastly beside their claim however that the new penology marks a fundamental rupture in the penal narratives of modernity.

Related to this issue, one of the larger criticisms that the new penology has faced is its absence in social practice and cultural discourse, a fundamental gap in the manner in which penology is practically implemented and popularly imagined. Lisa Miller argues in her work on the implementation of crime control programs at the community level that "the new conceptions of penology that have emerged over the past several years have been insufficiently attentive to politics on the ground level, particularly to the power of heterogenous communities to resist and reconfigure crime control policy and to infuse it with their own concerns" (Miller 2001, 169). Simon and Feeley (1994) ask in response to critiques of this nature, "why has the success of the new penology among insiders and specialists in criminal justice not been followed by a commensurate influence on public discourse?" (149). They then theorize this gap to be one that is increasing, reflecting an absence of narratives, representations, and organizing frames for public understandings of punishment. In the context of penological crisis, all major philosophies of punishment are subject to a high degree of discreditation—even the philosophical mainstays which have predominated penal thought and intent. No longer are the instrumentalist perspectives of rehabilitation or deterrence viable ends, as the project of punishment is cited as having failed in practice. In such terrain, a return to emotional and populist appeals for punishment, including retribution and revenge, becomes seriously foregrounded. Consequently, public policy and political discourse speak through a vocabulary which often denies the key discourses and objectives which make up the new penology and instead emphasizes "values and emotional appeals, while expert discourse emphasizes operational questions that public discourse ignores" (Simon and Feeley 1994, 151). Part of the reason for this gap is argued to be grounded in the American context with its individualistic emphasis upon volitional actors. Perceptions of neutrality and scientificity, a distinct "blindness of actuarial vision to the political and moral meaning of certain differences" (Simon 1988, 780), and a disregard for the persistent viability of the individual all fly in the face of the moral, rational actor and the dependence of frames of punishment upon the subjectivity of experience. Thus, the classical frames in which crime and punishment have been understood remain firmly ensconced in the individualistic cultural and scientific vocabularies surrounding punishment. As Simon (1988) argues, "while they provide a highly efficient means of management, actuarial practices also conflict with other powerful traditions in our cultural background," including "the strongly held value that people be considered primarily as individuals" (776). The success of the new penology as an organizing framework, critics argue, depends upon its ability to provide a (grand) narrative that accounts for crime through these classical frames and expresses the potential for more security through actuarial models. However, although the new penology implies an underlying logic for the expansion of the penal system, it remains unable to tap into or explain the rise of populist understandings of punishment centered upon retribution, a harsh punitiveness, and the persistent primacy of rational actor models.

This kind of critique is most apparent in the rise of retribution and the hardening of public attitudes toward offenders. Actuarial logics often mute the role of emotion, affect, and agency in understandings of crime, punishment, and social configuration. However, as predominant theorists of punishment, including Nietzsche and Durkheim, have insisted across time, the essence of punishment is, in part, passion. To deny this emotionality is to separate punishment as an institution from the primary motives and reasons which underscore its invocation: retribution—and a retribution that is more generally grounded in revenge. The vengeance which underlies the implied calm reason of systematic, procedural, proportional retribution cannot be repressed and will often defy a rational logic of any kind. To privilege an actuarial logic above such close-to-the-ground motives for punishment obscures the nature of punishment itself.

In part this critique is bound up with the contradictory nature of punishment, itself a fundamentally conflicted social institution. The constellation of penal practices takes place without an overarching theoretical framework for its understanding. This is what the new penology seeks to be. Yet one of its primary limitations has been its inability and the inability of any single theoretical account to explain the conflicting amalgam of values, practices, and motives in punishing. Feeley and Simon (1998) have attempted to reconcile the populist punitive perspectives with actuarial modes of justice through arguments that insist that the new penology "represents deeper 'pre-political' thought that cannot easily be associated with conventional political labels"

(392). They also mark shifts in constitutional law which reflect actuarial logics that they expect to surpass the "law and order" configurations of contemporary justice. Whether such an approach can capture the degree of vindictiveness current in popular thought and penal practice is open to interpretation.

Beyond this critique lies another key issue for new penologists, including the question of whether frontline actors and professionals in the justice system actually have internalized the routines, techniques, and objectives of a new penology. As Mona Lynch writes, "one site for examining whether the new penology is indeed emerging as a distinct penological operating system is at the place where strategy is put into penal practice: at the level of implementation. There is reason to think that the contact point between the institution (and its new penological policies) and the outside world (with its old-fashioned "modern" take on criminality) is one battleground where the sustainability of the new penology may be tested" (Lynch 1998, 842). Some research such as Vaughn and Smith's work on correctional medical workers whose ethics are impacted negatively by actuarial rationalities suggest that this internalization is a rising phenomenon but in a manner which culminates, through interactions with prison worker subcultures, not only in reconfigurations of practice at the aggregate level but also in distinct settings of harm and torture for individual offenders. However, other researchers argue that the shift toward a new penology is more rhetorical than practical. For example, McCorkle and Crank (1996) take a new institutionalist approach in their research on the operational environment of parole workers, arguing that "What might appear to be transformations in probation and parole over the past two decades are, upon closer examination, only 'ceremonial responses' to changes in its institutional environment" (3). Mona Lynch's analysis of parole agent identity argues similarly that frontline actors continue to be substantially informed by popular discourse on crime in their daily understandings of work. Thus, parole agents tend to see themselves more readily through the lenses of crime fighting and law enforcement. However, Lynch also finds that at the management level the new penology serves as an active template for agency goals, organization, and operations. Such critiques demand an account of the contradictory nature of punishment, which is often experienced and practiced as an amalgam of ideas, motives, emotions, and moralities. To reduce such complex processes in the daily operations of justice to actuarial logics couched in bureaucratic, procedural techniques is to risk the construction of a theoretical iron cage. In this regard, much of the new penology's future (as well as other social theories of punishment) will depend upon its ability to account for the broad diversity in reasons why people punish and how they punish including provisional maps of human agency. Otherwise, something imperative is lost in translation about the complex manner in which justice is conducted daily. Discretionary motives may not transpose well onto the risk assessments and classification schemes of actuarial models nor, as Pat Carlen argues in her discussion of suicide in a women's prison, may the targets of a new penology interpret it as such. In such contexts, she argues that "in the interest of developing a politics of penal probity, . . . it is necessary to take seriously the intentions of 'speaking subjects' at a particular moment in time" (Carlen 2001, 469), thus ushering in the possibility of a "third way" between the questions of "what works" and "nothing works." Otherwise, in a context where

> successive studies of governmentality may suggest that prevailing power relations ensure that all practices of imprisonment are always and already illegitimate, and, on the other, successive governments continue to evaluate women's prisons according to totally inappropriate criteria, present opportunities to recognize, record and extend the genuinely therapeutic practices which can reduce the damaging pain of women in penal custody will be lost. (Carlen 2001, 469)

Finally, a looming question for those who theorize and test the new penology is the task of contextualizing that work within the broader social structures from which actuarial models derive. For instance, much of the new penology occurs against the backdrop of social reorientations in the economy in conjunction with risk, uncertainty, sovereignty, and governance. As Baker and Simon (2002) write, the role of risk is manifested in two distinct cultural trends:

> The first follows logically from efforts to spread risk and consists of a wide variety of efforts to conceive and address social problems in terms of risk. For example, money management, social services, policing, environmental policy, tort law, national defense, and a host of otherwise unrelated fields have all come to share a common vocabulary of risk. The second cultural trend is a reaction against spreading risk, and it consists of various efforts to make people more individually accountable for risk. (1)

Similarly, it is not entirely clear how the new penology marks a fundamental rupture from disciplinary to actuarial modes. A more complex framework might work to explain how discourses, objectives, and techniques may both unite and diverge not only within rubrics of punishment but also in broader social orders that are not always consistent or easily reconciled. All of this should culminate in a broader theorization of punishment, in which, regardless of its criticisms, the new penology has played an important role.

Where Do We Go from Here?

Feeley and Simon's discussion highlights the amenability of punishment to a wide range of discontents within penological and criminological thought and practice, with the objective of their commentary arguably best envisioned not "so much as a theory or program conceived in full by any particular actors in the system, but as an interpretive net that can help reveal in the present some of the directions the future may take" (1992, 460). In this future, for Feeley and Simon, the essential elements of the new penology are powerful enough to risk becoming "permanent features of the criminal justice system" (1992, 470). This transformation in turn can potentially reshape the fundamental configurations not simply of punishment, but of justice, governance, and social relations. Thus, a reconfiguration of what it means to be social is implied as well. This transformation also reflects a fundamental shift in the organization of criminology through objectives similar to those of the new penology:

> The new penology produces representations of the system that facilitate objectives like deterrence (which demands only efficiently produced punishment) and incapacitation. The traditional appeal of modern penal reformers has been to emphasize the humanity of offenders and the cruelty of current penal practices. The new penology not only has trouble recognizing the cultural investment in the figure of the criminal, it has trouble with the concept of humanity. (Simon and Feeley 1994, 173)

On a more hopeful note, the intellectual introduction of a new penology was meant to provide and is, I believe, a particularly insightful lens through which to anticipate and work to prevent such permanent forms of configuration. Its invocation is grounded in the call to consider the unanticipated consequences of penological reform, whose contemporary correlates are grounded in penal expansion against a political and cultural backdrop of apathy and futility. Its insistence upon frames of social immobility provides an important opportunity to examine why we punish and the conditions under which we punish so very badly. The center of the new penology is revelatory of a fundamental problem with the project of punishment, one around which an entire social institution is destabilized while it simultaneously expands. Beyond this, it implies a fundamental transformation of social life with new innovations and limits. As knowledge concerning the features and qualities of particular groups grow more distinct in public records and classification schemes, "the ideological effects of actuarial practices . . . render more difficult the formation" of community and group mobilization where "the effect of actuarial practices is precisely to make it more difficult for groups to intensify their solidarity or to exercise political choice" (Simon 1988, 786–87). At the heart of the concerns surrounding the new penology is a stake then in the preservation and protection of human agency from forms of regulation and classification that may, at first glance, seem all too rational and logical. However, contemporary penal policy is clogged with irrationalities, including the inefficiency of an overcrowded and costly penal apparatus as well as the degree to which politicians and citizens are willing to allocate large sums of money toward punitive legislation and penal practices which have little crime control impact (three-strikes laws and supermax facilities). As David Shichor writes of three-strikes policy, the rationalization implied in the new penology resembles Ritzer's "McDonaldization" of punishment culminating in yet another iron cage where the irony of increased rationality is the production of fundamental irrationalities. For example, Shichor argues "the application of three-strikes laws results in inefficiency of the criminal justice process, punishments are not always clearly calculable, predictability of outcomes may be negatively affected by rational procedures, and the system may lose control over the nature of punishment. In short, as is the case with many other public policies, three-strikes laws could lead to a host of unintended consequences that may defeat the purposes for which they were intended" (Shichor 1997, 487).

In this manner, Simon argues in his early work,

> Today's actuarial practices presage the development of a third model of politics where neither status nor class provides the basis for engagement. Indeed, we have no real models of what aggregate politics look like, but extrapolating from current conditions leads to a disturbing picture. Actuarial practices can mobilize segments of the population and form majorities that have no patterns of shared experience or structures of association and no basis for understanding themselves as motivated by a common cause. (1988, 793)

This fear is bound up with a declining significance of moral and political identity and a "shallowing of the interiority of the individual subject" (Simon 1988, 793). In such contexts, actuarial techniques deny the moral and political significance of race, class, and gender, instead arguing these differences are no longer problematic, closing off significant social debates a priori. The very invisibility of such transformations also risks the potential erosion of fundamental standards for the protection of civil liberties. Jonathan Simon (1988) argues "Not only has the new penology escaped direct review, but its features have helped mask the decline of constitutional standards. Ironically, the more the state disavows goals of individualization and transformation, the more deference courts are invited to pay to their coercive uses of power" (467).

One final and potentially productive application of the new penology in the future is found in a post–9/11 context where distant, off-shore prisons such as Guantánamo and Abu Ghraib provide settings for the extrapolation of recent transformations in patterns of American punishment. At Abu Ghraib, the social networks of penality are complex and deep. Civilian interrogators are suspected to have played primary roles in the scandal, routinely brought in to question detainees at Abu Ghraib precisely in order to evade the rule of law (as they are exempt from both military and international law), implying another story of commercial contractors, the privatization of prisons, and the global expansion of the security sector. A recent estimate suggested that there are at least twenty thousand private military contractors in Iraq alone (Dworkin 2004). Before September 11, numerous private prison companies had begun to remodel themselves as private security agencies focused upon a global market and they were the first stocks to rise when the markets reopened. We also witness the inverse as well, as prisons at home become transnational sites for punishment. Within American borders, we find a longstanding history of the detention of foreign nationals outside the rule of law and not simply in times of crisis. Before September 11, 2001, it is estimated that over twenty thousand undocumented immigrants were held in custody for long periods of time and in harsh conditions, many placed outside of INS facilities in the general populations of jails and prisons, speaking little or no English. This process, as documented by Michael Welch, takes place while asylum seekers await background checks with little or no legal representation while facing no charges (Welch 2003). Since the 1980s, immigration policy has consistently hardened amidst documentation of human rights abuse (Human Rights Watch 1997; 1998). In the aftermath of September 11, the number of detainees held indefinitely without charges by American forces is estimated to be at or above fifty thousand (Schlesinger 2004). In conjunction with these developments, the war on terror brings about new patterns of penality in the offshore, off-limit prisons such as Guantánamo Bay, the myriad undisclosed locations at which detainees are held, the "rendering" of suspects or exporting of prisoners to other countries for torture, and U.S. "disappearances" that are occurring internationally (Brody 2004).

Abu Ghraib and Guantánamo, like the U.S. prison system at home, mark the kind of penal expansion that takes place in the context of wars with no end: wars on drugs, crime, and terror. In the U.S., where we imprison more than anyone in the world, this unprecedented use of the penal apparatus has largely taken place outside of public notice or interest, in disregard of decades of work by penal scholars and activists who have introduced a vocabulary of warning through terms like "penological crisis," "incarceration binge," "prison-industrial complex," and the new penology. Such massive expansion has direct effects upon the private lives of prisoners, correctional workers, their families and their communities. The new penology, however, maps a possibility that extends far beyond immediately apparent penal contexts into a fundamental reconfiguration of social life. Such unprecedented penal expenditures mark the global emergence of a new discourse of punishment, one whose racial divisions and abusive practices are revised into a technical, legal language of acceptability, one in which Americans are conveniently further distanced from the social realities of punishment through strategies of isolation and exclusion, all conducted in a manner and on a scale which exacerbates the fundamental class, race, and gender contradictions and divisions of democracy. In this respect, whatever our criticisms, the new penology merits our serious scientific attention as both a material practice and discursive language whose expansion and intensification potentially need recognize no limits, no borders, no bounds.

Notes

1. In 2003, the U.S. incarcerated 2.1 million people, or 1 in every 140 Americans. Nearly half of the prison population is African American. Another 18 percent are Hispanic or Latino. Currently, African American males have a one in three chance of serving time in their lifetime and one in seven is currently or permanently disenfranchised with no right to vote due to felony convictions. Beyond this, seventy percent of the prison population are illiterate and at least ten percent are mentally ill. Women constitute the most rapidly growing prison demographic group, again disproportionately African American and Latinas. Over half of the female prison population have not completed high school and have experienced some form of physical or sexual abuse prior to incarceration. Seventy-five percent used drugs regularly before their arrest. Ninety-five percent entered prison with incomes below ten thousand dollars. In the context of an emergent law and order society with its war on drugs and its "three strikes," "truth in sentencing," habitual offender, and mandatory minimum laws, contemporary patterns of imprisonment are defined by massively disproportional class, gender, and, especially, racial effects. African Americans, for instance, who constitute only thirteen to fifteen percent of the drug user population, account for 36 percent of all drug arrests and 63 percent of all drug offenders sentenced to imprisonment. These statistics are available at the U.S. Department of Justice, Bureau of Justice Statistics, Prison and Jail Inmates at Midyear 2003 (May, 2004), NCJ 203947. See <www.ojp.usdoj.gov/bjs/prisons.htm>. They are also drawn from reports and briefs published by The Sentencing Project, a nonprofit organization well known for its research and advocacy on criminal justice policy. See <www.sentencingproject.org>.

2. On race, see Bosworth 2004; Maur 1999; and Beckett 1997. On class, see Melossi and Pavarini 1981; Reiman 2005; and Western and Beckett 1999. For the reconfiguration of justice, see Feeley and Simon 1992; Simon 1993; and Beckett 1997. For the

reconfiguration of social life and culture, see Girling, Loader, and Sparks 1999; Garland 2000; Young 1999; and Wacquant 2000.

References

Baker, T., and J. Simon. 2002. "Introduction." Pp. 1–25 in T. Baker and J. Simon, eds., *Embracing Risk: The Changing Culture of Insurance and Responsibility*. Chicago: University of Chicago Press.

Bayens, G. J., M. W. Manske, and J. O. Smykla. 1998. "Research Note: The Impact of the 'New Penology' on ISP." *Criminal Justice Review* 23, no. 1: 51–62.

Beckett, K. 1997. *Making Crime Pay: Law and Order in Contemporary American Politics*. New York: Oxford University Press.

Bonger, W. [1916] 1969. *Criminality and Economic Conditions*. Bloomington: Indiana University Press.

Bosworth, M. 2004. "Theorizing Race and Imprisonment: Towards a New Penality." *Critical Criminology* 12: 221–42.

Brody, R. 2004. *The Road to Abu Ghraib*. Human Rights Watch. Retrieved June 28, 2005, <www.hrw.org/reports/2004/usa0604/>.

Carlen, P. 2001. "Death and the Triumph of Governance?: Lessons from the Scottish Women's Prison." *Punishment and Society* 3, no. 4: 459–71.

Christie, N. 1993/1994. *Crime Control as Industry: Towards Gulags, Western Style*. London: Routledge.

Cohen, S. 1985. *Visions of Social Control: Crime, Punishment, and Classification*. New York: Polity Press/Blackwell.

Colvin, M. 1992. *The Penitentiary in Crisis: From Accommodation to Riot in New Mexico*. Albany: State University of New York Press.

Davis, A. 1998. *The Angela Y. Davis Reader*. Malden, MA: Blackwell.

Durkheim, E. 1947. *The Division of Labor in Society*. Trans. G. Simpson. New York: The Free Press.

———. 1973. *Moral Education: A Study in the Theory and Application of the Sociology of Education*. New York: The Free Press.

Dworkin, A. 2004, April. *Security Contractors in Iraq: Armed Guards or Private Soldiers?* Retrieved June 28, 2005, <www.crimesofwar.org/onnews/news-security.-html>.

Edwards, W., and C. Hensley. 2001. "Contextualizing Sex Offender Management Legislation and Policy: Evaluating the Problem of Latent Consequences in Community Notification Laws." *International Journal of Offender Therapy and Comparative Criminology* 45, no. 1: 83–101.

Elias, N. [1939] 1978. *The Civilizing Process*. Oxford: Oxford University Press.

Feeley, M., and J. Simon. 1992. "The New Penology: Notes on the Emerging Strategy of Corrections and Its Implications." *Criminology* 30, no. 4: 449–74.

———. 1998. "Actuarial Justice: The Emerging New Criminal Law. P. 375 in P. O'Mally, ed., *Crime and the Risk Society*. Brookfield, VT: Ashgate.

The Final Report of the Independent Panel to Review DoD Detention Operations. 2004,

August. J. R. Schlesinger, chair. Retrieved June 28, 2005, <http://news.findlaw.com/hdocs/docs/dod/abughraibrpt.pdf>.

Foucault, M. [1977] 1991. *Discipline and Punish: The Birth of the Prison*. New York: Pantheon Books.

Garland, D. 1990. *Punishment and Modern Society: A Study in Social Theory*. Chicago: University of Chicago Press.

———. 1995. "Penal Modernism and Postmodernism." Pp. 181–209 in *Punishment and Social Control: Essays in Honor of Sheldon L. Messinger*. New York: Aldine de Gruyter.

———. 1996. "The Limits of the Sovereign State: Strategies of Crime Control in Contemporary Society." *British Journal of Criminology* 36, no. 4: 445–71.

———. 2001. *The Culture of Control*. Chicago: University of Chicago Press.

Girling, E., I. Loader, and R. Sparks. 1999. *Crime and Social Change in Middle England: Questions of Order in an English Town*. New York: Routledge.

Greenberg, D. 2002. "Striking Out in Democracy." *Punishment and Society* 4, no. 2: 237–52.

Human Rights Watch. 1997. *Slipping Through the Cracks: Unaccompanied Children Detained by the U.S. Immigration and Naturalization Service*. New York: Human Rights Watch.

———. 1998. *Locked Away: Immigration Detainees in Jails in the U.S.* New York: Human Rights Watch.

Irwin, J., and J. Austin. 2001. *It's About Time: America's Imprisonment Binge*. Belmont, CA: Wadsworth.

Kellough, G., and S. Wortley. 2002. "Remand for Plea: Bail Decisions and Plea Bargaining as Commensurate Decisions." *British Journal of Criminology* 42: 186–210.

Kempf-Leonard, K., and E. Peterson. 2000. "Expanding Realms of the New Penology: The Advent of Actuarial Justice for Juveniles." *Punishment and Society* 2, no. 1: 66–97.

Latour, B. 1993. *We Have Never Been Modern*. Cambridge, MA: Harvard University Press.

Lynch, M. 1998. "Waste Managers? The New Penology, Crime Fighting, and Parole Agent Identity." *Law and Society Review* 32, no. 4: 839–69.

Marquart, J. W., V. E Brewer, J. L. Mullings, and B. M. Crouch. 1999. "Health Risk as an Emerging Field within the New Penology." *Journal of Criminal Justice* 27, no. 2: 143–54.

Martinson, R. 1974. "What Works? Questions and Answers about Prison Reform." *Public Interest* 35: 22–54.

Mauer, M. 1999. *The Race to Incarcerate*. New York: New Press.

McCorkle, R., and J. P. Crank. 1996. "Meet the New Boss: Institutional Change and Loose Coupling in Parole and Probation." *American Journal of Criminal Justice* 21, no. 1: 1–25.

Melossi, D., and M. Pavarini. 1981. *The Prison and the Factory: Origins of the Penitentiary System*. London: MacMillan.

Miller, L. L. 2001. "Looking for Postmodernism in all the Wrong Places: Implementing a New Penology." *British Journal of Criminology* 41, 168–84.

Packer, H. 1968. *The Limits of the Criminal Sanction*. Stanford, CA: Stanford University Press.

Petrunik, M. G. 2002. "Managing Unacceptable Risk: Sex Offenders, Community Response, and Social Policy in the United States and Canada." *International Journal of Offender Therapy and Comparative Criminology* 46, no. 4: 483–511.

Reiman, J. 2005. *The Rich Get Richer and the Poor get Prison: Ideology, Class, and Criminal Justice.* 7th ed. Boston: Allyn and Bacon.

Rose, N. 2002. "At Risk of Madness." Pp. 209–37 in T. Baker and J. Simon, eds., *Embracing Risk: The Changing Culture of Insurance and Responsibility.* Chicago: University of Chicago Press.

Rothman, D. 1980. *Conscience and Convenience: The Asylum and Its Alternatives in Progressive America.* Toronto: Little Brown.

Rusche, G., and O. Kirchheimer. 1939. *Punishment and Social Structure.* New York: Columbia University Press.

Schlosser, E. 1998. "The Prison-industrial Complex." *The Atlantic Monthly* 282, no. 6: 51–77.

Shichor, D. 1997. "Three Strikes as a Public Policy: The Convergence of the New Penology and the McDonaldization of Punishment." *Crime and Delinquency* 43, no. 4: 470–92.

Silverstein, M. 2001. "The Ties That Bind: Family Surveillance of Canadian Parolees." *Sociological Quarterly* 42, no. 3: 395–420.

Simon, J. 1988. "The Ideological Effects of Actuarial Practices." *Law and Society Review* 22, no. 4: 771.

———. 1993. *Poor Discipline.* Chicago: University of Chicago Press.

———. 1998. "Managing the Monstrous: Sex Offenders and the New Penology." *Psychology, Public Policy, and Law* 4, nos. 1–2: 452.

Simon, J., and M. Feeley. 1994. "True Crime: The New Penology and Public Discourse on Crime." In T. G. Blomberg and S. Cohen, eds., *Punishment and Social Control.* New York: Aldine de Gruyter.

Taylor, I., P. Walton, and J. Young. 1975. *Critical Criminology.* London: Routledge and Kegan Paul.

Vaughn, M. S., and L. G. Smith. 1999. "Practicing Penal Harm Medicine in the United States: Prisoners' Voices from Jail." *Justice Quarterly* 16, no. 1: 175–231.

Western, B., and K. Beckett. 1999. "How Unregulated Is the U.S. Labor Market?: The Penal System as a Labor Market Institution." *American Journal of Sociology* 104, no. 4: 1030–60.

Wacquant, L. 2000. "The New 'Peculiar Institution': On the Prison as Surrogate Ghetto." *Theoretical Criminology* 4, no. 3: 377–90.

Welch, M. 2003. *Detained: Immigration Laws and the Expanding I.N.S. Jail Complex.* Philadelphia: Temple University Press.

Young, J. 1999. *The Exclusive Society.* London: Sage.

Part II

Applications of Theory

Introduction to Part II

Walter S. DeKeseredy and Barbara Perry

THE THEORETICAL APPROACHES featured in the first section of this book attest to the richness of critical criminology. Nonetheless, they are limited in value unless and until they are applied to the sorts of criminological dilemmas that face real people in their lived experiences. Consequently, this section offers a selection of chapters that illustrate the practical utility of critical criminological theory as applied to the analysis of substantive social issues of the day. If part I offered a glimpse of how critical criminologists "think," part II offers a look into some of the things that they "think about."

The social problems that critical criminologists have examined are legion, and range from violence against women, to street crime, to crimes of the state. In fact, critical criminologists such as Frank and Lynch (1992) have been among the first to take things like environmental devastation seriously, and to acknowledge such phenomena as "crime." Moreover, critical criminologists have championed scholarship accounting for both sides of the power equation: how crimes of the powerful go relatively unchallenged; and how the powerless become criminalized.[1] Similarly, critical criminology offers strong accounts of the victimization process, especially as it is experienced by the most vulnerable and marginalized sectors of the community.

The selections that follow constitute an interesting mix of foci. They are not the typical collection of topic areas, but represent a combination unique to this volume. For the most part, they delve into relatively un- or under-explored areas of inquiry, as many of the authors attest. While diverse in scope, however, the chapters do share some similarities. Foremost among these is a critical review and assessment of the literature in the field in question. Additionally, most of the authors suggest "ways forward," or offer an advanced analysis of their topic of choice.

Violence

It may seem counterintuitive to suggest that violence is a new area of inquiry. However, it is a topic that has not been extensively examined within critical criminology. Rather, critical criminologists have tended to examine particular types of violence. Walter S. DeKeseredy, Shahid Alvi and Martin D. Schwartz, for example, have done extensive theoretical and empirical work on violence against women specifically,[2] just as Benjamin Bowling (1993; 1998) has focused attention on racist violence. Work such as this does not attempt to account globally for the broader, comprehensive phenomenon of "violence." Alternatively, critical criminologists have imagined violence as one form of criminal activity. Even work like James Messerschmidt's (1999; 2004)—which Gregg Barak cites in chapter 6 as an exemplar of more critical approaches—treats violence as one choice along a continuum of frequently antisocial practices for negotiating self and identity.

Thus, Barak's critique and synthesis of the literature on violence is a welcome foray into rare territory. He suggests that both mainstream and critical approaches to violence have tended to be both excessively simplistic and one dimensional, focusing only on individual, *or* institutional, *or* structural dimensions of violence. As a corrective, Barak offers a richer reciprocal theory of violence that integrates multiple mechanisms and contexts for violence.

Hate Crime

Where Barak offers an assessment of the literature in the broad area of violence, in chapter 7, Barbara Perry focuses on a specific type of violence: hate crime. This, too, is a relatively underdeveloped field of inquiry, especially within the ranks of critical criminologists. Having said that, then, it is ironic that some of the earliest, ground-breaking work on hate crime came from a critical criminologist—Mark Hamm. In 1994, he published *American Skinheads: The Criminology and Control of Hate Crime*. While not the first book on hate crime, it was the first theoretically guided account of one arm of the hate movement. Sadly, critical criminologists have not built on Hamm's work, nor has Hamm remained active in this area. Perry is virtually alone in her critical orientation to bias-motivated crime.

Consequently, what Perry's chapter offers is not a litany of what we think we know. Rather, it is a synopsis of what we don't know about hate crime. There are curiously neglected areas in our scholarship and research, which must be avenues of new and expanded inquiry. Perry argues that among the most disappointing gaps in this area are the lack of critical reflection on the usefulness of the term "hate crime" as a descriptor of bias-motivated behavior, and the failure to theorize the phenomenon. Moreover, scholars have largely failed to examine the specificity of the bias crime experiences of diverse victim groups, instead leaving the impression that all victims experience the problem in much the same way. In light of these gaps, it is perhaps not surprising that little interest has been shown in scholarship that explores measures aimed at preventing and responding to hate crime. In short, there is much work left to be done on this phenomenon.

Women and Drugs

Gender is featured prominently in critical criminological literature. Masculinities studies, for example, attempt to account for men's over-representation in crime statistics; other work focuses on women's experience of crime, and especially of sexual and domestic violence. In chapter 8, Judith Grant, however, offers a different focus: women's use and abuse of drugs. Like Barak, Grant offers a critique of mainstream—or in this case, "malestream"—approaches to her field. She argues persuasively that both scholars and practitioners have failed to take seriously the fact that women experience substance abuse differently than men. While the context and meaning of drug abuse differs dramatically for men and women, Grant argues that there have been far too few attempts to listen to women's voices as they articulate their journeys of addiction and recovery. This, then, frames Grant's assessment of ways forward, highlighting the need for gender specific perspectives and research.

Rural Crime

Criminology generally tends to focus on urban patterns of crime and crime control. Critical criminology is no exception to this trend. In chapter 9, Joseph F. Donnermeyer, Pat Jobes, and Elaine Barclay offer a stimulating corrective to this trend, drawing attention to crime in the rural context. It is not surprising that urban patterns of crime and victimization have been at the forefront of scholarship. This is, after all, where crime is concentrated. Bourgois's (1995) ethnographic work on drug dealing in East Harlem is most memorable in this context. A recent contribution, this time based on the Canadian urban experience, is DeKeseredy, Alvi, Schwartz, and Tomaszewski's (2003) *Under Siege: Poverty and Crime in a Public Housing Community.*

Each in its own way provides insight into urban experiences of young men, in the first instance, and culturally and economically disadvantaged people living in public housing in the second.

Donnermeyer, Jobes and Barclay's chapter provides a conceptual overview for the examination of rural crime in the context of poverty and other community factors. "Community" is proposed as the generalizing concept for interpreting broad cultural, economic, and social changes that are affecting the behaviors and attitudes of individuals living in rural areas. This approach embraces the spirit of C. W. Mills's (1959) conceptual distinction between "public issues" and "personal troubles" for developing criminologically based theories about the relationship between crime and place within the rural context. Specifically, this chapter examines how aspects of social disorganization explain crime in diverse rural places—an intriguing departure from the University of Chicago–inspired origins of that perspective.

Mentally Ill Offenders

There is a lively strain of legal analysis within critical criminology, one that often focuses on the creation of criminal law, or on its application, especially in terms of its uneven consideration of the powerful and the powerless. In chapter 10, Bruce A. Arrigo moves us in a slightly different direction, emphasizing instead the intersection of criminal law and mental health law. He is particularly concerned with the ways in which the legal and psychiatric disciplines conspire to create marginalized communities of those deemed mentally ill. This chapter represents a strong example of the substantive applications of a critical criminological theory, in that Arrigo makes sense of the "doctrine of competency" through a postmodernist lens. In short, he illustrates how the combined discourse and practice of the applied logic of competency punish the mentally ill offender in unique and unparalleled ways.

Body Donation

The final chapter in this book also represents the conscious application of a particular theoretical model—constitutive criminology—to a particular substantive issue—body donation. It also involves the application of a case study methodology. The beauty of this chapter is that it reminds us that critical criminology is indeed theoretically, substantively, and methodologically diverse. Most of the topics addressed in this section can and have been studied from multiple perspectives as well as through multiple methodological lenses. Julie Borkin, Stuart Henry, and Dragan Milovanovic here provide a case study of a documentary as a means of theoretically understanding the controversial question of body donation.

Notes

1. Reiman's (2004) widely read and cited book *The Rich Get Richer and the Poor Get Prison* is a major example of such work.

2. For example, see DeKeseredy and Schwartz (1998), DeKeseredy, Schwartz and Alvi (2000), and Schwartz and DeKeseredy (1997).

References

Bourgois, P. 1995. *In Search of Respect: Selling Crack in El Barrio.* New York: Cambridge University Press.

Bowling, B. 1993. "Racial Harassment and the Process of Victimization." *British Journal of Criminology* 33: 231–50.

———. 1998. *Violent Racism: Victimization, Policing and Social Context.* New York: Oxford University Press.

DeKeseredy, W. S., S. Alvi, M. D. Schwartz, and E. A. Tomaszewski. 2003. *Under Siege: Poverty and Crime in a Public Housing Community.* Lanham, MD: Lexington Books.

DeKeseredy, W. S., and M. D. Schwartz. 1998. *Woman Abuse on Campus: Results from the Canadian National Survey.* Thousand Oaks, CA: Sage.

DeKeseredy, W. S., M. D. Schwartz, and S. Alvi. 2000. "The Role of Profeminist Men in Dealing with Woman Abuse on the Canadian College Campus." *Violence Against Women* 6: 918–35.

Frank, N., and M. Lynch. 1992. *Corporate Crime, Corporate Violence: A Primer.* New York: Harrow & Heston.

Hamm, M. 1994. *American Skinheads: The Criminology and Control of Hate Crime.* Westport, CT: Praeger.

Messerschmidt, J. W. 1999. *Nine Lives: Adolescent Masculinities, the Body, and Violence.* Boulder, CO: Westview.

———. 2004. *Flesh and Blood: Adolescent Gender Diversity and Violence.* Lanham, MD: Rowman & Littlefield.

Mills, C. W. 1959. *The Sociological Imagination.* New York: Oxford University Press.

Reiman, J. 2004. *The Rich Get Richer and the Poor Get Prison: Ideology, Class, and Criminal Justice.* 7th edition. Boston: Allyn & Bacon.

Schwartz, M. D., and W. S. DeKeseredy. (1997). *Sexual Assault on the College Campus: The Role of Male Peer Support.* Thousand Oaks, CA: Sage.

6

A Critical Perspective on Violence

Gregg Barak

THIS CHAPTER PROVIDES a critical perspective on violence by exploring the most prominent scientific or academic theories of violence in general rather than those of violence in particular. Over the course of my examination of general theories of violence, I maintain that a satisfactory picture of both the individual and collective pathways to violence requires nothing less than a theoretical framework that incorporates a reciprocal integration of interpersonal, institutional, and structural violence.

Nearly all mainstream or traditional explanations of violence begin as "ad hoc" explanations that try to account for the observed regularity of various forms of isolated and self-contained violent events in such singular entities as gender, class, or ethnicity as these are, in turn, related to differences in biology, psychology, sociology, culture, and mass communication. Accordingly, most conventional explanations of violence remain partial and incomplete as they separately emphasize different yet related phenomena of violence, without ever trying to provide for a comprehensive explanation or framework that encompasses the full range of interpersonal, institutional, and structural violence. In fact, most of these one-dimensional explanations of violence underscore the behavioral expressions of persons to the relative exclusion of the institutional and structural expressions (Barak 2003).

These "interpersonal" explanations of violence can typically be classified into one of four kinds, based not only on the etiology of individual violence as either *internal* or *external*, but on the particular focus or orientation assumed about the relationship between *human nature* and violence. Traditionally, these explanations of general violence are associated with theories that locate the origins of violence within the person or within the social environment. Concurrently, some ad hoc theories maintain that humans are naturally inclined to act violently, requiring little in the way of stimulation or motivation, and that violence is, ultimately, the product of a failure of constraint or control. Other ad hoc theories maintain that humans are naturally inclined to conform to the rules of custom and order, requiring much in the way of stimulation or motivation, and that violence is, ultimately, the product of unusual or "deviant" impulses. From this dualistic (either/or) noncritical perspective, violence is "normative" in one case and "aberrant" in another case. Dialectically, however, it may very well be the case that various forms of violence are normative and aberrant at the same time; depending on whether or not they are sanctioned or unsanctioned as culturally and socially appropriate or inappropriate.

Whatever the case, the problems associated with ad hoc interpersonal theories of antisocial and violent behavior as well as with the dualistic approaches are being tackled by the recent emergence and development of *life-course*, *developmental*, and/or *integrative* perspectives. These epistemological approaches when applied to violence assume a complexity of human interaction that cuts across both the behavioral motivations and cultural constraints existing inside or outside the person. When compared to the earlier and more traditional, ad hoc, and one-dimensional explanations of violence, life-course and integrative explanations of violence constitute models that are conceptually (more) dynamic, developmental, and multidimensional in nature.

Life-course models of violence focus attention on the developmental trajectories of persons toward and away from specific courses of behavior. Integrative explanations focus attention on the dynamic relationships between the internal and external influences of violence and, in some instances, nonviolence, and the pushes (motivation) toward and pulls (constraints) away from violence/nonviolence. The application of these pathways to violence and/or nonviolence recognizes the accumulative natures of these behaviors, the reciprocal consequences of abusive and nonabusive behavior, and the integral relationships between events, situations, and conditions in the course of one's personal and social experiences.

A Review of Mainstream General Theories of Violence

Ad hoc/mainstream/one-dimensional explanations of general violence break down into those theories that explain violence in one of two fundamental ways: First, in terms of "properties" or "processes" that are either external to individuals—*externally motivated*—or inside people—*internally motivated*.

In either circumstance, people are stimulated to act violently. Second, in terms of the failure, absence, or lack of *internally* or *externally grounded constraints* to inhibit or prohibit people from acting on their violent impulses. These constraints are typically represented as self-control and social control.

What these explanations of violence all have in common is the tendency to reduce violence to one primary variable or set of variables. These one-dimensional explanations of violence often acknowledge the importance of other variables, but rarely do they factor them into their examinations and analyses. For example, several explanatory frameworks have been advanced to make sense out of violence in general. These include: *exchange theory*, *subcultural theory*, *resource theory*, *patriarchal theory*, *ecological theory*, *social learning theory*, *evolutionary theory*, *sociobiological theory*, *pathological conflict theory*, *psychopathological theory*, *general systems theory*, and *inequality theory.* Out of these twelve theories, eight of them address only one of the four cells from a typology of interpersonal explanations of violence (see table 6.1).

Of the four remaining explanations of violence: *pathological conflict* theory takes into account both internally motivated and constrained variables; *ecological theory* takes into account both externally motivated and constrained

TABLE 6.1.
A Typology of Interpersonal Explanations of Violence: Unicellular Models

	Origin of Cause	
	External	**Internal**
Nature of Cause		
Motivation	*Sociobiological* *Social Learning* *Subcultural* *Patriarchal*	*Psychological*
Constraint	*Evolutionary* *Exchange* *Resource*	

variables; *inequality theory* takes into account both internally and externally motivated variables; and *general systems theory* takes into account both internally and externally motivated variables as well as externally constrained variables (see table 6.2).

In terms of these two typologies, *externally motivated* explanations of generalized family violence, for example, are represented not exclusively by the disciplines of social-psychology, social anthropology, and sociology. These explanations of violence as well as of aggression, vulnerability, and risk stress the importance of structural-functionalism and the processes of socialization. As categorized above, these explanations of violence are most commonly expressed by sociobiological, social learning, subcultural, and patriarchal theories.

The sociobiological theories are used to explain rape, child abuse, infanticide, and other forms of domestic violence (Alexander 1974; Daly and Wilson 1981; Lightcap, Kurland, and Burgess 1982). These explanations of intimate violence are based on the inclusive fitness theory, which postulates that individuals will behave in ways to increase the probability that their genes will be transmitted to future generations. There are, indeed, associations between cases of child abuse and paternal uncertainty, handicapped or stepchild status, and among poor families when the allocations of limited resources require the hierarchal ranking of offspring.

TABLE 6.2.
A Typology of Interpersonal Explanations of Violence: Multicellular Models

Nature of Cause	Origin of Cause: External	Origin of Cause: Internal
Motivation	Inequality Ecological	Inequality Pathological Conflict
	General Systems	General Systems

By contrast, the social learning or sociocultural theories of violence, of which the subcultural and patriarchal theories are simply a variation, are less about nature than they are about nurture. These explanations of aggression and violence address issues of gender-centric attitudes and maintain that these behaviors are learned and precipitated by a combination of contextual and situational factors (O'Leary 1988). The social context of the "dysfunctional" family, for example, produces stress, aggressive personalities, and violent behavior. Or the situational factors like alcohol or drug abuse, financial problems, or marital infidelity accommodate exercises in aggression and violence. Probably, the most familiar of these social learning theories is the intergenerational transmission of family violence explanation, which contends that people who have witnessed or suffered physical family violence when growing up have a greater likelihood of living in a violent domestic situation later on in life. There are also associations between those people who have been sexually abused, especially boys, becoming sexually abusing teenagers and adults (Straus, Gelles, and Steinmetz 1980; Pagelow 1981; Groth 1983; Kaufman and Zigler 1987).

The subcultural theories of violence such as the "culture of violence theory" (Wolfgang and Ferracuti 1967) argue that within large, complex, and pluralistic societies, subgroups learn and develop specialized norms and values through differential associations and organizations that emphasize and justify the use of physical force above and beyond that which is regarded as "normative" of the culture as a whole. Family and street violence, for example, are viewed as the products of an exaggerated ethos of masculinity or of machismo, characteristic of "lower class" society. The various patriarchal theories have been advanced mostly, but not exclusively, by feminist social and behavioral scientists, who argue that violence is used by men to control women, to suppress the latter's rebellion and resistance to male domination, and to enforce the differential status of men and women that have traditionally been translated into laws and customs, in order to serve the collective interests of men. These theories argue both in the past and present, but less so today, that the unequal distribution of power between the sexes has resulted in societies that have been dominated by men and that most women occupy subordinate positions of power, increasing their vulnerability to violence, especially within the family (Martin 1976; Dobash and Dobash 1979).

Externally constrained explanations of generalized family violence are represented not exclusively by anthropologists, sociologists, and economists (Berreman 1978; Lenski and Lenski 1970; Pryor 1977). Evolutionary theories maintain that aggression and violence in technologically developed and highly stratified societies, for example, are used during childhood socialization as means of securing youngsters' obedience and conformity both within the family and larger society. The argument assumes that:

> In simpler and less technologically advanced societies, independence and self-reliance are encouraged in youngsters. This also means less adult supervision, more individual freedom, and therefore less demand for obedience and submission and fewer occasions for punishment. Instead, in complex, advanced, and hierarchical societies, compliance and obedience are the preferred traits. One had only to think of an industrial assembly line or of a large legal firm working on an important case to realize the pressure toward unquestioning acceptance of assignments and directions along rank lines. (Viano 1992, 9)

The two other externally constrained explanations of family violence are of a negative kind. That is to say, exchange theory is essentially a cost-benefit analysis of violence. "People hit and abuse other family members because they can" (Gelles 1983, 157). Similarly, the resource theory argues that the family member with the most power or aggregate value of resources (e.g., money, property, prestige, strength) in society, traditionally the male, commands higher power in the marital and family relationships than other members, namely, women and children who are in subordinate and vulnerable positions (Blood and Wolfe 1960). Like exchange theory, resource theory views violence in the nuclear family as a product of a lack of external constraints.

Internally motivated explanations of generalized family violence are represented not exclusively by the fields of psychology, psychoanalysis, psychiatry, physiology, and biology. These explanations of family and domestic violence range widely in scope. Some of these explanations of violence may include those favoring: internalized feelings of shame and humiliation leading to feelings of anger, hostility, and rage (Hale 1994); Freudian systems of ego pathology and impaired object relationships in the development of sexuality or concerns about dominance, submission, and control as unresolved conflicts originating during the anal period of development; pathophysiological models such as "cognitive fracture," where it is hypothesized that "hyperaroused orbitofrontal and medial prefrontal cortices tonically inhibit the amygdala and are no longer regulated by visceral and somatic homoeostatic controls ordinarily supplied by subcortical systems" (Fried 1997, 1845); abnormal trace-metal concentrations such as the presence of elevated serum copper and depressed plasma zinc in the blood of violence-prone individuals (Walsh et. al. 1997); and general psychopathology models such as those involving the American Psychiatric Association's label of "conduct disorder," where repetitive acts of patterned aggression toward animals and people are significant to the diagnosis (*Diagnostic and Statistical Manual of Mental Disorders*, edition IV).

All of these explanations despite their differences, share in common the attempt to account for personality dynamics and psychopathology that are unique to violent assailants. In other words, affected individuals, regardless of their particular origin of violence, are suffering from some kind of physiological and/or psychological imbalance/s expressed by combinations of obsessive ideation, compulsive repetition, poor impulse control, rapid desensitization to violence, diminished affective reactivity, failure to adapt to changing stimulus-reinforcement associations, hyperdependence, depression or anxiety, low self-esteem, paranoia, dissociation from their own feelings, antisocial tendencies, failure to empathize, fear of intimacy, and so forth.

Moving in a more inclusive direction, then, are the four other explanations of violence. Three of these consider two cells and one considers three cells from the typology of interpersonal violence. Each of these theories—pathological conflict, ecological, inequality, and general systems—is an improvement over the one-dimensional ad hoc theories of violence already discussed.

Pathological or social conflict theories are not exclusively represented by social psychologists, cultural anthropologists, and sociologists. These models of violence as pathological conflict, whether addressing marital disputes or large-scale conflicts, focus attention on communication processes and the tensions between the *internal constraints* or "bonds" and "attachments" among individuals, especially families as well as the larger communities, on the one hand, and the *internal motivations* of "abandonment," "shame," and "alienation," on the other hand. Pathological or emotional conflict in the forms of aggression and violence occur, whether individual or collective, when unacknowledged humiliation, dissociation, or depression is transformed into reactive anger and rage (Retzinger 1991; Gilligan 1997).

Ecological theories are not exclusively represented by such disciplines as mental health, social work, ecology, sociology, and criminology. These explanations of aggression are sensitive to social milieus such as neighborhood context, social support networks, poverty, and value systems that may coalesce to breakdown the *external constraints* to violence while simultaneously legitimating the *external motivations* to violence. For example, child abuse has been associated with the isolation of the nuclear family in contemporary advanced societies, on the one hand, and with the associated rationales for using violence against children, on the other hand (Garbarino 1977).

Inequality theories are advanced by virtually all of the disciplines of the behavioral and social sciences. These explanations of aggression and violence are related to the differential ways in which inequalities, privileges, hierarchies, discriminations, and oppressions, on the one hand, *externally motivate* some people to abuse, exploit, and generally take advantage of those labeled as socially inferior and, on the other hand, *internally motivate* those persons subject to the labels of inferiority to resist and rebel violently against their statuses. These explanations of violence are grounded in the political economies of private property and capitalist development (Iadicola and Shupe 1998).

Finally, general systems theories are also advanced by several of the social and behavioral sciences. These explanations of aggression and violence focus on positive feedback loops involving the interactions of individuals, families, and societal spheres (Straus 1978). These theories assume that optimal levels of violence are necessary or needed to maintain and reproduce the system. With the exception of internally constrained mechanisms of violence, these explanatory models take into account various sets of behavioral factors, including: high levels of conflict inherent in the family; the integration of violence into personality and behavioral scripts; cultural norms that legitimate violence; and the sexist organization of families and society (Viano 1992).

A Critique of Mainstream Theories of Violence

There are at least six problems with most of these types of ad hoc explanations of interpersonal violence. First, they are overly deterministic and one-dimensional, focusing on a limited rather than a broadened number of specific empirical regularities of violence. Second, they overemphasize one of the four binary combinations—EM, IM, EC, IC—to the relative neglect of the other three. Third, they represent one-directional and linear formulations of violence that split "causation" into either/or categories of internally and externally motivated or constrained acts of violence. Fourth, they are generally static and stable models of violence, locating the etiology of violence or antisocial behavior mostly in the early years of life. Fifth, they ignore and lack any explanation for the interconnections between individual forms of violence, on the one hand, and institutional and structural forms of violence, on the other hand. Sixth, they fail to consider the factors or properties involved in the desistance of antisocial behavior and violence (Barak 2003).

As already noted, all of these one-dimensional ad hoc explanations of violence are too narrowly focused, each excluding more variables of importance to violence than they include. With respect to some forms of violence, each of these explanations may be partially correct, plausible, and in some way or another empirically demonstrated (i.e., correlated), however, there remain many cases with respect to each of these that do not square with their models. In sum, the dynamics of violence are far more complex in nature than any of the ad hoc one-dimensional explanations imply. It may, therefore, make more sense to talk about these ad hoc relationships (correlations) as properties of violence. In other words, it may be more viable to view violence as a product of the interactive processes created by the four cells of interpersonal violence in relation to a reciprocal set of cells operating at the institutional and structural levels of society, as each of these intersects with the other spheres of violence.

In the next section, I turn to an overview of the recent development of those "critical" theories that accommodate, at a minimum, explanations of violence (and sometimes of nonviolence) inclusive of the four cells at the interpersonal, if not, also at the institutional and/or structural levels of social intercourse.

Critical Developments in Violence Theorizing

It has been written that "life-course theories systematically examine the multitude of causal influences that shape offending behavior over time" (Piquero and Mazerolle 2001, 87). As part of the development of a newly emerging and dynamic paradigm in the study of human behavior and social change, the life-course and integrative explanations bring together the interdisciplinary nature of the interaction between biography and history. At the same time, these reciprocal explanations of human interaction reject the ad hoc, one-dimensional, and overdetermined explanations of antisocial and violent behavior.

The "life-course" or "developmental" as well as "integrative" studies of human behavior and social structure have tried to address the ongoing interaction between individuals and their social environments over time. These overlapping and converging orientations to the interplay of human agency and historical conditions, appreciate the diverse ways in which individual lives are linked and connected through social integration with, and unlinked and disconnected through social separation from, families, communities, nations, and the world. In contrast to the ad hoc theories discussed above, each of the developmental models or theories of human behavior and social interaction provides an explanation capable of taking into account the four dimensions of the interpersonal typology of violence.

Two central concepts currently lie beneath the analysis of life-course dynamics: trajectories and transitions. A "trajectory" is a pathway or a line of development over the life span. Trajectories might include, for example, the growth (or lack) of self-esteem, depression, aggression, passivity, marriage, parenthood, a career, and so on. Trajectories or pathways by definition refer to long-term patterns and sequences of behavior. By contrast, a "transition" refers to a change of state or condition that is abrupt or involves shorter time spans. Transitions, such as a first marriage, a first child, or a first job, are specific life events that are viewed as embedded in trajectories or pathways of longer duration.

More specifically, the life course "can be viewed as a multilevel phenomenon, ranging from structured pathways through social institutions and organizations to the social trajectories of individuals and their developmental pathways," both subject to changing conditions and future options as well as to short-term transitions that are usually chronologically grounded (Elder 2001, 4). In the developmental scheme of things, life course analyses assume that earlier trajectories and transitions have implications for subsequent experiences and events. In fact, theoretically informed panel studies have already begun to "document the mechanisms of reciprocal influence between social and developmental trajectories" (Elder 2001, 5). At the same time, however, the majority of young antisocial children do not become adults who engage in antisocial behavior. Hence, the contradictory realities of continuity and change "are best seen as two aspects of a single dialectical process in which even major transformations of individuality emerge consequentially from the interaction of prior characteristics and circumstances" (as cited in Sampson and Laub 1992/2001, 33).

Taken together, the life-course/developmental and integrative perspectives on antisocial behavior, regardless of orientation, share in common a concern for the dynamic, interacting, and unfolding nature of biological, psychological, and social processes through time. In opposition to the time-invariant or static interpretations of the ad hoc explanations of violence, the life-course perspectives focus "on systematic change, especially how behaviors set in motion dynamic processes that alter future outcomes" (Sampson and Laub 1996/2001, 147). Nevertheless, within most of the research, so far, there has been a tendency to attribute continuity to time-stable personality traits and social-psychological processes over structured mechanisms of social allocation or inequality, even though both are capable of producing differentiating tendencies in successive cohorts (Dannefer 1987).

In the rest of this section, attention is paid to four related and developing theoretical articulations of the life-course and/or integrative perspective and to some of the supportive research findings:

Life-Course Persistent Antisocial Behavior

Terrie Moffitt (1993/2001), a psychologist, has offered a two-pronged theory of "adolescence-limited" and "life-course-persistent" antisocial behavior. Her contentions are that both of these types of antisocial offenders have unique natural histories and etiologies. In the case of the adolescence-limited theory of antisocial behavior, "a contemporary maturity gap encourages teens to mimic antisocial behavior in ways that are normative and adjustive" (Moffitt 2001, 91). In the case of the life-course-persistent theory of antisocial behavior, "children's neuropsychological problems interact cumulatively with their criminogenic environments across development, culminating in a pathological personality" (Moffitt 2001, 91). Comparatively, the antisocial behavior of the first group is temporary, situational, and less extreme than the antisocial behavior of the second group, represented by a relatively small number of males whose behavioral problems are acute, stable, and persistent over the life course.

Research studies have shown that antisocial behavior is stable across time and circumstances for a small percentage of people, ranging from 3 percent to 9 percent, yet decidedly unstable for most, but not necessarily all, other groups of birth cohorts, such as those who are regarded as being at moderate risks (Fergusson et al. 1991). Epidemiological research has also shown that there are virtually no persons diagnosed with adult antisocial personality disorder who did not have conduct disorder as children (Robins 1966; 1978). Other research has found continuity between disobedient and aggressive behavior at age 3 to later childhood conduct disorder and finally to arrest in early teen years (White et al. 1990), and between those who were first arrested between the ages of 7 and 11 and those who were also arrested as adults (Loeber 1982). Moreover, research reveals that life-course persistent antisocial persons lie at home, cheat at school, fight at bars, steal or embezzle at work, drive drunk, batter spouses, and abuse and neglect children (Farrington 1991; Farrington and West 1990; Loeber and Baicker-McKee 1989; Sampson and Laub 1990). Finally, research has also born out the relative distinctions between life-course-persistent and adolescent-limited wrongdoers and the career relationships between serious, violent, and chronic juvenile and adult offenders (Kempf-Leonard et al. 2001).

In short, "continuity is the hallmark of the small group of life-course-persistent antisocial persons. Across the life course, these individuals exhibit changing manifestations of antisocial behavior: biting and hitting at age 4, shoplifting and truancy at 10, selling drugs and stealing cars at age 19, robbery and rape at age 22, and fraud and child abuse at age 30; the underlying disposition remains the same, but its expression changes form as new social opportunities arise at different points in development" (Moffitt 2001, 100). At the core of Moffitt's explanation of life-course-persistent antisocial behavior is a theory that "emphasizes the constant process of reciprocal interaction between personal traits and environmental reactions to them"(2001, 111).

Moffitt locates the roots of stable antisocial behavior in factors that are present before or soon after birth. She hypothesizes that "the etiological chain begins with some factor capable of producing individual differences in the neuropsychological functions of the infant nervous system" (2001, 102). Whether such factors as disruption in the ontogenesis of the fetal brain due to physical injury, poor prenatal nutrition, maternal drug abuse during pregnancy, pre- or postnatal exposure to toxic agents are the proximate elements associated with elevated rates among violent offenders and subjects with antisocial personality traits (Fogel et al. 1985; Kandel et al. 1989; Paulhus and Martin 1986), or whether neuropsychological development is disrupted later by neonatal deprivation of nutrition, stimulation, and even affection (Cravioto and Arrieta 1983; Kraemer 1988; Meany et al. 1988), or later yet, by more deliberate child abuse and neglect cases associated with brain injuries and histories of delinquents with neuropsychological impairment (Lewis et al. 1979; Milner and McCanne 1991; Tarter et al. 1984), Moffitt argues there is good evidence to believe that "children who ultimately become persistently antisocial do suffer from deficits in neuropsychological abilities" (2001, 102).

Moffitt cites research demonstrating: the intergenerational transmission of severe antisocial behavior, especially involving aggression; the resemblance between parents and children on temperament and personality as well as on cognitive ability; and the stacking of the social and structural aspects of the environment against those children who enter the world at risk. She refers to this negative covariation in the nature of the child-environment relationship as providing a source of interactional continuity. She then turns her attention to the reciprocal relationships between the emergence of antisocial behaviors and what she refers to as the problem of parent-child interactions.

More specifically, Moffitt identifies three person-environment interactions that she believes are important in promoting an antisocial style and maintaining its continuity across the life course. These interactions are: *evocative*, *reactive*, and *proactive*. Of the three types of interactions, Moffitt suggests that evocative interaction is perhaps the most influential. Evocative interaction refers to when a child's behavior evokes distinctive responses from others. The point being that children with neuropsychological problems evoke challenges for even the most resourceful, loving, and patient families (Tinsley and Parke 1983). Similarly, numerous studies have shown that the problem behaviors of toddlers, for example, affect the parents' disciplinary strategies as well as subsequent interactions with adults and peers (Bell and Chapman 1986; Chess and Thomas 1987). The other two types of interaction are triggered by early behavioral difficulties and are maintained through the development of persistent and repetitive antisocial behavior, a function over time of the evoking responses exacerbating the child's tendencies. In other words, "the child acts; the environment reacts; and the child reacts back in mutually interlocking evocative interaction" (Caspi et al. 1987, 308).

Moffitt continues that once the evocative interactions are set in motion, that reactive and proactive interactions promote the further extension or continuity and pervasiveness of antisocial behavior throughout the life course, so long as the same underlying constellation of traits that got a person into trouble as a child remain intact. In other words, reactive interactions over time become conditioned defensive responses. In new or ambiguous interpersonal situations, for example, hyperactive or aggressive children are more likely (than nonaggressive) to attribute harmful intent to others and to act accordingly (Dodge and Frame 1982). Proactive interactions refer to the fact that antisocial individuals appear to selectively affiliate with others of similar personality configurations, including the nonrandom mating patterns of spouses who have both been convicted of crimes (Buss 1984; Baker et al. 1989). Finally, Moffitt's theory of life-course persistent antisocial behavior argues that these early causal sequences are dominated by chains of cumulative and contemporary continuity that restrict a person's behavioral repertoire and opportunities to succeed positively in life.

Informal Social Control and Cumulative Disadvantage

Robert Sampson and John Laub (1990; 1992/2001; 1993; 1996/2001), who were among the first in the early 1990s to popularize the life-course perspective in the field of criminology, have consistently focused their developmental work "on continuities and discontinuities in deviant behavior over time and on the social influences of age-graded transitions and salient life events" (1992/2001, 21). The life-course perspective argues that there is both stability of individual differences over time as well as changes in adolescence or adulthood that cannot be explained by early childhood development, or by the pathways first traveled and experienced in life.

Criminologists Sampson and Laub (1996/2001) have provided a theory of "informal social control and cumulative disadvantage" that I believe nicely complements Moffitt's two-pronged theory of antisocial behavior. Their explanation of antisocial behavior argues that there are important events and conditions that alter and redirect deviant pathways. Their theory is built upon three related themes or arguments: First, that structural factors or conditions such as poverty or racism impact the development of social bonds. Second, that a combination of social conditions and labeling processes can lead to cumulative disadvantage and the stability of antisocial behavior across the life span. Third, that the development of social capital later in life, especially during adulthood, can alter antisocial trajectories toward conformity. What holds this theory of "cumulative disadvantage" together is "a dynamic conceptualization of social control over the life course, integrated with" what they argue is "the one theoretical perspective in criminology that is inherently developmental in nature—labeling theory" (Sampson and Laub 1996/2001, 147).

While it is certainly true that the labeling perspective is developmental in nature because of its emphasis on processes such as "primary" and "secondary" deviance, to say that there are no other theories in criminology that are developmental is to reflect narrowly on the field of criminology. It is to reflect only about the sociological contributions to crime and deviance, ignoring the biological, psychological, and evolutionary models that are more often than not developmental in their structural approaches. Nevertheless, I believe that Sampson and Laub are correct for emphasizing the interactive nature of labeling, identity formation, exclusion from normal routines and conventional opportunities, and the increased contact with and relative support from other deviant or antisocial subgroups, as converging to create a "cumulative disadvantage."

Specifically, they argue that "the cumulative continuity of disadvantage is thus not only a result of stable individual differences in criminal propensity, but a dynamic process whereby childhood antisocial behavior and adolescent delinquency foster adult crime through the severance of adult social bonds" (Sampson and Laub 1996/2001, 155). In the process, they link the pathways of cumulative disadvantage and the constraints of subsequent development to four key institutions of social control—family, school, peers, and state sanctions—and to the causal sequential link in a chain of adversity between early childhood delinquency and adult criminal behavior. Following the lead of Gerald Patterson (1993; Patterson et al. 1989; Patterson and Yoerger 1993) and his colleagues, Sampson and Laub talk in terms of a "cascade" of secondary problems (e.g., school failure, peer rejection, depressed mood, and involvement with deviant peers) and of antisocial traits as a "chimera" of socially constructed and interactive aspects of racial, socioeconomic, and structural locations.

Gender Diversity and Violence

James Messerschmidt (1993; 1997; 2000; 2004) utilizes structured action theory in combination with an analysis of "doing" masculinities and femininities to derive his gender-based "sociobiological" theory of violent behavior among adolescent boys and girls. "Structured action theory has a long-established emphasis on the salience and fluidity of gender (as well as of race, class, age, and sexuality) and, therefore, offers" a theoretical model for exploring violence in relationship to both the body and society (Messerschmidt 2004, 146). Moreover, a "structured action theory acknowledges that both boys and girls are capable of 'doing' masculinities and femininities as well as other forms of gender embodiment" (Messerschmidt 2004, 146).

The key to understanding the various forms of gender construction and their relation to violence, lies in the way in which embodied social actions are structured by specific gender (as well as race, age, class, and sexuality) relations within particular social settings. Messerschmidt argues that the interactive and reciprocally gendered relations in the family, school, and street settings, provide the necessary motivation for violent and nonviolent behavior among boys and girls alike. By scrutinizing the life-histories of small samples of both boys and girls, grounded in the personal choices, experiences, and transformations that occur during early and late childhood, including adolescence, he identifies the social processes involved in youths becoming violent or nonviolent participants. In short, to understand male or female adolescent roles of violence/nonviolence, one must appreciate how structure and action are woven inextricably into the ongoing activities of violent predispositions, masculinity and femininity challenges, motivations, opportunities, and the resulting violent or nonviolent behaviors.

Messerschmidt demonstrates how the predispositions to violence and nonviolence arise from the reciprocal interplay of home, school, and street, and from the possibilities and pressures embedded in those interactions. More specifically, adolescent boys and girls in relation to their bodies, to their socialization experiences, and to the constructions of hegemonic, subordinate, and oppositional masculinities as well as to the alternate constructions of femininity, adopt violent or nonviolent behaviors in the course of doing different types of gender.

For example, in his discussions on embodied violence, Messerschmidt reveals the interactive life-course experiences of the home and the school or the street. With respect to two of his male subjects, he concluded that both were gender conformists. Yet, at the same time, they produced in particular settings specific but different types of embodied masculine practices through the use of different forms of assaultive violence and nonviolence: Both Lenny and Perry embodied situationally complicit (yet subordinate) masculinities at home, yet because Lenny did not experience masculinity challenges in this setting—as Perry did—he constructed a nonviolent masculine self, whereas Perry eventually embodied a violent masculine self in this milieu. Outside the home context different types of masculinities by Lenny and Perry emerged from practices that likewise reflected different social circumstances and different bodily resources (Messerschmidt 2004, 118).

With respect to two of his female subjects, Messerschmidt (2004, 128) similarly concluded that: "The life history data highlight the time- and place-specific aspects of Tina and Kelly doing gender through assaultive violence and nonviolence, depending upon the particular gender relations and their position in those relations. Indeed, such gender relations specific to certain settings resulted in both girls embodying nonviolence in different contexts—Kelly at home and Tina on the street—as well as assaultive violence in the same (the school) and different (the home vs. the street) milieus." In addition, in specific settings each of the girls embodied power and powerlessness. Finally, making matters more complicated, Messerschmidt also discovered what Jody Miller (2001; 2002) had found in her examinations of girls, gangs, and gender: namely, that gender diversity rather than gender dichotomy captures the complexity of what some have referred to as a "third gender."

A Reciprocal Theory of Violence and Nonviolence

Gregg Barak's (2003; 2004; 2005a; 2005b) reciprocal theory of violence and nonviolence is derived from an extension of the same logic used by the more traditional integrative, pathway, and multidimensional life-course theories. At its core, my approach to violence maintains that the key to understanding the dialectics of violence and nonviolence can be discovered, on the one hand, in the adversarial and mutualistic tendencies of social intercourse and, on the other hand, in the reciprocal relations of violent and nonviolent properties and pathways. More specifically, the reciprocal theory argues that the struggle between violence and nonviolence is a struggle about the contradictory relations or tensions between adversarialism and mutualism, which universally intersect virtually all individuals, groups, and nation-states alike, as these express themselves as competing properties. In addition, my theory contends that there are also pathways for culturally organizing personal and societal identities that, ultimately, navigate and guide individual, institutional, and structural behavior with respect to non/violent outcomes.

Found throughout families, neighborhoods, classrooms, boardrooms, workplaces, country clubs, or in a variety of settings involving other groups of people or institutions such as the military, law enforcement, judiciary, mass media, and the church, there are a diversity of violent and nonviolent expressions. There are also common or established "properties" and "pathways" that operate across a two-sided continuum of interpersonal, institutional, and structural relations of social and cultural organization that simultaneously promote violence (adversarialism) and nonviolence (mutualism). The interconnections between the interpersonal, institutional, and structural spheres constitute a reciprocal playing field where the constellations of pathways to non/violence are mutually reinforced, resisted, or negotiated.

Properties of violence refers to the essential attributes, characteristics, elements, factors, situations, routines, hot spots, conditions, and so on identified by any of the ad hoc, life-course/developmental, and integrative theories of antisocial behavior. These properties of violence, unsanctioned and sanctioned, may include negative emotional states involving feelings of alienation, shame, humiliation, mortification, rejection, abandonment, denial, depression, anger, hostility, projection, and displacement. They may also include a lack of emotional states associated with the properties of nonviolence such as empathy and compassion stemming from positive experiences of love, security, attachment, bonding, identification, altruism, mutualism, and so on.

When the properties of violence or "emotional pathogens" as James Gilligan (1997) refers to them, form in the familiar, subcultural, and cultural interactions between individuals and their social environments, and these states of being are not checked or countered by the states of being associated with the properties of nonviolence, then the potential for violent interactions involving the battered psyches of persons, groups, and nation-states alike, persists. That is to say, feelings of shame and humiliation, or of self-esteem and well-being, may be experienced by individuals, families, communities, tribes, nations, and other social groupings or subcultural stratifications based on age, gender, class, religion, ethnicity, sexuality, and so on. In short, to the extent that individuals and groups feel abandoned by or bonded with their parents, peers, schools, communities, and nation-states, or to the extent that people experience connection or disconnection, they will be prone to relate or not relate, to identify or not identify, to empathize or not to empathize, to take or not take responsibility, to project or not project hostility and aggression, to make war or love, to make violence or nonviolence, to be anxious and uptight, or to be contented and calm.

As for the production of violence, over time and space, the transitions or trajectories toward or away from non/violence accumulate, forming an array of divergent pathways that may facilitate or impede one state of being over the other. It makes sense, therefore, to view adversarialism, violence, and abuse, or mutualism, nonviolence, and empathy, as occurring along a two-sided continuum where the actions of individuals, groups, and nation-states are capable of stimulating, accommodating, or resisting pathways to one or the other. In terms of time and place, these pathways refer to the spatial webs of violence and nonviolence expressed at the familiar, subcultural, and cultural levels of social, political, and economic organization.

All combined, there are nine possible pathways to violence and nine possible pathways to nonviolence. In the structural spheres of violence and nonviolence alone, for example, there are the same informational, financial, and media networks that form an underside of global capitalism, global terrorism, and global peacemaking. Whether operating for prosocial, antisocial, or no particular purposes, these expanding infrastructures have created virtual realities in which once-secure societies now find themselves becoming "permeable webs that both allow and require new communication systems, circulation patterns and organizational structures" (Taylor 2001, B14). As societies and people adapt, as we find ourselves moving from industrial to network organization, and as the new technologies interact with both isolated individuals and collective villages of globalized culture, pathways to violence and nonviolence are reproduced.

Conclusion

This chapter has presented an overview of ad hoc, life-course/developmental, and integrative models of explaining violence and violent behavior. Comparatively, it was argued that the ad hoc theories—exchange, subcultural, resource, patriarchal, ecological, social learning, evolutionary, sociobiological, pathological conflict, psychopathological, general systems, and inequality—are inadequate explanations because, for the most part, they each ignore more relevant variables than they explore. Eight of these explanations address only one of the four interpersonal dimensions of internal as well as external motivation and constraint. Explanations derived from models of inequality, ecology, and pathological conflict address two of the four interpersonal dimensions, while general systems explanations address all but the internal constraints.

By contrast, the life-course/developmental and integrative models were judged to be superior explanations, as most of these tried to account for all four dimensions of the interpersonal typology of violence. Such models as Moffitt's two-pronged theory of adolescence-limited and life-course-persistent antisocial behavior, Sampson and Laub's theory of informal social control and cumulative disadvantage, and Messerschmidt's theory of gender diversity and violence, all recognize the interactive, reciprocal, and dialectical relationships leading to violent and nonviolent behavioral outcomes. While these models are, indeed, an improvement over the primarily ad hoc one-dimensional models, these explanations also reveal themselves to be incomplete. Though they usually account for internal as well as external motivations and constraints at the interpersonal level, they generally ignore similar interactive, reciprocal, and dialectical relationships involving the structural and at times, the institutional, domains of violence. Finally, omitted from these explanations of violence are the reciprocal or mutually reinforcing relationships between the spheres of interpersonal, institutional, and structural violence and nonviolence.

As a more comprehensive explanation of violence, the reciprocal theory of violence and nonviolence was introduced. This model argues that both the properties of and pathways to violence or nonviolence, across both the spheres of interpersonal, institutional, and structural relations and the domains of family, subculture, and culture, are accumulative, mutually reinforcing, and inversely related.

References

Alexander, R. D. 1974. "The Evolution of Social Behavior." *Annual Review of Ecology and Systematics* 5: 325–83.

Baker, L. A., W. Mack, T. E. Moffitt, and S. A. Mednick. 1989. "Etiology of Sex Differences in Criminal Convictions in a Danish Adoption Cohort." *Behavior Genetics* 19: 355–70.

Barak, G. 2003. *Violence and Nonviolence: Pathways to Understanding*. Thousand Oaks, CA: Sage.

———. 2004. "A Reciprocal Approach to Terrorism and Terrorist-like Behavior." Pp. 33–49 in M. Deflem, ed., *Terrorism and Counter-terrorism: Criminological Perspectives*. Amsterdam: Elsevier.

———. 2005a. "A Reciprocal Approach to Peacemaking Criminology: Between Adversarialism and Mutualism." *Theoretical Criminology* 9.

———. 2005b. "Applying Integrated Theory: A Reciprocal Theory of Violence and Nonviolence. In S. Henry and M. Lanier, eds., *The Essential Criminology Reader*. Boulder, CO: Westview.

Bell, R. Q., and M. Chapman. 1986. "Child Effects in Studies Using Experimental or Brief Longitudinal Approaches to Socialization." *Developmental Psychology* 22: 595–603.

Berreman, G. E. 1978. "Scale and Social Relations." *Current Anthropology* 19: 225–37.

Blood, R. O., and D. M. Wolfe. 1960. *Husbands and Wives: The Dynamics of Married Living*. Glencoe, IL: The Free Press.

Buss, D. M. 1984. "Toward a Psychology of Person-environment Correspondence: The Role of Spouse Selection." *Journal of Personality and Social Psychology* 53: 1214–21.

Caspi, A., G. H. Elder, and D. J. Bem. 1987. "Moving against the World: Life-course Patterns of Explosive Children." *Developmental Psychology* 23: 308–13.

Chess, S., and A. Tomas. 1987. *Origins and Evolution of Behavior Disorders: From Infancy to Early Adult Life*. Cambridge, MA: Harvard University Press.

Cravioto, J., and R. Arrieta. 1983. "Malnutrition in Childhood." Pp. 32–51 in M. Rutter, ed., *Developmental Neuropsychiatry*. New York: Guilford Press.

Daly, M., and M. I. Wilson. 1981. "Abuse and Neglect of Children in Evolutionary Perspective." Pp. 405–16 in R. Alexander and D. Tingle, eds., *Natural Selection and Social Behavior: Recent Research and New Theory*. New York: Chiron.

Dannefer, Dale. 1987. "Aging as Intracohort Differentiation: Accentuation, the Matthew Effect, and the Life Course." *Sociological Forum* 2: 211–36.

Dobash, R. E., and R. P. Dobash. 1979. *Violence Against Wives*. NY: Free Press.

Dodge, K. A., and C. K. Frame. 1982. "Social Cognitive Biases and Deficits in Aggressive Boys." *Child Development* 53: 629–35.

Elder, G. 2001. "Time, Human Agency, and Social Change." Pp. 3–30 in A. Piquero and P. Mazerolle, eds., *Life-Course Criminology: Contemporary and Classic Readings*. Belmont, CA: Wadsworth.

Farrington, D. P. 1991. "Antisocial Personality from Childhood to Adulthood." *The Psychologist* 4: 389–94.

Farrington, D. P., and D. J. West. 1990. "The Cambridge Study of Delinquent Development: A Long-term Follow-up of 401 London Males." Pp. 117–38 in H. J. Kerner and G. Kaiser, eds., *Kriminalitat*. New York: Springer-Verlag.

Fergusson, D. M., L. J. Horwood, and M. Lloyd. 1991. "A Latent Class Model of Child Offending." *Criminal Behavior and Mental Health* 1: 90–106.

Fogel, C. A., S. A. Mednick, and N. Michelson. 1985. "Minor Physical Anomalies and Hyperactivity." *Acta Psychiatrica Scandinavica* 72: 551–56.

Fried, I. 1997. "Syndrome E." *The Lancet* 350: 1845–47.

Garbarino, J. 1977. "The Human Ecology of Child Maltreatment: A Conceptual Model for Research." *Journal of Marriage and Family* 39: 721–35.

Gelles, R. 1983. "An Exchange Social Theory." Pp. 151–65 in D. Finkelhor, R. J. Gelles, G. T. Totaling, and M. A. Straus, eds., *The Dark Side of Families: Current Family Violence Research*. Beverly Hills, CA: Sage.

Gilligan, J. 1997. *Violence: Reflections on a National Epidemic*. New York: Vintage Books.

Groth, A. N. 1983. "Treatment of the Sexual Offender in a Correctional Institution." Pp. 160–76 in J. G. Greer and I. R. Stuart, eds., *The Sexual Aggressor: Current Perspectives in Treatment*. New York: Van Nostrand Reinhold.

Hale, R. 1994. "The Role of Humiliation and Embarrassment in Serial Murder." *Psychology: A Journal of Human Behavior* 31: 17–23.

Iadicola, P., and A. Shupe. 1998. *Violence, Inequality, and Human Freedom*. Dix Hills, NY: General Hall.

Kandel, E., P. A. Brennan, and S. A. Mednick. 1989. "Minor Physical Anomalies and Parental Modeling of Aggression to Predict Violent Offending." *Acta Psychiatric Scandinavica* 78: 1–5.

Kaufman, J., and E. Zigler. 1987. "Do Abused Children Become Abusive Parents?" *American Journal of Orthopsychiatry* 57: 316–31.

Kempf-Leonard, K., P. E Tracy, and J. C. Howell. 2001. "Serious, Violent, and Chronic Juvenile Offenders: The Relationship of Delinquency Career Types to Adult Criminality." *Justice Quarterly* 18: 449–78.

Kraemer, G. W. 1988. "Speculations on the Neurobiology of Protest and Despair."

Pp. 101–47 in P. Simon, P. Soubrie, and D. Widlocher, eds., *Inquiry into Schizophrenia and Depression: Animal Models of Psychiatric Disorders*. Basel, Switzerland: Karger.

Lenski, G., and J. Lenski. 1970. *Human Societies: An Introduction to Macrosociology*. New York: McGraw-Hill.

Lewis, D. O., S. S. Shanok, J. H. Picus, and G. H. Glaser. 1979. "Violent Juvenile Delinquents: Psychiatric, Neurological, Psychological, and Abuse Factors." *Journal of American Academy of Child Psychiatry* 2: 307–19.

Lightcap, J. L., J. A. Kurland, and R. L. Burgess. 1982. "Child Abuse: A Test of Some Predictions from Evolutionary Theory." *Ecology and Sociobiology* 3: 61–67.

Loeber, R. 1982. "The Stability of Antisocial and Delinquent Child Behavior: A Review." *Child Development* 53: 1431–46.

Loeber, R., and C. Baicker-McKee. 1989. "The Changing Manifestations of Disruptive Antisocial Behavior from Childhood to Early Adulthood: Evolution of Tautology?" Unpublished manuscript. Western Psychiatric Institute, University of Pittsburgh, PA.

Martin, D. 1976. *Battered Wives*. San Francisco: Glide.

Meany, M. J., D. H. Aitken, C. van Berkel, S. Bhatnagur, and R. M Sapolsky. 1988. "Effect of Neonatal Handling on Age-related Impairments Associated with the Hippocampus." *Science* 239: 766–68.

Messerschmidt, J. 1993. *Masculinities and Crime: Critique and Reconceptualization of Theory*. Lanham, MD: Rowman & Littlefield.

———. 1997. *Crime as Structured Action: Gender, Race, Class, and Crime in the Making*. Thousand Oaks, CA: Sage.

———. 2000. *Nine Lives: Adolescent Masculinities, the Body, and Violence*. Boulder, CO: Westview.

———. 2004. *Flesh and Blood: Adolescent Gender Diversity and Violence*. Lanham, MD: Rowman & Littlefield.

Miller, J. 2001. *One of the Guys: Girls, Gangs, and Gender*. New York: Oxford University.

———. 2002. "The Strengths and Limits of 'Doing Gender' for Understanding Street Crime." *Theoretical Criminology* 6, no. 6: 433–60.

Milner, J. S., and T. R. McCanne. 1991. "Neuropsychological Correlates of Physical Child Abuse." Pp. 131–45 in J. S. Milner, ed., *Neuropsychology of Aggression*. Norwell, MA: Kluwer Academic.

Moffitt, T. [1993] 2001. "Adolescence-limited and Life-course-persistent Antisocial Behavior: A Developmental Taxonomy." In A. Piquero and P. Mazerolle, eds., *Life-Course Criminology: Contemporary and Classic Readings*. Belmont, CA: Wadsworth.

O'Leary, D. K. 1988. "Physical Aggression between Spouses: A Social Learning Theory Perspective." Pp. 31–55 in V. B. Van Hasselt, ed., *Handbook of Family Violence*. New York: Plenum.

Pagelow, M. D. 1981. *Women-battering: Victims and Their Experiences*. Beverly Hills, CA: Sage.

Patterson, G. R. 1993. "Orderly Change in a Stable World: The Antisocial Trait as a Chimera." *Journal of Consulting and Clinical Psychology* 61: 911–19.

Patterson, G. R., B. D. DeBaryshe, and E. Ramsey. 1989. "A Developmental Perspective on Antisocial Behavior." *American Psychologist* 44: 329–35.

Patterson, G. R., and K. Yoerger. 1993. "Developmental Models for Delinquent Behavior." Pp. 140–72 in S. Hodgins, ed., *Mental Disorder and Crime*. Newbury Park, CA: Sage.

Paulhus, D. L., and C. L. Martin. 1986. "Predicting Adult Temperament from Minor Physical Anomalies." *Journal of Personality and Social Psychology* 50: 1235–39.

Piquero, Alex, and P. Mazerolle, eds. 2001. *Life-course Criminology: Contemporary and Classic Readings*. Belmont, CA: Wadsworth.

Pryor, F. L. 1977. *The Origins of the Economy*. New York: Academic Press.

Retzinger, S. M. 1991. *Violent Emotions: Shame and Rage in Marital Quarrels*. Newbury Park, CA: Sage.

Robins, L. N. 1966. *Deviant Children Grown Up*. Baltimore: Williams and Wilkins.

———. 1978. "Sturdy Childhood Predictors of Adult Antisocial Behavior: Replications for Longitudinal Studies." *Psychological Medicine* 8: 611–22.

Sampson, R., and J. Laub. 1990. "Crime and Deviance over the Life Course: The Salience of Adult Social Bonds." *American Sociological Review* 55: 609–27.

———. [1992] 2001. "Crime and Deviance in the Life Course." In A. Piquero and P. Mazerolle, eds., *Life-Course Criminology: Contemporary and Classic Readings*. Belmont, CA: Wadsworth.

———. 1993. *Crime in the Making: Pathways and Turning Points through Life*. Cambridge, MA: Harvard University Press.

———. [1996] 2001. "A Life-course Theory of Cumulative Disadvantage and the Stability of Delinquency." Pp. 133–61 in T. P. Thornberry, ed., *Developmental Theories of Crime and Delinquency: Advances in Criminological Theory*. Somerset, NJ: Transaction Books.

Straus, M. 1978. "Wife-beating: How Common and Why?" *Victimology* 2: 443–59.

Straus, M., R. J. Gelles, and S. K. Steimetz. 1980. *Behind Closed Doors: Violence in the American Family*. New York: Anchor.

Tarter, R. E ., A. M. Hegedus, N. E. Winsten, and A. L. Aterman. 1984. "Neuropsychological Personality and Familiar Characteristics of Physically Abused Delinquents." *Journal of American Academy of Child Psychiatry* 23: 668–74.

Taylor, M. C. 2001, December 14. "Unplanned Obsolescence and the New Network Culture." *The Chronicle of Higher Education*: B14–16.

Tinsley, B. R., and R. D. Parke. 1983. "The Person-environment Relationship: Lessons from Families with Preterm Infants." Pp. 93–110 in D. Magmusson and V. I. Allen, eds., *Human Development in Interactive Perspective*. San Diego, CA: Academic Press.

Viano, Emilio, ed. 1992. *Intimate Violence: Interdisciplinary Perspectives*. Washington, DC: Hemisphere Publishing.

Walsh, W. J., H. R. Isaacson, F. Rehman, and A. Hall. 1997. "Elevated Blood Copper/Zinc Ratios in Assaultive Young Males." *Psychology and Behavior* 62: 327–29.

White, J., T. E. Moffitt, F. Earls, L. N. Robins, and P. A. Silva. 1990. "How Early Can We Tell? Preschool Predictions of Boys' Conduct Disorder and Delinquency." *Criminology* 28: 507–33.

Wolfgang, M., and F. Ferracuti. 1967. "The Subculture of Violence: Toward an Integrated Theory of Criminology." London: Tavistock.

7

Missing Pieces: The Paucity of Hate Crime Scholarship

Barbara Perry

GIVEN THE RELEVANCE of key critical criminological concepts to the phenomenon of hate crime, it is curious that this problem has not been an object of extensive critical inquiry. Conceptually, it lies at the intersection of several themes which are currently to the fore: violence, victimization, race/ethnicity, gender, sexuality, and difference, for example. In spite of the centrality of violence as a means of policing the relative boundaries of identity, few attempts have been made to critically investigate the place of hate crime in the contemporary arsenal of oppression. Critical criminology has remarkable potential to help us to understand hate crime, since it is explicitly concerned with the importance of power in the context of crime and social control. However, critical scholars have largely neglected this field of inquiry. Granted, they are not alone in this, in that hate crime generally has only recently been the focus of serious academic inquiry generally. Nonetheless, it is disturbing that the stuff of hate crime—racism, nationalism, homophobia, sexism, xenophobia—has been undertheorized by critical scholars. This is overwhelmingly the case in criminology, where the most neglected field of inquiry has been "the relationship of crime and minority groups within society" (Flowers 1990, xiii). More specifically, with respect to race and ethnicity, at least, criminologists have been most consumed with efforts to examine minority patterns of offending and criminal justice processing, rather than their victimization; similarly, they have rarely made the explicit attempt to examine victimization based on the victim's status or group membership.

I have had occasion to reflect on the limitations of hate crime scholarship in the process of producing two books in the field. Together, the projects have indirectly led me to this paper. In the first, *In the Name of Hate: Understanding Hate Crime*, I directly confronted the lack of theorizing the problem by offering the theoretically grounded argument that hate crime is one resource for "doing difference," and for punishing those who "do difference differently." The second book, *Hate and Bias Crime: A Reader*, featured what I then saw as the most important extant work in the field. It was during the course of pulling the reader together that I began to identify a number of themes that could be said to constitute the "missing pieces" in hate crime scholarship. I use these here as the organizational tools for what follows. Specifically, I suggest that the following four areas are most in need of further critical review:

1) definitions and measurement of hate crime
2) conceptualizations of the causes and consequences of hate crime
3) analysis of particular victim groups
4) responses to hate crime.

To be fair, these lapses are attributable to the relative novelty of hate crime as a recognized social problem. The literature and public discussions of hate crime are not much beyond their adolescence, having little more than two or three decades longevity. In the U.S., for example, recognition of the social problem now known as hate crime can only be traced to the early 1980s, when the civil rights, women's rights and victims' rights movements seemed to provide the context for an anti–hate crime movement (Jenness 1995; Jenness and Broad 1998). While the term has evolved to the point of entering the popular lexicon, the phenomenon it describes remains underexplored. In this paper, then, I offer ways in which we might continue the scholarly initiatives begun in the 1980s.

Critical Scholarship on Hate Crime: Unfulfilled Promise

Critical criminology has a great deal to recommend it as an explanatory framework for hate crime. It explicitly confronts at least two of the primary conceptual "facts" associated with the phenomenon: marginalization and power. Both themes are crucial to a fully political understanding of hate crimes, given that they are themselves exercises of power intended to assert the marginal status of victims, and simultaneously, the relatively privileged status of the offenders. Moreover, the understanding of hate crime requires consideration of the specific sociohistorical context in which it emerges—an approach which is also a hallmark of recent critical theorizing. For Gilroy (1982, 281) this involves paying attention to "the construction, mobilization and pertinence of different forms of racist ideology and structuration in specific historical circumstances." In so doing, critical criminology points to the official ideologies and practices which might make minorities vulnerable to popular forms of repression as well.

However, critical analyses of the relationship between minority groups and crime have been most concerned with the way in which marginalization contributes to crime. What of the obverse? What of the way in which crime contributes to marginalization? This is what hate crime accomplishes. It constructs the relative identities of both offender and victim by simultaneously asserting one and subordinating, if not annihilating another.

The most sophisticated critical exegesis on hate crime is undoubtedly Mark Hamm's (1994a) exploration of U.S. skinheads. This is an explicit attempt to not only expose the skinhead culture, but also to theorize its motives and structure. Hamm is unafraid to approach the issue in an innovative and eclectic manner, both methodologically and theoretically. The very nature of the skinhead subculture required an unorthodox style of research. Hamm was faced with the task of overcoming the paranoia, resistance and violence of this movement. What emerged, then, was a rich ethnography, which drew its sample from a diverse range of sources.

A complex and surprising picture of the skinhead subculture emerges from Hamm's interviews. While skinhead culture appears to be a working-class phenomenon (subcultural), it is also characterized by *synanomie* rather than *anomie*. That is, skinheads appear to be "hyperactively bonded to the dominant social order" (Hamm 1994a, 212). These are not the alienated, disenfranchised misfits of the media stereotypes. Rather, they are relatively successful "hyperconformists" who use beer as a catalyst for violence. This in itself forces us to reevaluate popular conceptions of who hate crime offenders are.

While inspiring this question, Hamm's account does not necessarily provide a generalizable response. Hamm falls short of providing a comprehensive approach to hate crime generally. Not all perpetrators resemble skinheads in manner or motivation. Not all are exposed to the vitriol of Metzger. Not all are committed to the philosophy of neo-Nazism. To be fair, this was not Hamm's intent. His research was explicitly motivated by an interest in understanding terrorist youth subcultures. What Hamm offers, then, is a starting point for analysis, based on the recognition that skinheads represent a "subculture whose rituals and symbols reveal a basic truth about the values of society at large" (Hamm 1994a, 215). Subsequent theorizing must make clear what that "basic truth" is, and how it informs the bigotry and actions of those not associated with organized hate groups.

Hamm's efforts are illustrative of the one area of strength in critical scholarship around hate crime. If there is one subject in the broad field of hate crime literature that has received extensive attention it is hate groups. I write here of the hate movement/hate groups, by which I mean a shorthand for an array of organizations known variously as hate groups, racialist groups, militias, separatist organizations, the patriot movement, or extremist groups. I fully recognize the distinctions between these, but nonetheless use the terms hate group or hate movement for the sake of simplicity and consistency.

Indeed, there is some very exciting work that explores the connections between identity and hate-group membership. For example, Randy Blazak's and Kathleen Blee's works specifically address the process of "becoming a racist," although with considerably different emphases. Blazak is specifically concerned with the recruitment of young, disaffected, and "anomic" youth who join violent Skinhead groups as a means of reclaiming some power. In contrast, Blee offers an intriguing examination of women who affiliate with KKK and neo-Nazi groups. The two approaches complement one another. Blee's work answers the question implicitly raised by Blazak's work: why would women join and remain in organizations that are, by and large, male oriented and male dominated? These scholars have begun a dialog that must be continued, helping us to understand what kinds of people are vulnerable to the siren call of the movement. Nonetheless, Blazak and Blee are among only a small handful of critical scholars in the field.

Area 1: Defining and Measuring Hate Crime

The first issue I see warranting critical reflection may, at first blush, seem little more than a question of semantics. I am referring here to the use of the term "hate crime" itself. The phrase is fraught with dilemmas and difficulties. Laypeople as well as professionals and scholars tend to take it far too literally, often insisting that all (violent) crimes are "about hate," or alternatively, that perpetrators don't necessarily "hate" their victims. A letter to the editor of the *Arizona Republic* (April 17, 1999) illustrates the point: "All crimes are hate crimes. They say to the victim: I don't care about your rights, your loss, your injury, your pain, your death or those who love you." This is to oversimplify the concept through very prosaic interpretations of the concept. It is, then, unfortunate that the term "hate crime," coined by Representatives Conyers, Kenally, and Briggs in their 1985 sponsorship of a hate crime statistics bill, has stuck. While it has a dramatic ring to it, the phrase conjures up particular motivations and emotions. Moreover, it tends to:

> individualize racist [and other forms of] violence, to present it as an act of pathological individuals. It encourages a view of racism and violence as the result of the presence of pathological individuals, rather than as embedded in institutional practices of offending communities, in locales and habitual ways of dealing with the world, and especially dealing with problematic situations. (Ray and Smith 2001, 221)

Too often, the term assumes the status of the trivial, akin to "dislike," thereby allowing critics a basis on which to oppose hate crime regulation. Such critics argue that "hate" crime refers to "thought" or "attitude" or "belief." The reduction of the concept of "hate" crime to its basest interpretation is vividly illustrated in the Andrew Sullivan's contention that

> hate is a vague, complex and highly personal emotion and does not pertain to a particular set of beliefs. Thus labeling violent acts committed against certain victims of "hate crimes" is deeply problematic and possibly unconstitutional. (1999)

Such simplistic and reductionist accounts, I would argue, are consciously used to minimize the import and impact of violent and discursive forms of bigotry. They occlude the distinction between the popular "dictionary" meaning of hate, and the sociological meanings that informed the adoption of the term in the first place. In such cases, "hate" is divorced from its cultural and political context. However, the sorts of violence we have in mind are not "about" hate, but "about" the cultural assumptions we make with respect to difference. In short, bias-motivated violence is a reflection not of individual values or sentiments, but of culturally normative values of domination and subordination. It resonates with a network of norms, assumptions, behaviors, and policies which are structurally connected in such a way as to reproduce the identity based hierarchies that characterize so many Western cultures. In this respect then, hate crime is as normal and as usual as alternative mechanisms of oppression, such as cultural stereotyping or employment segregation.

A consideration of the language of hate crime also raises subsequent questions about how we define the concept. Recent legislation at both state and federal levels in the U.S., as well as elsewhere, is a manifestation of the shifting conceptualization of bias-motivated violence. Most notably the Hate Crime Statistics Act of 1990 (HCSA) was the first piece of federal legislation to explicitly institutionalize this new understanding. As is typical of governmental decrees, the HCSA provides a narrow legalistic definition of hate crime: "crimes that manifest evidence of prejudice based on race, religion, sexual orientation or ethnicity."

For the most part, states which subsequently (or previously) introduced hate crime legislation have followed suit, adopting a similar definition. According to these definitions, the hate crime designation may only be applied where a "predicate offence," or underlying crime is committed, as a result of bias or prejudice. This is not to say that even legal definitions are consistent. They are not. What constitutes a hate crime differs dramatically between jurisdictions. Across the U.S., there are dramatic differences in how bias is defined, what classes of victims are protected, and the extent of bias motivation necessary for classification (e.g., "in whole or in part," or "primarily" motivated by bias). The matter is even more complex when one considers international differences. For example, while the U.S. emphasizes individual acts, German legislation tends to emphasize the organized hatred and violence associated with Nazi and neo-Nazi organizations, as well as "incitement to hatred." In short, "crimes motivated by a victim's race, ethnicity, or religion are defined at least nine different ways in seven different nations around the world" (Hamm 1994b, 174).

While narrow, legalistic definitions may be deemed necessary within the law enforcement community, it is not particularly satisfying from a social science perspective. As with "crime" in general, it is difficult to construct an exhaustive definition of the term "hate crime." Crime—hate crime included—is relative. It is historically and culturally contingent. What we take as hate crime today in the United States, in another time, in another place, may be standard operating procedure. Michalowski (1985), for example, reminds us that it is a myth that "there exists some universally consistent definition of theft and violence as criminal acts." On the contrary, both as a category and as a social phenomenon in and of itself, hate crime is "dynamic and in a state of constant movement and change, rather than static and fixed" (Bowling 1993).

Bowling's comments suggest yet another important consideration in defining crime. That is, crime is best understood as a process rather than an event. It does not occur in a cultural or social vacuum, nor is it "over" when the perpetrator moves on. For this reason, we must define hate crime in such a way as to give the term "life" and meaning, in other words, as a socially situated, dynamic process involving context and actors, structure and agency. While this is a heavy order for any single definition to fill, it is nonetheless possible to construct a conceptual definition which allows us to account for the predominant concerns raised by Bowling: historical and social context; relationships between actors; and relationships between communities. Seen in this context, it is apparent that our understanding of hate crime is furthered by a definition which recognizes the ways in which this particular category of violence facilitates the relative construction of identities, within a framework of specific relations of power. This allows us to acknowledge that bias-motivated violence is not "abnormal" or "anomalous" in many Western cultures, but is rather a natural extension of the racism, sexism and homophobia that normally allocates privilege along racial and gender lines. As expressions of hate, such acts of intimidation necessarily "involve the assertion of selves over others constituted as Other" (Goldberg 1995), where the self is thought to constitute the norm.

In light of this caveat, it is equally important to distinguish hate crime from its non–bias-motivated counterparts. A potential starting point may be the distinction drawn by Berk, Boyd and Hamner (1992) between symbolic and actuarial crimes, and between expressive and instrumental motives. Symbolic crimes are purposefully directed toward a victim because of her/his group membership and the way in which the perpetrator perceives the group; actuarial crimes, on the other hand, use the victim's status as a predictor of his/her practical value as a victim. In a parallel manner, expressive motives are characterized by a wish to send a message to the victim and his/her community, whereas instrumental motives seek objective ends—money, for example. Similarly, a Harvard Law Review note (1995) suggests a subtle distinction between "rational targeting"—in which offenders "will use common sense to select victims who offer the highest benefit and lowest cost" (1929) and "racist violence"—motivated by prejudice "based on the view that (the victims) do not merit treatment as equals or that they deserve blame for various societal ills" (1930). Extant cases might be investigated as a means of highlighting the unique dynamics that characterize ethnoviolence as a distinct class.

One consequence of the varied and divergent definitions used to conceptualize bias-motivated crime is that the confusion inevitably complicates the process of gathering data on hate crime. Berk, Boyd and Hamner (1992) astutely observe that "much of the available data on hate-motivated crime rests on unclear definitions; it is difficult to know what is being counted as hate-motivated and what is not." As a result, while both academic and media reports make the claim that ethnoviolence represents a "rising tide," the truth is we don't know whether in fact this is the case or not (Jacobs and Potter 1998). For the most part, existing methodologies are both too new and too flawed to give us an accurate picture of changes over time. For example, because the U.S. hate crime data are collected in the same way as the other Uniform Crime Report (UCR) data, they are fraught with the same well-documented deficiencies (Bureau of Justice Assistance 1997). A recent analysis of the first decade of data gathering under the HCSA documents the many limitations that continue to inhibit accurate counting (McDevitt et al. 2000). Among the problems: lack of law enforcement agency policies on investigating and recording hate crime; lack of intensive training on hate crime; and police officers' lack of understanding of or sympathy for hate crime as an offense category.

Overall, the UCR and its counterparts in other countries provide little more than starting points for any discussion of hate crime. Given the problems noted above, we are well advised to supplement these official sources of information with data available from the growing number of nongovernmental bodies devoted to tracking and responding to hate crime. Generally, these agencies tend to gather information specific to one target group—the Anti-Defamation League (ADL) on anti-Semitism, or the NGLTF on anti-gay violence for example—and are thus limited in scope. In short, each of these bodies brings with it unique strengths and weaknesses. For example, in an assessment of several unofficial data analysis efforts, Ilarraza, Angel and Becker (2001) conclude, "The results of our effort to identify and assess the extent and content of unofficial hate crime data suggest the presence of several important issues which must be taken into account when using 'alternative data sources' as evidence of the extent and nature of hate crime in America." Among the limitations they identify are such issues as inconsistency in defining hate crime; the lack of national level data; and the failure to follow rigorous research practices.

One way forward is to work with the sorts of agencies noted above to conduct rigorous assessments of their data gathering efforts, and to then assist them in enhancing their internal methodologies. Beyond that, there is no single approach that I would propose as *the* way to proceed. On the contrary, I would concur with Bowling's (1993) recommendation that, given the complexity of hate crime as a process, we should proceed in a multidimensional way:

> Surveys could be complemented by ethnography, life history research, case studies and other methods to research aspects of victimization and offending. The combination of methods will clearly be contingent on the nature of the research subject. Different combinations will have advantages for different forms of crime and for different moments in crime processes. (248)

Moreover, returning to the processual understanding of hate crime noted earlier, it is apparent that, whatever the method employed, it is crucial that it "allow for the relationships between victim, offender, and statutory agents (police, courts, housing authority, etc.) to be charted; and that these relationships should be set in the context of family, 'community' and neighbourhood, race, class, and age divisions" (Bowling 1993). While qualitative approaches are probably most suited to these dynamic characteristics of hate crime, I would encourage others to also develop creative quantitative approaches that seek to uncover some of these contextual cues.

With data in hand, scholars will be in a much better position to contribute to our understanding of other dimensions of hate crime. In particular, enhancing the empirical base of "facts" about hate crime will help us to fill another notable void in the literature: analyses of the causes and consequences of hate crime.

Area 2: Causes and Consequences

In my book (Perry 2001), I observed that the social sciences had failed us with respect to enhancing our theoretical understanding of hate crime. It is disturbing that, in a 2002 publication, Kellina Craig (2002) could still claim—quite accurately—that efforts to explain hate crime theoretically remain rare. In part, the limitations of definition and measurement highlighted above help to explain the limited attempts thus far to theorize hate crime. In the absence of empirical information about bias-motivated violence, it is difficult to construct conceptual frameworks. Without the raw materials, there is no foundation for theorizing. Additionally, the relatively recent recognition of hate crime as a social problem (Jenness and Broad 1998) also contributes to the lack of theoretical accounts. To be sure, racially, religiously, and gender-motivated violence has long been part of the history of all nations, yet it has not been readily acknowledged as problematic until recent decades.

To date, the theoretical literature on hate crime has been dominated by psychological and social-psychological accounts; that is, the emphasis has been on individual level analyses. Such accounts "seek to understand the psychological causes that compel people to commit hate crimes. Sometimes these causes are sought in enduring psychological orientations or propensities; in other cases, hate crime is said to arise because individuals with certain kinds of beliefs and aversions find themselves in situations where these psychological attributes are brought to the fore" (Green et al. 2001, 484). This is not to say that broader social or cultural conceptualizations are not available. In fact, Green et al. (2001) recently published an overview of hate crime literature in which they identified an additional five macro-level theories found in the hate crime literature: historical-cultural, sociological, economic, political and synthetic accounts.

Nonetheless, the entries within each class of theories are limited. There is ample room for more—and more sophisticated—analyses if we are to fully understand and confront the problem. One option is to let broader empirical work guide our theory-making as we engage in the process of constructing grounded theory—what processes, relationships, motives, and so forth are suggested by the empirical patterns of crime? Alternatively, we can let extant theory guide our research. Personally, I would like to see more theoretically grounded work which takes as its frame the cultural, social and political processes that underlie hate crime. Hate crime is at once part of and symptomatic of larger patterns of intergroup conflict, and especially of subordination. Racial violence, therefore, is in fact a social practice embedded in broader patterns of oppression which systematically restrict the capacities and autonomy of its victims. For example, Young (1990) operationalizes oppression in a way that provides a very useful framework for contextualizing bias-motivated violence. She articulates five interrelated "faces of oppression" by which we might characterize the experiences of common target groups: exploitation (e.g., employment segregation); marginalization (e.g, impoverishment); powerlessness (e.g., underrepresentation in political office); cultural imperialism (e.g., demeaning stereotypes); and violence (e.g., hate crime). Together, structural exclusions and cultural imaging leave minority members vulnerable to systemic violence, and especially ethnoviolence. The former makes them vulnerable targets, the latter makes them "legitimate" targets. Moreover, violence is very likely to emerge in contexts wherein the formerly disadvantaged challenge the other bases of oppression, as when they seek to empower themselves economically or socially through rights claims.

This specific model suggests two directions for further theoretical work: examining the concrete connections between systematic violence and other forms of oppression; and especially testing the link between victim group mobilization, activism, and visibility on the one hand, and retaliatory victimization on the other. I have begun to apply this model to an understanding of the victimization of Native Americans in the U.S. (Perry 2002; forthcoming). Similar work, exploiting or building upon alternative theoretical models can and should also be undertaken.

Another related area that remains underdeveloped is the question of the consequences of hate crime. Running through much of the literature—even through court decisions on hate crime—is the assumption that such offences are qualitatively different in their effects, as compared to their non–bias-motivated counterparts. For the sake of simplicity, I identify two interrelated dimensions of the impact of hate crime for individuals and collectives: impact on immediate victims; and impact on other members of the victim's group. Only one of these has received serious attention, and that very narrowly.

It is the first of these that has garnered scholarly attention. Research suggests that first and foremost among the impacts on the individual is the physical harm: bias-motivated crimes are often characterized by extreme brutality (Levin and McDevitt 1993). Additionally, the empirical findings in studies of the emotional, psychological, and behavioral impact of hate crime are beginning to establish a solid pattern of more severe impact on bias crime victims, as compared to non-bias victims (see, e.g., Herek et al. 2002; McDevitt et al. 2001). Such comparative analyses of bias- and non–bias-motivated victims must be replicated to enhance the credibility of such findings.

A largely unknown aspect of the victim's experience is the impact of victimization on his/her perceptions of the offender and his/her group. If we are to understand the collective and cumulative effects of ethnoviolence on broader intergroup relationships, it is important to first understand how victimization—even the act of offending—affects the perceptions of the individuals directly involved in the offense. This is something about which we have little if any information. When we move beyond the experiences of the immediate victim, we enter the realm of speculation. Many scholars—myself included!—point to the "fact" that hate crimes are "message crimes" that emit a distinct warning to all members of the victim's community: step out of line, cross invisible boundaries, and you too could be lying on the ground, beaten and bloodied (see, e.g., Iganski 2001). Consequently, the individual fear noted above is thought to be accompanied by the collective fear of the victim's cultural group, possibly even of other minority groups likely to be victims. Weinstein (as cited in Iganski 2001), refers to this as an *in terrorem* effect: intimidation of the group by the victimization of one or a few members of that group. Yet I know of no study that explicitly surveys large numbers of victims' reference communities to determine the veracity of this assumption. If we are to argue for the classification of hate crime as a distinct form of victimization, it is incumbent upon us to establish the disparate impact it has on those other than the victim.

One related area that has received scant attention has been the observation that anxiety triggered by the victimization of one's cultural group can easily erupt into periods of retaliatory violence. In the U.S., Chief Justice Rehnquist acknowledged this writing for the majority in *Wisconsin v. Mitchell* (1993) He argued for the recognition of hate crime as a special class of offence because of the likelihood that it would, in fact, initiate yet more violence. This effect was evident in New York following the murder of a young African American man by a crowd of Italian youth in Bensonhurst in 1989, where the murder was followed by days of racial skirmishes. A more recent example occurred in Carson City, Nevada, in 2002, where a group of twelve American Indian males attacked two Latino males, apparently in response to an earlier assault on a Native American in which they were thought to have taken part. McDevitt et al. (2001) include a retaliatory motive in their typology of hate crime offenders, based on their observation that a notable proportion of offenders reported that their offence was a response to a prior (perceived or real) offence perpetrated against them. But again, the efforts to establish this link are few, and tend to rely on anecdotal evidence.

Even if the victim's cultural group does not directly retaliate against the hate crime perpetrators or their reference community, it is argued, hate crime may yet have deleterious effects on the relationships between communities. Cultural groups that are already distant by virtue of language differences, or differences in values or beliefs are rendered even more distant by virtue of the fear and distrust engendered by bias-motivated violence. Intergroup violence and harassment further inhibit positive intergroup interaction. Again, explorations of changing intergroup dynamics in the face of bias-motivated violence will confirm—or deny—that such a relationship exists.

Alternatively, one possibility is that hate crime acts as a catalyst to positive change. That is, patterns of persistent violence, or highly publicized cases—like the 1998 Matthew Shepard or James Byrd cases—often have the unintended effect of mobilizing victim communities and their allies. Again, anecdotally, there is some evidence that this occurs. This was the case in New York City, for example, where Haitians accompanied by other Caribbeans demonstrated angrily, vocally and visibly against the racist violence represented by Abner Louima's brutal beating at the hands of police officers in 1997. While innumerable victims had previously remained silent out of fear and intimidation, the publicity surrounding Louima's victimization galvanized the community into action. We might choose to look more closely at such examples to determine the circumstances that ensure positive mobilization, rather than retaliation or withdrawal.

Clearly, the broader social effects of hate crime must be examined both theoretically and empirically. How can we measure the impact of hate crime on the broader public? How does it affect perceptions of the liberties held dear in democratic states? To what extent is hate crime a reflection of broader hatreds, and to what extent does it exacerbate or alleviate these? Any combination of these questions provides a valuable starting point in our efforts to test widely held assumptions about the societal impact of ethnoviolence.

Area 3: Victims of Hate Crime and Bias-motivated Crime

To date, hate crime literature has tended to be very broad and nonspecific in its focus. That is, little scholarship devotes attention to specific categories of victims. Extant literature has tended to discuss hate crime in generic terms, as if it were experienced in the same ways by women, by Jews, by gay men, by Latino/as, by lesbians. Even racial violence is collapsed into one broad category, as if all racial and ethnic groups experience it in the same way. Consequently, we do not have a very clear picture of the specific dynamics and consequences that may be associated with victimization on the basis of different identity positions. The possible exceptions here are anti-gay victimization, which has been widely examined by the likes of Gregory Herek et al. (2002) in the U.S., and European work on immigrants.

Official data and anecdotal evidence both point to the staggeringly high rates of victimization of racial minorities in most Western countries. In spite of this, little effort has been made to tease out the effect of racial animus in this context. Moreover, it is increasingly the case that racial violence is often inseparable from anti-immigrant violence, given the popular elision between race and immigration status. One intriguing element of racist violence that is especially underexamined is what appears to be—from official data sources—high numbers of anti-white violence (although whites remain underrepresented as victims). These are certainly data that play into the rhetoric of extremist groups arguing for the recognition of whites as a victimized, disadvantaged group. However, scholars have made virtually no attempt to understand the dynamics of anti-white victimization, or the dynamics of reporting by white victims. It may be that white victims are more likely to report their victimization, seeing it as an affront to the racial order. Or, in fact, it might be a form of ethnic bias—anti-Italian, or anti-Polish—that does not fit neatly into the limited Hispanic/non-Hispanic ethnic categories in most official data bases. The truth is, as scholars, we have hardly acknowledged, let alone explored, this apparent anomaly.

Complaints by the white supremacist movement notwithstanding, in the U.S., the limited data available suggests that African Americans are the most frequent victims of racial violence. Frantz Fanon was no stranger to this reality: As an active and outspoken critic of Western racial politics, he often found himself accused of racial transgressions. Thus, he recalls (2000), "I was expected to act like a black man—or at least like a nigger. I shouted a greeting to the world and the world slashed away my joy. I was told to stay within my bounds, to go back where I belonged." There is—as many black or Asian or Native or Hispanic people know—danger in nonconformity and in challenging borders. The white gaze is upon them, judging them against their own whiteness, but also against imposed standards of behavior and demeanor. It is this normativity which most intrigues me: the extent to which the array of violent practices—verbal taunts, disparate treatment in public and private, assaults, police brutality—continue to be everyday experiences for African Americans, as well as for most racial and ethnic minority groups. We might borrow from Georges-Abeyie's (2001) conceptualization of petit apartheid, or from Russell's (1998) analyses of micro- and macro-aggressions, for example, to further our understanding of the cumulative, ongoing nature and impact of ethnoviolence as experienced by so many ethnic and racial minority groups.

A related area for further inquiry involves religiously motivated violence. Two issues, it seems to me, warrant particular attention. The first of these is anti-Semitic violence. Given the absolute absence of literature on violence against Jews in the U.S. or Canada, the field is wide open. One specific issue of concern has emerged out of recent Anti-Defamation League annual audits. An overview of recent audits reveals an especially disturbing trend: since 1991, anti-Semitic violence has been increasingly more likely to involve personal rather than property crimes. Historically, this has been a group victimized by crimes against property, such as synagogue or cemetery desecrations. However, the tide has turned in recent years. Additionally, the decline in the number of anti-Semitic incidents beginning in 1995 has corresponded to an increase in the intensity of the violence associated with the incidents.

The second class of victimization I would like to see explored concerns anti-Muslim violence. Many Christian Americans have long been hostile to what they perceive as Islamic fundamentalism, which in turn is increasingly associated with terrorism in the American psyche. Especially in the aftermath of the September 11, 2001, attacks on New York City and Washington, DC, Americans have come to associate the fundamentalism of Islam with fundamentalist violence—believing they will do anything that they deem to be the "will of Allah." Consequently, Muslims are suspected of being foreign and domestic terrorists. As I argue elsewhere (Perry 2003), the history of anti-Arab sentiment and discrimination has conditioned the contemporary wave of retaliatory violence against those perceived to be Muslim, or Middle Eastern. But again, there is ample room for alternative analyses and interpretations of anti-Muslim violence. Scholars have only just begun to think about this class of victims, largely motivated by recent events.

As I noted at the outset of this section, anti-gay violence has probably been the most widely examined form of ethnoviolence, both empirically and theoretically. In spite of the relative depth of the scholarship on anti-gay violence, a significant gap does exist: violence against lesbians, specifically, has not been of great concern to researchers. In part, this may be because anti-lesbian victimization appears to be less pervasive than violence against gay men. Yet such quantitative distinctions do not excuse our failure to take seriously the sharply gendered nature of anti-gay violence.

Von Schulthess's (1992) study of anti-lesbian violence in San Francisco reveals close links between anti-woman and anti-lesbian violence. In fact, she argues that anti-lesbian violence is an extension of misogynistic sentiment generally. This confusion may, in fact, deflate the numbers of *reported* anti-lesbian hate crimes. Victims and law enforcement authorities alike are often unable (or unwilling) to identify assaults as anti-lesbian. They may, instead, be perceived as anti-woman. For example, Brownworth (1991, 52) quotes a lesbian victim, who makes clear the difficulty of distinguishing the motive in this context:

> Was my attack anti-lesbian? Or was it anti-woman? . . . I was raped because as a woman I'm considered rapeable, and as a lesbian I'm considered a threat. How can one separate these two things?

Lesbians and nonlesbians alike frequently report this confusion (Pharr 1988; NGLTF 1994). Sexual harassment—wolf whistles, and "come-ons," for example—often escalates into lesbian baiting and, worse, violence. Thus the two are difficult to untangle.

Given the depth of cultural heterosexism, it is perhaps not surprising that there has consistently been resistance to including sexual orientation as a protected class in hate crime legislation. What is, perhaps, surprising is that similar controversy has swirled around the inclusion of gender as a protected category. There is a tragic irony in the fact that, on December 6, 1989, in Montreal, Canada, Marc Lepine lined up female engineering students against a wall, opened fire and killed 14 while shouting his intent to "kill the feminists." Just four months later, on April 23, 1990, the U.S. Congress signed into law the Hate Crime Statistics Act mandating the collection of data on crime motivated by prejudice on the basis of race, ethnicity, religion and sexual orientation. In light of the international publicity assigned the former, the failure of the latter to include gender is telling. Perhaps more clearly than any other case, the Lepine murders demonstrate that much violence against women is indistinguishable from other hate crimes. It, too, is intended to intimidate and control the larger class of people—women—not just the victims. This very argument provides the basis for future scholarship. There is still considerable resistance to the inclusion of gender-motivated violence as a "hate crime."

Just as there is a reluctance to consider violence against women as hate crime so too has there been a reticence to recognize people with disabilities as potential victims of bias-motivated violence. A bare handful of articles have explicitly addressed bias-motivated violence against persons with disability. Moreover, these have not typically been grounded in empirical investigations of such victimization. Consequently, we know very little about the extent, nature, or impact of violence against this population. This is ironic given that, in the U.S., at least, people with disabilities represent one of the largest minority groups—an estimated 20 percent of Americans have some form of recognized disability (Grattet and Jenness 2001b, 667). Additionally, the victimization experienced by people with disabilities parallels that of other targeted communities, to the extent that such violence is

> produced by a whole series of ideological structures that legitimize oppressive behavior. Indeed, disabled people face a pattern of oppressive societal treatment and hatred, much as women face misogyny, gay men and lesbians face homophobia, Jews face anti-Semitism and people of color face racism. (Waxman 1991, 187)

Finally, we have not attempted to understand the specificity of violence experienced by people who occupy multiple positions of culturally defined inferiority: women with disabilities, or gay men of color. For example, Sheffield (1987) argues that the good/bad woman dichotomy that often underlies violence against women is especially problematic for women of color, who, according to strictures of the racial hierarchy, can never achieve "goodness." It is the presumption of the inherent inferiority of black women that long left them vulnerable to unpunished and unpunishable rape at the hands of white men. That black women, especially, are uniquely vulnerable to gendered violence is implicit in Adisa's observation that

> African American women are more likely to be raped than any other woman, are least likely to be believed, and most often watch their rapists treated with impunity or mild punishment. (1997, 196)

It is the intersection of race, gender and sexuality—and frequently class—which shapes the victimization of black women and other women of color (Crenshaw 1994; Collins 1993). In other words, race conditions the gender imagery to which women are held accountable, especially in terms of their sexuality. While both white women and women of color are vulnerable to gendered violence, the cultural permission for such victimization varies dramatically. White women are often victimized because they are perceived to have crossed some boundary of appropriate feminine behavior; women of color because they are perceived to be, "by nature," sexually available and provocative. In short, white men's subordination of white women and women of color "involves holding them accountable to normative conceptions of essential womanly nature in different ways" (West and Fenstermaker 1993, 168). My perceptions here are speculative, and theoretically grounded. What is needed is explorations that seek to either confirm or negate their validity. It is important to look both theoretically and empirically at the cultural and structural practices that leave people vulnerable to violence on the basis of overlapping identities.

Related to this is another area of victimization that remains underdeveloped: minority-on-minority violence. It is ironic that at the same time that policy makers, scholars and commentators point to the increasing diversity of most industrialized nations, they stubbornly persist in collapsing racial and cultural relations into a black-white binary. If we are to make sense of the current state of racial and cultural conflict, it is imperative that we broaden our understanding to recognize these countries for what they are: multicultural, multiracial and multiethnic communities, characterized by multiple and crosscutting coalitions and cleavages. The politics of difference, in other words, is also inscribed in the interethnic relations of oppressed groups. Cornel West insists that

> although this particular form of xenophobia from below does not have the same institutional power of those racisms that affect their victims from above, it certainly deserves attention as a struggle within the politics of identity formation. (1994, 109)

It is particularly important to acknowledge this in our conversations about hate crime, where minority-on-minority violence is not unheard of. Two especially dramatic conflicts in the U.S. highlight this often overlooked reality: the Crown Heights violence between black and Jewish people in 1991; and the black-Asian-Hispanic conflicts that exploded in the Los Angeles riots of 1992. While obviously revealing the long-standing tensions among and between these similarly marginalized groups, these incidents represent efforts to negotiate identity and place in the U.S. In these events—and others like them—the actors either created or accepted opportunities to do difference, and especially race, through violence. What is needed are efforts to make sense of this intercultural violence between and among subordinate groups. The task is hampered by the paucity of literature in the area. Scholars have been slow to address the occurrence of hate crime in this context. My intent is to draw attention to the issue, and to stimulate dialogue and inquiry. We might choose to explore illustrative sets of relationships, such as prejudice- and hate-motivated violence in the U.S. and Europe among and between: African Americans/Afro Caribbeans and Asians; Jews and African Americans/Afro Caribbeans; Afro Caribbeans and Nigerians; or gay men within communities of color, for example.

Area 4: Responding to Hate Crime

In the extant scholarship, there is little consensus as to how to respond to or prevent bias-motivated crimes. Throughout the literature, authors often suggest resolutions that derive logically from their analyses. However, for the most part, these recommendations come by way of a conclusion, and are thus not fully developed. Hence, this section encourages researchers to explicitly address interventions intended to ameliorate the incidence or impact of hate crime. Initiatives might range from broad summaries of "promising practices," to very specific strategies like victim-offender mediation. Moreover, the focus might include assessments (e.g., Jacobs and Potter 1998, on hate crime legislation), or speculative recommendations for alternative approaches (e.g., Cogan 1996, on social change).

Not surprisingly, the American literature, in particular, is dominated by attention to legislative responses. No dimension of hate crime has garnered as much scholarly attention as has its legal regulation. Nor has any area engendered so much controversy. While scholars can agree, in principle, that hate crime is grounded in bigotry (whether individual or cultural), there is no such consensus as to how, or even whether hate crime should be regulated legally. Nonetheless, as is typical in the United States, the most widespread response to hate crime has been statutory. Very little literature is available on approaches outside of the criminal justice system.

However, as many authors argue, hate crime legislation is not without serious limitations. James Jacobs and Kimberly Potter (1998) are among the number of scholars critical of legislation that appears to criminalize "thought" rather than "action." He raises the question of the constitutionality of hate crime legislation, as well as its potentially divisive impact on intergroup relations. From this perspective, the "identity politics" inherent in hate crime legislation seriously threatens First Amendment guarantees to freedom of speech, as well as equal protection provisions.

Another point of contention within the hate crime canon is the existence of inconsistencies in protected classes, as Grattet and Jenness (2001a; 2001b) make clear. Where traditionally oppressed groups are excluded from the legislation—as is often the case with women and gay men and lesbians—the implication is that they are not worthy of the same protections afforded racial minorities. Moreover, the groups that are protected vary dramatically across jurisdictions, so that there is no shared national vision of who should be extended the protections of the law. The law may or not have some impact on offenders—actual or potential—or on victims' feelings of empowerment or on public consciousness. But it must not be the focus of attention. The peculiarly American obsession with legal solutions must not blind us to other fruitful avenues toward the prevention of hate crime or the amelioration of its effects.

I would like to see hate crime scholars wield their pens in the interests of alternative responses to hate crime within and beyond the criminal justice system. As in most areas, the typical response to offenders has been punitive. We can explore, theorize, and test nonpunitive measures that are likely to have more positive outcomes for the victims and offenders alike. Shenk (2001), for example, encourages us to extend the currently popular restorative justice model to the area of hate crime. Literature like Shenk's that justifies consideration of nonpunitive approaches must be followed up by scholarship that critically assesses the impact and effectiveness of such measures when and if they are adopted.

Under the current regime, and given the presence of hate crime legislation, an immediate question that arises is that of the role of police in invoking the relevant statutes. Numerous scholars have noted the extent to which law enforcement officers are frequent perpetrators of violence and brutality against people of color and gay men and lesbians. In addition to outright bias, many officers remain insensitive or poorly trained—either of which can contribute to inadequate enforcement of hate crime measures (see Bell 2002). Add to that prosecutorial reluctance to proceed with hate crime charges (see Grattet and Jenness 2001a) and the limitations of hate crime legislation are readily apparent. Consequently, it is vital that legislative initiatives be accompanied by provisions for effectively training law enforcement and prosecutors in the identification, investigation, and prosecution of hate crime (see, e.g., Wessler 2000). However, such training must itself become a focus of investigation. The assumption seems to be that if the training is offered, that is enough. Police will be equipped to deal with hate crime. Much more assessment of such programs is needed. In 2002, I sat in on a day-long training session offered by a well known and well respected antiprejudice organization. I came away from the session thinking that it was no wonder police found such trainings to be a waste of time. It was very vague, with few concrete suggestions for how police might improve their investigations, or even their interactions with victims. If it was frustrating for me, it must have been much worse for the officers. It is this sort of content based assessment that might become one avenue for exploration.

Law enforcement officers are not the only people in need of education around hate crime and the prejudices that underlie it. As a means of preventing hate crime, antiprejudice and antiviolence projects have begun to spring up across the U.S. and Canada, especially in elementary and secondary schools, but also in college and university settings. Federal, state and local governments continue to support such initiatives through promotional and funding activities. For example, the Office of Juvenile Justice and Delinquency Prevention (OJJDP) sponsored the development of a Healing the Hate curriculum directed toward youthful hate crime offenders. Similarly, the U.S. Department of Education is mandated by the Safe and Drug Free Schools and Communities initiative to support the development of hate crime prevention curricula, as well as training programs for teachers and administrators. Together, the OJJDP and the Department of Justice fund the National Center for Hate Crime Prevention. Working in partnership with such agencies as the ADL, the Center for Democratic Renewal, and the International Association of Chiefs of Police, the Center is dedicated to interventions for youth, in particular. The Center provides training, workshops, technical support, interventions, and information for youth, practitioners and communities.

As with police training programs, there have been few if any academic assessments of such initiatives. The starting point for such evaluation research lies within the organizations and programs themselves. They must take the initiative in clearly defining expected outcomes of hate crime prevention and response efforts. Useful program evaluation relies on clear and measurable definitions of outcomes. In addition to reducing the incidence of hate crime positive outcomes could include "changes in attitudes of children or community members who participate in hate crime prevention training, improved conflict resolution skills, increased victim satisfaction, enhanced perceptions of safety and well-being, reduced recidivism rates, and positive changes in the behavior or attitudes of offenders" (IACP 1999). It is also important to keep in mind, however, that "in jurisdictions where the rate of hate crime reporting has been low, a desirable short-term or interim outcome may well be to increase the rate of reported hate incidents or crimes" (IACP 1999).

The last decade of the twentieth century saw a flurry of hate crime legislation and other state activities, none of which has had an appreciable effect on the frequency or certainly the severity of hate crime. Such initiatives are insufficient responses to bias-motivated violence, in that they do not touch the underlying structures that support hate crime. Abdicating responsibility for countering such violence to the state, then, will not be a sufficiently effective long term strategy. Alternatively, I encourage advocacy scholarship that is grounded in the theoretical models urged previously. Such literature would stimulate thinking about creative, democratic approaches to the elimination of hate crime and of the cultural and social processes that underlie it. This is the other side of the equation: not evaluating what exists, but rather advocating for alternative approaches, which may or may not be outside the formal criminal justice system.

Valerie Jenness and Kendal Broad's (1998) work on antiviolence projects reveals that widespread ethnoviolence has in fact mobilized identifiable social movements. In particular, she draws attention to the success of feminist and gay and lesbian organizations in developing "collective action frames" that have redefined hate crime as a legitimate social problem. In fact, Jenness and Broad (1998, 174) conclude that "anti-violence projects across the United States have provided and continue to provide the structural basis for the mobilization around violence and victimization." Such bodies serve two primary roles: lobbying for the elimination of discriminatory law and practice; and monitoring and responding to hate crime.

The social movements and organizations referred to above will continue to stimulate change for the communities for which they speak. However, it is becoming increasingly important that they recognize their shared objectives, and engage in coalition building. The victim groups addressed throughout this paper have often experienced a similarity (but not sameness) of oppression. In other words, blacks, Jews, Asians, homosexuals and others have all suffered various degrees of discrimination and victimization. Racial and ethnic communities, and gender communities alike have been marginalized and are victims of bias-motivated violence. Yet rather than acknowledging this and forming coalitions, they have often resorted to conflict among themselves. While recognizing the distinct nature and impact of hate crimes upon different victim groups, expressed above, intercultural coalitions must challenge the essentialist assumptions about identity that insist on irreconcilable differences between races, between genders, between race and gender. The social change advocated by Jeanine Cogan (1996), for example, will require that we see race, class, gender and sexuality as "categories of connection" rather than as categories of opposition.

Conclusion

Clearly, there is extensive room for critical scholarship on hate crime. Such work can further both the substantive field and the distinct approach known as critical criminology. Scholars within this orientation are in a position to clarify the links between power and victimization, while at the same time broadening the scope of inquiry within the model. At the outset, I noted that critical analyses of race and crime, in particular, had emphasized the processes of criminalization. Hate crime, however, illustrates the obverse: the processes of victimization. It uncovers yet another mechanism by which identities are negotiated through deviance.

It is my belief that as critical, humane scholars we have some responsibility through our scholarship—and our praxis—to engage in work that counters the cycles of violence and oppression that affect too many people. We can begin this process by creating a dialogue that culminates in the sorts of inquiries that can uncover the underlying motives, cultures, conditions, and dynamics of animus based victimization. Such work has barely begun within our circles. It is hoped that the present paper has provided some challenges that readers will take up as part of their research agendas on the interstices of difference and justice.

References

Adisa, O. P. 1997. "Undeclared War: African American Women Writers Explicating Rape." Pp. 194–208 in L. O'Toole and J. Schiffman, eds., *Gender Violence: Interdisciplinary Perspectives.* New York: New York University Press.

Anti-Defamation League. 1999, May 17. *Frontline*, Letter to the Editor. New York: ADL *Arizona Republic*: 3.

Bell, J. 2002. *Policing Hatred: Law Enforcement, Civil Rights and Hate Crime.* New York: New York University Press.

Berk, R., E. Boyd, and K. Hamner. 1992. "Thinking More Clearly about Hate-motivated Crimes." Pp. 123–43 in G. Herek and K. Berrill, eds., *Hate Crimes: Confronting Violence against Lesbians and Gay Men.* Newbury Park, CA: Sage.

Bowling, B. 1993. "Racial Harassment and the Process of Victimization." *British Journal of Criminology* 33, no. 2: 231–50.

Brownworth, V. 1991, November 5. "An Unreported Crisis." *The Advocate*: 50, 52.

Bureau of Justice Assistance. 1997. *A Policy Maker's Guide to Hate Crimes.* Washington, DC.

Cogan, J. 1996. "The Prevention of Anti-lesbian/gay Hate Crimes through Social Change and Empowerment." Pp. 219–38 in E. Rothblum and L. Bond, eds., *Preventing Heterosexism and Homophobia.* Thousand Oaks, CA: Sage.

Collins, P. H. 1993. "The Sexual Politics of Black Womanhood." Pp. 85–104 in P. Bart and E. Moran, eds., *Violence Against Women.* Newbury Park, CA: Sage.

Craig, K. 2002. "Examining Hate-motivated Aggression: A Review of the Social Psychological Literature on Hate Crimes as a Distinct Form of Aggression." *Aggression and Violent Behavior* 7: 85–101.

Crenshaw, K. W. 1994. "Mapping the Margins: Intersectionality, Identity, and Violence against Women of Color." Pp. 93–118 in M. Albertson Fineman and R. Mykitiuk, eds., *The Public Nature of Private Violence.* New York, NY: Routledge.

Fanon, F. 2000. "The Fact of Blackness." In L. Back and J. Solomos, eds., *Theories of Race and Racism.* London: Routledge.

Federal Bureau of Investigation. 2000. *Hate Crime Statistics, 1999.* Washington, DC.

———. 2001. *Hate Crime Statistics, 2000.* Washington, DC.

Flowers, R. 1990. *Minorities and Criminality.* Thousand Oaks, CA: Sage.

Georges-Abeyie, D. 2001. "Foreword: Petit Apartheid in Criminal Justice: The More 'Things' Change, the More 'Things' Remain the Same." Pp. ix–xiv in D. Milovanovic and K. Russell, eds., *Petit Apartheid in the U.S. Criminal Justice System*. Durham, NC: Carolina Academic Press.

Gilroy, P. 1982. "The Myth of Black Criminality." *Socialist Register*. London, UK.

Goldberg, D. T. 1995. "Afterword: Hate or Power?" Pp. 267–76 in R. K. Whillock and D. Slayden, eds., *Hate Speech*. Thousand Oaks, CA: Sage.

Grattet, R., and V. Jenness. 2001a. "The Birth and Maturation of Hate Crime Policy in the United States." *American Behavioral Scientist* 45, no. 4: 668–96.

———. 2001b. "Examining the Boundaries of Hate Crime Law: Disabilities and the "Dilemma of Difference.'" *Journal of Criminal Law and Criminology* 91: 653–97.

Green, D., L. McFalls, and J. Smith. 2001. "Hate Crime: An Emergent Research Agenda." *Annual Review of Sociology* 27: 479–504.

Hamm, M. 1994a. *American Skinheads: The Criminology and Control of Hate Crime*. Westport, CT: Praeger.

———. 1994b. "Conceptualizing Hate Crime in a Global Context. Pp. 173–94 in *Hate Crime: International Perspectives on Causes and Control*. Cincinnati: Anderson.

Harvard Law Review Note. 1995. "Racial Violence against Asian Americans." *Harvard Law Review* 106: 1926–43.

Hate Crime in America Summit Recommendations. 1998. Alexandria, VA: IACP. Retrieved November 18, 2001, <www.theiacp.org/documents/index.cfm?fuse action = documentanddocument_ty pe _id = 1anddocument_id = 160>.

Herek, G., J. Cogan, and R. Gillis. 2002. "Victim Experiences in Hate Crimes based on Sexual Orientation." *Journal of Social Issues* 58, no. 2: 319–39.

Hesse, B., D. Rai, C. Bennett, and P. McGilchrist. 1992. *Beneath the Surface: Racial Harassment*. Aldershot, UK: Avebury Press.

Iganski, P. 2001. "Hate Crimes Hurt More." *American Behavioral Scientist* 45, no. 4: 626–38.

Ilarraza, F., D. Angel, and P. Becker. 2001. "Hate Crime Data and Its Sources: An Assessment." *Journal of Social and Behavioural Sciences* 38, no. 2: 128–38.

International Association of Chiefs of Police. 1999. *Hate Crime in America Summit: Recommendations*. Washington, DC: IACP.

Jacobs, J., and K. Potter. 1998. *Hate Crimes: Criminal Law and Identity Politics*. New York: Oxford University Press.

Jenness, V. 1995. "Social Movement Growth, Domain Expansion, and Framing Processes: The Gay/lesbian Movement and Violence against Gays and Lesbians as a Social Problem." *Social Problems* 42, no. 1: 145–70.

Jenness, V., and K. Broad. 1998. *Hate Crimes: New Social Movements and the Politics of Violence*. New York: Aldine de Gruyter.

Levin, J., and J. McDevitt. 1993. *Hate Crimes: The Rising Tide of Bigotry and Bloodshed*. New York: Plenum.

McDevitt, J., J. Balboni, S. Bennett, J. Weiss, S. Orchowsky, and L. Walbotet. 2000. *Improving the Quality and Accuracy of Bias Crime Statistics Nationally: An Assessment of the First Ten Years of Bias Crime Data Collection*. Boston: Center for Criminal Justice Policy Research.

McDevitt, J., J. Balboni, L. Garcia, and J. Guet. 2001. "Consequences for Victims: A Comparison of Bias- and Non–bias-motivated Assaults." *American Behavioral Scientist* 45, no. 4: 697–713.

Michalowski, R. 1985. *Order, Law and Crime.* New York: Random House.

National Gay and Lesbian Task Force. 1994. *Anti-gay/lesbian Violence, Victimization and Defamation in 1993.* Washington, DC: NGLTF Policy Institute.

Perry, B. 2001. *In the Name of Hate: Understanding Hate Crimes.* New York: Routledge.

———. 2002. "From Ethnocide to Ethnoviolence: Layers of Native American Victimization." *Contemporary Justice Review* 5, no. 3: 231–47.

———. 2003. "Backlash Violence: Anti-Muslim/Anti-Arab Hate Crime in the Aftermath of 9/11." In B. Perry, ed., *Hate and Bias Crime: A Reader.* New York: Routledge.

———. 2003. *Hate and Bias Crime: A Reader.* New York: Routledge.

———. Forthcoming. "Normative Violence: Everyday Racism in the Lives of Native Americans." In A. Aguirre and D. Baker, eds., *Structured Inequality in the United States: Critical Discussions on the Continuing Significance of Race, Ethnicity, Gender and Class.* 2nd ed. New York: Prentice-Hall.

Pharr, S. 1988. *Homophobia: A Weapon of Sexism.* Inverness, CA: Chardon Press.

Ray, L., and D. Smith. 2001. "Racist Offenders and the Politics of "Hate Crime." *Law and Critique* 12: 203–21.

Russell, K. 1998. *The Color of Crime.* New York: New York University Press.

Sheffield, C. 1987. "Sexual Terrorism: The Social Control of Women." Pp. 171–217 in B. Hess and M. M. Ferree, eds., *Analyzing Gender.* Newbury Park, CA: Sage.

Shenk, A. 2001. "Victim-offender Mediation: The Road to Repairing Hate Crime Injustice." *Ohio State Journal on Dispute Resolution* 17, no. 1: 185–217.

Sullivan, A. 1999, September 26. "What's So Bad About Hate?" *The New York Times,* A6.

von Schulthess, B. 1992. "Violence in the Streets: Anti-lesbian Assault and Harassment in San Francisco." Pp. 65–75 in G. Herek and K. Berrill, eds., *Hate Crimes: Confronting Violence against Lesbians and Gay Men.* Newbury Park, CA: Sage.

Waxman, B. 1991. "Hatred: The Unacknowledged Dimension in Violence against Disabled People." *Sexuality and Disability* 9, no. 3: 185–99.

Wessler, S. 2000. *Promising Practices against Hate Crime: Five State and Local Demonstration Projects.* Portland, ME: Center for the Study and Prevention of Hate Crime.

West, C. 1994. *Race Matters.* New York: Vintage.

West, C., and S. Fenstermaker. 1993. "Power, Inequality and the Accomplishment of Gender: An Ethnomethodological View." Pp. 151–74 in P. England, *Theory on Gender / Feminism on Theory.* Hawthorne, NY: Aldine de Gruyter.

Wisconsin v. Mitchell (92-515), 508 U.S. 47. 1993.

Young, I. M. 1990. *Justice and the Politics of Difference.* Princeton, NJ: Princeton University Press.

8

Women and Drugs: A Feminist Perspective

Judith Grant

> [There is the need to] explore the ways in which the experiences of women substance users can be recognized and valued. [One way to begin is to create] a critical framework in which the production of feminist knowledge becomes a real possibility within this field. We need images of women substance users that empower rather than stigmatise or victimise them. [We need to gain] a distinct view of the way "masculinist" ways of thinking can be appropriately challenged in the substance use field (Ettorre 1992, 16)

A FEMINIST PERSPECTIVE on women's use of drugs has emerged in the past decade as a response to what Ettorre (1992) identified above. However, much more needs to be done. For example, the climate of domestic drug policy in Canada and the United States at the beginning of the twenty-first century is divided into two specific modes of regulation—criminalization or medicalization; each mode is based on the model of addiction as either a crime or a disease (Adrian et al. 1996; Campbell 2000; Goode 1999). Specifically, our knowledge of women and their use of controlled substances is somewhat limited to these modes of regulation highlighted mainly through government funded studies, quantitative studies published in scholarly journals, and/or views developed through the popular media (Rosenbaum 1998).

For example, the literature often centres on narrow theoretical frameworks focusing on only psychological and psychiatric issues, often ignoring the social and cultural context in which addiction arises and is maintained. Further, reliance on quantitative methods frequently fails to examine meaning, motivation, and coping strategies of the addict contributing little to our understanding of the problem of addiction/recovery from the addict's perspective (Goode 1999; Rosenbaum 1981). Also, much of the literature generates a stereotypical image of women who use controlled substances, thus distorting their experiences and minimizing their challenges (Campbell 2000; Plant 1997). Further, Campbell argues that

> [p]opular culture, legal discourse, the scientific discourse of addiction research, and therapeutic discourse exhibit a series of assumptions about addicted women's characteristics and needs. (2000, 23)

Historically, concerns about women and their use of controlled substances has had an intensely moral tone around essentially moral issues: the supposed effects of alcohol and other drug use on women's "maternal instincts," their abilities to care for children and partners, and their sexualities and destruction of "female purity" (Blackwell et al. 1996, 229). Moreover, female users of controlled substances have generally been considered more pathological than male users (Clark 1996). For example, in the nineteenth and early twentieth century, they were described as "morphinist mothers" and "opium vampires." In the 1950s, they were seen as the "enemies within" and the "girl drug addicts," in the 1970s, as "heroin mothers," and, in more recent memory, as "crack moms" (Campbell 2000, 12). Women's use of controlled substances has historically been equated with "failure" as women, wives, and mothers: they have been seen as polluted, deviant, outcasts, or nonwomen (Ettorre 1992; Schur 1984).

The addiction and recovery field has primarily used males as its reference and standard in research, theory and practice (Goode 1999; Rosenbaum 1981; 1998). Traditionally, the definition of this subject area has been determined by a male focus of interest, reducing women to a side issue from the start (Rosenbaum 1981; 1998; Smith 1987). In much of the literature there is little discussion on women's experiences specifically as such experiences relate to addiction and recovery (Murphy and Rosenbaum 1999; Rosenbaum, 1981; 1998).

As Denzin (1987a, 12) argues, the literature concerned with theories of substance use offers very few insights into the phenomenon of addiction and recovery as a form of lived experience that "traps the individual in a self-destructive cycle of existence." Studies that do include women's experiences do so in juxtaposition with men's processes with the underlying assumption that women's experiences are similar (Campbell 2000; Raine 2001). Women's situations and needs have been largely unacknowledged, making their views a "non-field" (Ettorre 1992, 3). Few studies take into account the overall context of women's lives as they process addiction and recovery, suggesting that the extant addiction/recovery literature documents a "masculinist" truth (Ettorre 1992, 146), which blocks women out of the picture (Addiction Research Foundation 1994; Adrian et al. 1996).

Such a "masculinist truth" (Ettorre 1992, 146) suggests that by centering on men within the addiction/recovery field, scientific research tends "to uphold traditional, patriarchal images of men and women" (Ettorre 1992, 17). As a result, distorted views of women are presented. Ettorre (1992) argues that, traditionally, the lack of knowledge about women and their use of controlled substances has led clinical workers (e.g., psychologists and psychiatrists) to assume that substance use is primarily a "man's disease" or a "male problem." Women have been effectively ignored and excluded from analysis, especially in the alcohol field. For example, explanations of social drinking are based on assumptions such as "'developing a taste for drink, a palate, is a male attribute,' 'real men drink real ale' or within the drug culture men learn to drink, while women do not" (Ettorre 1992, 17).

Alcohol and drug use continues to afflict both Canadian and American society to a great extent (U.S. Department of Health and Human Services Substance Abuse and Mental Health Services Administration [SAMHSA] 2000; Adrian et al. 1996), resulting in serious consequences for those afflicted and for their families (Abbott 1995). For example, in the United States, 52 million women ages 12 and older reported using an illicit drug at some point in their lives (SAMHSA 2004). Among pregnant women aged 15 to 44, 4 percent reported using illicit drugs while pregnant (SAMHSA 2004). Approximately 38 percent of female high school students reported using marijuana (Centers for Disease Control and Prevention [CDC] 2004), and of the 22,000 persons who died of drug-induced causes in 2001, 34 percent were female (CDC 2003).

Of the 670,000 individuals admitted to emergency departments nationwide in the United States due to drug use, some 308,000 were women, a 22 percent increase from 1995 (SAMHSA 2004). Women also accounted for 30 percent of the nationwide admissions to all forms of treatment during 2002 (SAMHSA 2004). Additional data show that more than half of treatment admissions for sedatives in 2002 involved women (SAMHSA 2004).

In 2001, 17,000 females were arrested for drug offense charges (Bureau of Justice Statistics [BJS] 2003). Female offenders in prisons in the United States accounted for 8 percent of all federal prisoners serving time for drug offenses (BJS 2003). A median of 68 percent of adult female arrestees tested positive for either cocaine, marijuana, methamphetamine, opiates, or PCP during 2003. Overall, between 1995 and 2001, drug offenses accounted for 12 percent of the total prison population growth among female inmates (BJS 2003). Nearly one in three women serving time in state prisons said they had committed the offense that brought them to prison in order to obtain money to support their need for drugs (BJS 1999).

Of the approximately 40,000 new HIV infections that occur each year in the United States, about 30 percent occur among women (CDC 2001). From 1985 to 2002, the proportion of adult and adolescent AIDS cases in the United States reported in women increased from 7 percent to 26 percent (CDC 2001). Among teenage women ages 13 to 19, the cumulative number of AIDS cases multiplied more than 16 times between 1989 and 1997; for women ages 20 to 24, the number multiplied more than nine times during that period. Injection drug use accounted for 28 percent and 14 percent of cases in women in these age groups respectively. Women constitute the fastest-growing group of new HIV cases in the United States (CDC 1996). Overall, the direct and indirect costs of drug use totaled more than $294 billion (U.S. dollars) in the United States in 2001 (Office of National Drug Control Policy [ONDCP] 2001).

Drug use among Canadian women continues to be a serous issue as well (Adrian et al. 1996). In a 2002 Canadian Community Epidemiology Network on Drug Use (CCENDU) national report, the percentage of female drinkers increased in Canada, most pronouncedly among 20- to 24-year-olds (Dell and Garabedian 2003). Among Canadian women who were pregnant, 17–25 percent reported drinking alcohol during pregnancy. A larger proportion of women than men (23 percent versus 17 percent) report using at least one mood-altering prescription drug, although, in the general population, women are half as likely as men to be current users of cannabis or any other illegal drug. Women are less likely than men to report legal problems but are more likely to report harm to home life as a result of their substance use (Dell and Garabedian [CIDPC] 2003).

In Canada, of the 18,124 cumulative AIDS cases in adults, 7.9 percent occurred among women. The proportion of AIDS cases among women (relative to all reported AIDS cases in adults for which gender and age are known) has increased over time from 5.6 percent before 1992 to 8.3 percent in 1995 and peaked at 16.4 percent in 1999. In 2001, the proportion of AIDS cases among women remained at 16 percent (Centre for Infectious Disease Prevention and Control [CIDPC] 2003).

Annual productivity losses in Canada due to substance use have been estimated at $4.1 billion (Canadian dollars) for alcohol and $823.1 million for illicit drugs (Canadian Centre on Substance Abuse [CCSA] 1999). Substance use cost more than $18.4 billion to the Canadian economy in 1992, representing 2.7 percent of the gross national product in that year (CCSA 1999).

Substance use among women is a major health, legal, economic, and social issue in North America (Adrian et al. 1996; Campbell 2000; Goode 1999).

Such use among women has serious implications both for society and for women struggling with their addictions. Issues of concern include the increase in HIV/AIDS among women as a consequence of unsafe sex; family disruptions; impaired performance at work, resulting in some cases in loss of employment; growth in the female population in U.S. prisons; depression; victimization due to disproportionate vulnerability to attack; increased mental and social problems; and physiological risks, such as reproductive problems, physical disabilities, and, finally, death (Abbott 1995). Furthermore, the use of alcohol and drugs during pregnancy not only affects mothers but also often has a profound and irreversible effect on their fetuses (Abbott 1995). The cost of substance use among women is high in both personal and social terms for both the United States and Canada in the twenty-first century.

Men and women face very different challenges in addiction and recovery (Abbott 1995; Adrian et al. 1996; Campbell 2000; Ettorre 1992; Goode 1999; Plant 1997; Van Den Bergh 1991). Both in the United States and in Canada, addiction policy researchers argue that a full understanding of the problems associated with substance use among women requires an analysis of the status of women within a feminist theoretical framework (Blackwell et al. 1996; Campbell 2000; Ettorre 1992). Too often, as Blackwell et al. (1996, 230) argue, "the authors of substance abuse literature inappropriately extrapolate from men's experiences in order to understand those of women." A feminist framework favours sound empirical research that seeks to gain an understanding of the daily realties faced by women substance users. Further:

> A feminist framework rejects the value of research that consists of an extrapolation of research conducted on men, or that is founded on assumptions based on traditional feminine roles. (Blackwell et al. 1996, 231)

From a feminist perspective, attempts to treat substance use problems in women should be directed at the whole woman, "taking into account her history and her life circumstances and not just her substance use" (Blackwell et al. 1996, 240). Many feminist scholars are uncomfortable with the medical model, the disease model, and the Alcoholics Anonymous (A.A.) or 12-step model (Ettorre 1992). Both Canadian and American feminist scholars (Blackwell et al. 1996; Campbell 2000; Ettorre 1992) favor evaluating the larger sociopolitical context in which women in general and, more specifically, women who seek help for substance use currently live. Further research should focus on women's individual experiences in addiction and recovery processes in order to provide insights into their individual needs and concerns.

Within the field of addiction, men are socially dominant and active participants in the drug-using culture, whereas women are socially subordinate and relatively passive participants (Goode 1999). When women are considered within the addiction field, they have been seen to have a greater problem and to be more deviant or more psychologically disturbed than male counterparts (Schur 1984). Further, if women are in partnerships with men who use controlled substances, "they are seen as 'etiological agents,' that is, helping to cause the addiction or complicating the illness" (Ettorre 1992, 4). Ettorre (1992, 3) argues that a feminist critique on substance use does not exist and that the development of a gender-sensitive perspective on addictions remains in an "infancy stage" of development.

The main objective of this chapter is to provide the following: 1) an exploration of what a feminist perspective entails on the issues of women's use of drugs, 2) a critique of the relevant feminist literature on these issues and 3) suggestions for new directions in research, theory and policy as such directions pertain to women's need and concerns. First, however, an overview of feminist theory is highlighted in order to provide a framework for this chapter.

Feminist Theory

"Feminist" emerged into widespread usage in the Western world in the 1890s. It emerged as a way to identify individuals who supported an increased public role for women along with women's right to define themselves as autonomous beings. In the intervening years the definition has expanded and altered to include political, cultural, economic, sexual, racial, and ethical dimensions (Elliot and Mandell 1995). It has further been argued that a feminist perspective should be involved in changing society, raising feminist consciousness, and working to reduce gender inequality (Chafetz 1988).

Chafetz (1988) argues that there are three specific elements which render a theory feminist: 1) Gender comprises a central focus or subject matter of the theory. Feminist theory seeks to understand the gendered nature of virtually all social relations, institutions, and processes. 2) Gender relations are viewed as a problem. Therefore, feminist theory seeks to understand how gender is related to social inequalities, strain, and contradictions. 3) Gender relations are not viewed as either natural or immutable. Rather, the gender-related status quo is viewed as the product of sociocultural and historical forces which have been created and are constantly re-created by humans, and therefore can potentially be changed by human agency. Bologh states:

> Feminist theorizing promises not only to fill the gaps in knowledge about women but to provide an alternative perception of the world that men, because of their (dominant) position, could not possess. (1984, 382)

Overall, feminist theories tend to be explicitly political in inspiration and in their advocacy for social change (Chafetz 1988; Elliot and Mandell 1995). As Chafetz (1988, 6) argues, "The politics of feminist theories are only more self-conscious and explicit, not more intrusive or biasing, than those of most other theories."

Feminist Perspectives on Addiction and Recovery

Van Den Bergh (1991) provides a useful beginning to an understanding of feminist scholarship as she argues that although there are many different definitions of feminism, there are several premises common among them that have relevance to defining a feminist perspective on addiction and recovery: reconceptualizing power, eliminating false dichotomies and artificial separations, valuing process as equally important to product, validating renaming, and believing that the personal is political.

Overall, a feminist perspective on addiction examines societal inequalities that engender the sense of emptiness and despair that Van Den Bergh (1991, 3) argues constitutes "the genesis of any addictive behavior." Within patriarchy the social, political and economic forces create conditions conducive to the development of addictive behaviour (Connell 1987; Denzin 1987a; Ettorre 1992; Van Den Bergh 1991). This is especially true for women who historically have experienced discrimination and powerlessness in a capitalist system (Ettorre 1992; Lerner 1993; Schur 1984).

The feminization of poverty, sexual victimization and objectification as well as institutionalized sexism and racism can be associated with limiting women's control over their lives. Addiction then can be said to originate from a sense of powerlessness and one's addiction can be for the purpose of feeling powerful (Denzin 1987a; Raine 2001; Van Den Bergh 1991).

Reconceptualizing power within a feminist perspective argues that we need to rename power as energy of influence and responsibility that one uses in order to gain access to rights, resources, and opportunities (Van Den Bergh 1991). This means that addicts, particularly women, need to take responsibility for making things happen in their lives rather than being reactive, thus helping them build more of an internal loci of control within recovery, along with the building of feelings of autonomy in their lives (Nol 1991).

Eliminating false dichotomies is a reaction to patriarchal dynamics based on a "divide and conquer" model (Van Den Bergh 1991, 6). The tendency to dichotomize and compartmentalize sets up the conditions for a feeling of emptiness, void or vacuum, common within addiction (Denzin 1987a; Van Den Bergh 1991). A feminist perspective sees interconnectedness and relatedness as valuable. For example, health has been separated into discrete categories (e.g., mental, physical and spiritual). Within the feminist lens one's well being is interrelated between those categories, not as separate domains. Further, within recovery, the feminist perspective suggests that healthy recovery promotes choices (Ettorre 1992; Van Den Bergh 1991). For example, recovering individuals may make use of Alcoholics Anonymous (A.A.) and/or Narcotics Anonymous (N.A.). Others may self-recover while others may make use of in-patient facilities. A feminist view argues that there is no "right" way to proceed, common to all as people process their recovery.

Valuing process equally to product means that the way in which one pursues a goal is as important as the goal's outcome. Within patriarchy, a focus on ends rather than means is a common theme. There is a demand for perfectionism that can lead to anxiety, frustration and despair (Van Den Bergh 1991), culminating in addiction. A feminist principle applied to recovery suggests that recovery is an ongoing process in which individuals practice dealing with life on life's terms. It is crucial to accept that recovery is a process that involves pain, fear and anger. What are also valuable are the steps taken in moving toward one's goal (Van Den Bergh 1991), not just the goal itself.

Within our patriarchal culture, individuals can feel powerless and inadequate and experience a loss of self-definition and meaning (Denzin 1987a; Haas 2003; Van Den Bergh 1991). Addiction then can become a way to escape from such feelings. Nol argues, "unmet self-object needs impair the development of a core sense of self for addicts" (1991, 38). In the place of the self is a profound psychological emptiness. Therefore, it is the pain of this emptiness that the adult person attempts to soothe through their use of drugs, alcohol or other external means.

Within recovery, discovery of self is a fundamental goal (Denzin 1987b; Van Den Bergh 1991). A feminist perspective argues that renaming means having the right to define one's own direction, reality or indicators of success rather than conforming to conventional norms. To rename one's experiences is to get back to one's authentic self (Denzin 1987b; Haas 2003; Van Den Bergh 1991). Most basically, "a feminist approach encourages a woman to accept herself, and self-acceptance is the cornerstone of recovery" (Downing 1991, 58).

Finally, seeing the personal as political means that one needs to see one's experiences as the individualized outcome of social inequalities. This perspective means that the beliefs and values one holds, the goals that one sets and the way one pursues one's life can be considered political statements (Van Den Bergh 1991). Finally, as Van Den Bergh highlights:

> Using a feminist perspective to treat addictions starts with seeing the addicted person as someone split off from her or his authentic self. Recovery becomes a process of rediscovering oneself and reclarifying one's meaning and purpose in living. In that process differences become accepted, as do deviations from conventional norms, and an emphasis is placed on being rather than doing, living rather than competing. (1991, 27)

Often, the primary approach to substance use treatment has been based mainly on the biopsychosocial model. A feminist approach expands on the underpinnings of this model and its overall vision (Van Den Bergh and Cooper 1986). The major components of the model (the biological, the psychological and the social) are strongly intertwined. The feminist model attempts to reinforce this systemic interactional perspective through a greater explication of the combined social and cultural contexts related to women's lives.

Therefore, this model challenges historical beliefs that have assigned greater value to particular physical, cultural, and behavioural expectations (Lerner 1993). For example, certain values have been applied differently to females and males, to ethnic group members, and to disenfranchised members. Our white, male-dominated society places greater value on male attributes such as being competitive, independent, and rational, and less value on traditionally female attributes such as being cooperative, dependent, and emotional. The feminist approach challenges such gender and cultural disparities (Abbott 1995). As Fine succinctly argues:

> Through the critical and collective insights gathered at the margins, such insights speak to feminist research that can reframe those who have been cast as the Other, dismantle the partitions, and, more important, resuscitate buried images of strength, power and critique from those formerly deported to silence and shadows. A feminist approach that builds on empowerment, equality, inclusion, and respect for diversity advances accessibility for treatment and ultimately to addiction reduction. (1987, 99)

A feminist approach is concerned with ending domination and resisting oppression so as to provide equality of opportunity regardless of one's demographics or background. Feminism as a model of analysis is the antithesis of a patriarchal, capitalist perspective. It is a "liberation" philosophy promoting both nurturance of the self as well as concern with collective well being (Van Den Bergh 1991, 5). Van Den Bergh argues:

> The feminist approach includes working collaboratively, collectively and cooperatively; valuing personal experiences; encouraging growth and development;

> caring for others, building supportive relationships as well as believing in the interconnectedness of people and events. (1991, 5)

Through using a feminist approach, we can attempt to provide a new way of seeing and transforming traditional views of women's lives into "gender-illuminating notions" (Ettorre 1992, 18). Without such notions, women who use substances remain isolated and excluded from proper understanding and treatment (Ettorre 1992).

The foregoing discussion has considered feminist perspectives on women's addiction and recovery processes. The following section highlights present feminist scholarship on such processes for women.

Feminist Scholarship on Women's Addiction and Recovery Processes

Although there are very few studies that consider gender differences in individuals' processes of addiction and recovery (Abbott 1995; Bepko 1989; Campbell 2000; Goode 1999; Murphy and Rosenbaum 1999; Rosenbaum 1981; 1998), there are many studies on women's patterns of drug use. Such studies show why women turn to and ultimately leave their use of substances, but there is little research on how women experience or "make meaning" of such processes for themselves. Prior research has not adequately mapped out the details of formerly addicted women's social worlds (Murphy and Rosenbaum 1999).

For example, gender-specific characteristics of drug dependency show that women more than men use licit drugs such as tranquilizers, sedatives, psychoactive drugs, hypnotics, and stimulants (Abbott 1995; Nelson-Zlupko et al. 1995). Research also indicates that women are more frequently involved in multiple substance use (Celentano and McQueen 1984).

Research in the treatment tradition suggests that alcoholic women suffer from lower self-esteem, more anxiety and a greater sense of powerlessness and inadequacy about their drinking than male alcoholics (Beckman 1978; 1980; Ettorre 1992). Too, other studies consider high rates of incest and other forms of early sexual and family violence among drug-dependent women (Blood and Cornwall 1996; Miller and Downs 1993; Raine 2001; Ryan and Popour 1983). Further studies focus on the issues of psychological problems such as conflict and powerlessness in women's lives (Raine 2001).

Additional studies on women and alcohol tend to suggest that women use alcohol as an avenue for relieving stresses, discomforts and the strains of everyday life (Reed 1985). A study on Canadian women (Pihl et al. 1986) reports that alcohol use in women is related to such reasons as "relaxation," "to forget," and "to forget cares due to tension." Women are also more likely to be in relationships with drug-using partners or spouses (Reed 1985), and they suffer in problematic relationships (Lammers et al. 1995; Long and Mullen 1994). Other research documents that substance-using women experience higher levels of guilt, shame and depression, and anxiety about addiction than men (Blume 1990; O'Connor et al. 1994; Reed 1985; Underhill 1991; Wilsnack and Beckman 1984). Too, other scholars argue that addicted women come from families in which drugs are used as a primary coping strategy by one or more family members (Nelson-Zlupko et al. 1995; Weinberg 1994).

There is also a suggestion from some studies that women are more likely than men to use alcohol to change negative moods (Grover and Thomas 1993; Rubonis et al. 1994). Studies on lesbian women in relation to sex-role conflict have also been carried out (Bloomfield 1993; Hall 1993).

Little is known about black women in Canada and their use of controlled substances, but one recent Canadian study (Bernard 2001) that considers black women and their experiences with crack cocaine addiction argues that these women suffer stigma and shame from their communities. A loss of their children contributes to damaged self-esteem and shameful existence, and a lack of support and disconnection from families exacerbates their sense of hopelessness.

And, too, a study on older women (aged 65 and over) on use of alcohol and drug use (Graham et al. 1995) was carried out in Canada. This study shows that drinking is associated with being single, younger, not religious, in better health and smoking. The use of psychoactive prescription drugs (e.g., sleeping pills) tends to be associated with being widowed, older, less educated, more religious, in poorer health, with higher stress, lower income and less social support.

Feminist scholars argue that researchers have oftentimes misjudged the scope of gender socialization on lived experience (Lopata 1987; O'Leary et al. 1985). With increased attention in feminist work to women's self-changes in the past few decades, one might anticipate substantial work on the processes for women formerly addicted to controlled substances. Such is not the case. While work on female addicts remains sparse, there are three significant studies that consider women's lives through a feminist lens: women on heroin (Rosenbaum 1981), pregnant women on drugs (Murphy and Rosenbaum 1999), and the social context for women alcoholics (Raine 2001).

Arguing that women "have been invisible at worst or peripheral at best" in the field, Rosenbaum (1981, 18) considers 100 women heroin addicts in one of the first studies done specifically on women. Rosenbaum's (1981, 8) research was planned on the "fundamental assumption that the definitions, meanings, and categories employed by actors themselves are important factors in structuring their activities." Her methodology was guided by a combination of the philosophy of phenomenology and the theoretical perspective of symbolic interactionism.

According to Rosenbaum (1981), heroin addiction has a significant impact on women's sense of their identities. Women heroin users sustain identities that are directly related to the methods they use to support themselves and their habits. It is not the use of heroin per se, but women's involvement in the social world of heroin buyers and sellers and their own buying activities that begin to mold their identities as addicts. The longer women become part of this social world of heroin users, the more isolated they become (Rosenbaum 1981) from the world of nonusers. Women's behaviour and self-identification are organized around their roles as addicts within a social world of heroin use. As their entire world, activities, and social interactions consist of other addicts and heroin-related activities, women come to see themselves as junkies.

As a result of this identification, women find it increasingly difficult to leave the addict world (physically and psychologically) (Rosenbaum 1981). As addicts spend more time with other addicts, they avoid interaction with nonaddict significant others such as family, children, and partners. Correspondingly, nonaddict significant others increasingly avoid addicts. Overtime, addicts' involvement in criminal activity increases while their involvement in other nonaddict activities such as school, employment, and church attendance decreases.

Rosenbaum (1981, 60) argues that individuals are "inundated" into the heroin world. Because of women's lifestyles, they build safe social networks for themselves. Isolating themselves from nonaddicts, women associate with people who are "all right"—namely, other addicts. For these women, heroin addicts with children, inundation generates a general inability to fulfill their responsibilities as mothers.

Further, in their study which looks at the experiences of 120 pregnant women on drugs, Murphy and Rosenbaum (1999, 65) argue that pregnant women on heroin see pregnancy as a chance at motherhood, one of the "only conventional, socially sanctioned" identities available to them. Mothering roles provide a potential source of hope and pride for women offering them "an ideal image of self as competent mother" (Murphy and Rosenbaum 1999, 65), a view that contradicts their salient identities as heroin addicts.

Another important study is Raine's (2001) work in Great Britain on women's perspectives on alcohol use and the centrality of gender in their lives. Raine's (2001) central argument is that cultural, social and economic inequalities that women experience because they are women are crucial to an understanding of their drug use. She shows how women's "chaotic lifestyles are gender-related" (Raine 2001, 124). Such factors are victimization, self-harm, lifestyle consequences of drug use, and the frequently negative influence of male partners. She further integrates her analysis with women's experiences in treatment and how without a wider social change in the gender order, changes will be difficult. Ussher highlights this argument when she states:

> What is needed is a change in the wider social sphere, empowerment of individual women (and arguably some men) and a reconceptualisation of masculinity and femininity, leading to more egalitarian relationships between men and women. (1998, 159)

In her work on women and substance use, Ettorre (1992) also calls for a feminist analysis, arguing that few if any feminist scholars have written about women and addiction. She proposes a more critical approach which views substance use as a complex social issue with political implications. In her work, she challenges the "masculinist ways of thinking" (Ettorre 1992, 11) through arguing for a feminist perspective as well as a women-centred response rooted in the identity and consciousness of women substance users. Further, she states that there is a need for approaches on substance use highlighting the social construction of gender in the field. For example, Ettorre (1992) suggests we need images of women substance users that empower rather than stigmatize or victimize them. We also need to learn how to recognize these images while we are creating an alternative framework sensitive to the needs of women.

As reviewed above, various scholars (Ettorre 1992; Murphy and Rosenbaum 1999; Raine 2001; Rosenbaum 1981; Van Den Bergh 1991) call for further work on feminist scholarship on women and their issues within addiction and recovery. Much of the literature (Campbell 2000; Goode 1999; Murphy and Rosenbaum 1999; Raine 2001; Rosenbaum 1998) argues that many of the problems of women's lifestyles are gender-related, for example, victimization, self-harm and self-hate, along with lifestyle consequences of addiction. Overall, a centrality of gender is underresearched in the addiction/recovery literature (Goode 1999).

As this section has highlighted, competent research on women's issues regarding addiction and recovery need to be expanded. Therefore, what suggestions can be made for future research, theory and policy in women's lives; where do we need to go in order to enhance research, theory and policy on these issues? The following section attempts to answer these questions.

Suggestions for New Directions in Research, Theory and Policy

As argued, the increase in competent research on women, addiction and recovery has a distance to go before it can be termed sufficient. Therefore, what new directions are needed in order to enhance the field of addiction and recovery in women's lives?

First, more research needs to be undertaken in order to enrich the literature on women's addiction and recovery processes. Most empirical research on women gives very little information about women's true consciousness or women's individual and social history (Fine 1992). Therefore, more attention should be focused on women's experiences in order to continue to close the gap in the literature that has considered, mainly, a "masculinist" truth (Ettorre 1992, 146) about such processes. Bringing women's experiences into the description of social life creates a necessary balance to scientific inquiry, and feminist perspectives bring an experiential and more holistic approach that transforms such inquiry into a more integrated paradigm (Fine 1992).

Second, little is known about how individuals start and stop their use of controlled substances (McIntosh and McKeganey 2002; Woodward et al. 1997), particularly as to how such processes occur in women's lives. Therefore, future research should be undertaken that considers such self-changes as individuals process these experiences. As Fine argues,

> Knowledge is best gathered in the midst of social change projects. Such research is important as it is at once disruptive, transformative, and reflective; about understanding and about action; not about freezing the change but always about change. (1992, 227)

Third, as Ettorre (1992, 3) argues, the development of a gender-sensitive perspective on addiction/recovery remains in "the infancy stage." Therefore, more studies would contribute to this area in the literature and research fields. Finally, most addiction/recovery studies are limited to studies that do not (nor have not) considered individuals' subjective experiences (McIntosh and McKeganey 2002). It must be remembered, "The individual is a participant in that interaction as much as anyone else involved" (Anderson 1991, 351).

Further, of necessity is a policy base that respects women's differences and women's knowledge production. According to Kandall:

> Up to the 1980s drug treatment programs have focused almost entirely on men and thus based their treatment approach on a confrontational, male-orientated model, one that was soon recognized as counterproductive, and even poten-

> tially destructive, for most women. Traditionally, women who used drugs had been regarded as "sicker," more deviant, and more difficult to treat than addicted men, a partial explanation of why treatment options for addicted women were so limited until the mid-1970s. (1996, 199)

A respect for women's multiple voices is needed along with integrating their legitimacy in policy making. Women's addiction and recovery needs to be situated in the context of women's subordination and social constraints (Goode 1999). The social and cultural factors that lead to women's addiction/recovery processes should be of consideration in the field. Provisions in policy work that recognize that women suffer greater social exclusion, stigma and isolation than male addicts in addiction/recovery should be established. Through policy work we can strengthen women's economic security, their right to education, access to proper childcare, health care and reproductive rights. Increased spending at the community level for these factors needs to be more thoroughly implemented. There is the need to integrate theory and praxis when working with women as they process their addiction/recovery processes thereby helping to integrate a more holistic theory of women's lives into training modules for counselors and therapists in addiction and community centres.

Finally, addiction centres and shelters need to work together in validating women's experiences of drug use and violence in their lives. A consideration of the fact that women in shelters and women in addiction centres may be using controlled substances in order to "cope" with former or present violence is important. Work on violence issues should be of primary concern before women's addiction/recovery issues are considered.

Conclusion

As the foregoing discussion highlights, we need to expand the addiction and recovery fields as they relate to women's lives. Research reveals that addiction and recovery processes present challenges to women that differ from those confronted by men (Abbott 1995; Campbell 2000; Goode 1999; Van Den Bergh 1991). Gender differences exist with regard to alcohol and degree of drug use and associated behaviours (Grella and Joshi 1999), as well as to rates of use for various drugs, biological impacts, risk factors, nature of substance use problems, and recommended responses (Dell and Garabedian 2003; Goode 1999).

In order to provide meaningful, evidence-based care to women, researchers need to attend to women's experiences, their understanding of issues, and the social interactions within which they gain meanings and insights about their situations (Crooks 2001). Feminist work is ideal for investigating "relatively uncharted waters" (Crooks 2001, 12), that is, when important variables in the addiction and recovery field have yet to be determined.

As previously argued, much of what is known about women's experiences in the addiction/recovery field fails to address how they think, how they organize ideas, and what is meaningful to them (Crooks 2001; Ettorre 1992; Rosenbaum 1998). The "multifocal nature of womanhood" (Crooks 2001, 14) as it relates to formerly addicted women's lives has received little attention. Therefore, both hearing women's voices and understanding women's experiences from their own perspectives are important.

Various studies have been conducted on women's ways of knowing and how women perceive themselves to be heard, valued, and respected (Code 1991; Gilligan 1993; Smith 1987). "Gaining a voice" arose as a central metaphor of women's experiences and development (Crooks 2001, 15). Of special importance to research on women's issues are the developmental categories of silences, subjective knowledge, and constructed knowledge (Code 1991; Crooks 2001). Experiences as women are situated and embedded in a social context and are variously located in society (Smith 1987). Smith (1987, 105) argues, "[a] sociology for women preserves the presence of subjects as knowers and as actors." We start, therefore, with women's experiences; we begin in the particularities of women's actual everyday worlds. We start from the "standpoint of women" (Smith 1987, 122) and from where we are in the everyday world. We start "talking about a world that actually happens and can be observed" (Smith 1987, 123).

Feminism means giving women a voice because it assists in "continually bringing into being as it is and as it is becoming, in the daily practices of actual individuals" (Smith 1987, 125). Ways of knowing are important in feminist work. Therefore, both subjective and constructed knowledge provide the data for study and are key to identifying and expanding further work on women's processes and change in addiction and recovery.

Note

1. The terms "controlled substances" and/or "drugs," as used in this chapter include all drugs, licit and illicit (prescription and nonprescription), including alcohol.

References

Abbot, A. A. 1995. "Substance Abuse and the Feminist Perspective." Pp. 258–78 in N. Van Den Bergh, ed., *Feminist Practice in the 21st Century*. Washington, DC: National Association of Social Workers Press.

Addiction Research Foundation (ARF) Task Group on gender-focused research. 1994. *Gender Issues in Addictions Research.* Toronto, Ontario: Addiction Research Foundation.

Adrian, M., C. Lundy, and M. Eliany, eds. 1996. *Women's Use of Alcohol, Tobacco and Other Drugs in Canada.* Toronto, Ontario: Addiction Research Foundation.

Anderson, T. 1991. "Identity Transformation in Drug Addiction." Unpublished doctoral dissertation, American University, Washington, DC.

Beckman, L. 1978. "Self-esteem of Women Alcoholics." *Journal of Studies on Alcohol* 39, no. 3: 491–98.

———. 1980. "Perceived Antecedents and Effects of Alcohol Consumption." *Journal of Studies on Alcohol* 41, no. 5: 518–30.

Bepko, C. 1989. "Disorders of Power: Women and Addiction in the Family." Pp. 406–26 in M. McGoldrick, C. Anderson and F. Walsh, eds., *Women in Families.* New York: W. W. Norton.

Bernard, W. T. 2001. *Including Black Women in Health and Social Policy Development: Winning over Addictions—Empowering Black Mothers with Addictions to Overcome Triple Jeopardy.* Halifax, Nova Scotia: Maritime Centre of Excellence for Women's Health.

Blackwell, J., W. E Thurston, and K. Graham. 1996. "Canadian Women and Substance Abuse: Overview and Policy Implications." Pp. 228–46 in M. Adrian, C. Lundy, and M. Eliany, eds., *Women's Use of Alcohol, Tobacco and Other Drugs in Canada.* Toronto, Ontario: Addiction Research Foundation.

Blood, L., and A. Cornwall. 1996. "Childhood Sexual Victimization as a Factor in the Treatment of Substance Misusing Adolescents." *Substance Use and Misuse* 31, no. 8: 1015–39.

Bloomfield, K. 1993. "A Comparison of Alcohol Consumption between Lesbians and Heterosexual Women in an Urban Population." *Drug and Alcohol Dependence* 33: 257–69.

Blume, S. 1990. "Alcohol and Drug Problems in Women: Old Attitudes, New Knowledge." Pp. 183–98 in H. Milkman and L. Sederer, eds., *Treatment Choices for Alcoholism and Substance Abuse.* Lexington, MA: Lexington Books.

Bologh, R. W. 1984. "Feminist Social Theorizing and Moral Reasoning on Difference and Dialectic." In R. Collins, ed., *Sociological Theory.* San Francisco: Jossey-Bass.

Bureau of Justice Statistics (BJS). 1999, December. *Women Offenders.*

———. 2003, November. *Compendium of Federal Justice Statistics.*

Campbell, N. 2000. *Gender, Drug Policy, and Social Justice: Using Women.* New York: Routledge.

Canadian Centre on Substance Abuse (CCSA). 1999. CCSA Canadian Profile 1999. Ottawa, Ontario. Retrieved, November 19, 2004, .

Celentano, D. D., and D. McQueen. 1984. "Multiple Substance Use among Women with Alcohol-related Problems." In S. C. Wilsnack and L. J. Beckman, eds., *Alcohol Problems in Women.* New York: Guilford Press.

Centers for Disease Control (CDC). 1996. *HIV/AIDS Surveillance Report* 9 (2001): 2. Atlanta, GA.

———. 2001. "HIV and AIDS: United States, 1981–2001." *MMWR* 50: 430–34.

———. 2003. *Deaths: Final Data for 2001.* Contributors: E. Arias, R. N. Anderson, H. C. Kung, S. L. Murphy, and K. D. Kochanek. Hyattsville, MD: National Center for Health Statistics Division of National Statistics.

———. 2004, May 21. *Youth Risk Behaviour Surveillance, United States, 2003* 53, no. 2:1–96. Contributors: J. A. Grunbaum, L. Kann, S. Kinchen, J. Ross, J. Hawkins, and R. Lowry, et al. Hyattsville, MD: National Center for Chronic Disease Prevention and Health Promotion. Division of Adolescent and School Health.

Centre for Infectious Disease Prevention and Control (CIDPC). 2003, April. *National HIV Prevalence and Incidence Estimates for 1999: No Evidence of a Decline in Overall Incidence.* Ottawa, Ontario: Public Health Agency of Canada.

Chafetz, J. S. 1988. *Feminist Sociology: An Overview of Contemporary Theories.* Itasca, IL: F. E. Peacock Publishers, Inc.

Clark, J. 1996. "The Historical Context of Medicalization and Gender: Its Relationship to Alcohol and Other Drug Use in Canada." Pp.14–20 in M. Adrian, C. Lundy, and M. Eliany, eds., *Women's Use of Alcohol, Tobacco and Other Drugs in Canada.* Toronto, Ontario: Addiction Research Foundation.

Code, L. 1991. "Women and Experts: The Power of Ideology." Pp. 173–221 in *What Can She Know? Feminist Theory and the Construction of Knowledge.* Ithaca, NY: Cornell University Press.

Connell, R. W. 1987. *Gender and Power.* Cambridge: Polity Press.

Crooks, D. 2001. "The Importance of Symbolic Interaction in Grounded Theory Research on Women's Health." *Health Care for Women's International* 22, nos. 1–2: 11–28.

Dell, C. A., and K. Garabedian. 2003. *Canadian Community Epidemiology Network on Drug Use (CCENDU): 2002 National Report.* Ottawa, ON: Canadian Centre on Substance Abuse.

Denzin, N. K. 1987a. *The Alcoholic Self.* Newbury Park, CA: Sage.

———. 1987b. *The Recovering Alcoholic.* Newbury Park, CA: Sage.

Downing, C. 1991. "Sex Role Setups and Addiction." Pp. 47–60 in N. Van Den Bergh, ed., *Feminist Perspectives on Addiction.* New York: Springer.

Elliott, P., and N. Mandell. 1995. "Feminist Theories." Pp. 3–31 in N. Mandell, ed., *Feminist Issues: Race, Class, and Sexuality.* Scarborough, Ontario: Prentice Hall Canada.

Ettorre, E. 1992. *Women and Substance Use.* London: MacMillan.

Executive Office of the President, Office of National Drug Control Policy. 2001. *The Escalating Costs of Drug Abuse in the US, 1992–2002.* Washington, DC.

Fine, M. 1987. "Silencing and Nurturing Voice in an Improbable Context: Urban Adolescents in Public Schools." In H. Giroux and P. McLaren, eds., *Schooling and the Politics of Culture.* Albany: State University of New York Press.

———. 1992. *Disruptive Voices: The Possibilities of Feminist Research.* Ann Arbor: University of Michigan Press.

Gilligan, C. 1993. *In a Different Voice: Psychological Theory and Women's Development.* Cambridge, MA: Harvard University Press.

Goode, E. 1999. *Drugs in American Society.* 5th ed. Boston: McGraw-Hill.

Graham, K, V. Carver, and P. J. Brett. 1995. "Alcohol and Drug Use by Older Women: Results of a National Survey." *Canadian Journal of Aging* 14: 769–91.

Grella, C., and V. Joshi. 1999. "Gender Differences in Drug Treatment Careers among Clients in the National Drug Abuse Treatment Outcome Study." *American Journal of Drug and Alcohol Abuse* 25, no. 3: 385.

Grover, S. M., and S. P. Thomas. 1993. "Substance Use and Anger in Mid-life Women." *Issues in Mental Health Nursing* 14: 19–29.

Haas, J. 2003. *Seeking Bliss: The Study of Addiction and Recovery.* Victoria, BC: Mosaic.

Hall, J. M. 1993. "Lesbians and Alcohol: Patterns and Paradoxes in Medical Notions and Lesbians' Beliefs." *Journal of Psychoactive Drugs* 25: 109–19.

Kandall, S. 1996. *Substance and Shadow: Women and Alcoholism in the United States.* Cambridge, MA: Harvard University Press.

Lammers, S. M. M., D. E. H. Mainzer, and H. M. M. Breteler. 1995. "Submission and Rebellion: Excessive Drinking of Women in Problematic Heterosexual Partner Relationships." *International Journal of the Addictions* 30: 901–17.

Lerner, G. 1993. *The Creation of Feminist Consciousness: From the Middle Ages to Eighteen-seventy.* New York: Oxford University Press.

Long, A., and B. Mullen. 1994. "An Exploration of Women's Perceptions of the Major Factors That Contributed to Their Alcohol Abuse." *Journal of Advanced Nursing* 19: 623–39.

Lopata, H. 1987. "Women's Family Roles in Life Course Perspective." In B. Hess and M. Ferree, eds., *Analyzing Gender.* Newbury Park, CA: Sage.

McIntosh, J., and N. McKeganey. 2002. *Beating the Dragon: The Recovery from Dependent Drug Use.* Harlow, England: Prentice-Hall.

Miller, B. A., and W. R. Downs. 1993. "The Impact of Family Violence on the Use of Alcohol by Women." *Alcohol Health and Research World* 17: 137–143.

Murphy, S., and M. Rosenbaum. 1999. *Pregnant Women on Drugs: Combating Stereotypes and Stigma.* New Brunswick, NJ: Rutgers University Press.

Nelson-Zlupko, L., E. Kauffman, and M. M. Dore. 1995. "Gender Differences in Drug Addiction and Treatment: Implications for Social Work Intervention with Substance-abusing Women." *Social Work* 40, no. 1.

Nol, J. 1991. "Self Object Search: Role of Addictions in a Patriarchal Culture." Pp. 31–44 in N. Van den Bergh, ed., *Feminist Perspectives on Addictions.* New York: Springer.

O'Connor, L. E., J. W. Berry, D. Inaba., J. Weiss, and A. Morrison. 1994. "Shame, Guilt and Depression in Men and Women in Recovery from Addiction." *Journal of Substance Abuse Treatment* 11: 503–10.

Office of National Drug Control Policy (ONDCP). 2001. "The Economic Costs of Drug Abuse in the United States 1992–2002." *Drug Facts.*

O'Leary, V., R. K. Unger, and B. Wallston, eds. 1985. *Women, Gender and Social Psychology.* Hillsdale, NJ: Lawrence Erlbaum Associates.

Olenick, N. L., and D. Chalmers. 1991. "Gender-specific Drinking Styles in Alcoholics and Nonalcoholics." *Journal of Studies on Alcohol* 52, no. 4: 325–30.

Pihl, R. O, D. Murdoch, J. E. Lapp, and R. Marinier. 1986. "Psychotrope and Alcohol Use by Women: One or Two Populations?" *Journal of Clinical Psychology* 42, no. 6: 991–99.

Plant, M. 1997. *Women and Alcohol: Contemporary and Historical Perspectives.* London: Free Association Books.

Raine, P. 2001. *Women's Perspectives on Drugs and Alcohol: The Vicious Circle.* Hampshire, England: Ashgate.

Reed, B. G. 1985. "Drug Misuse and Dependency in Women: The Meaning and Implications of Being Considered a Special Population or Minority Group." *International Journal of Addictions* 20, no. 1: 13–62.

Rosenbaum, M. 1981. *Women on Heroin.* New Brunswick, NJ: Rutgers University Press.

———. 1998. *Women and Drugs: Twenty-five Years of Research and Policy.* San Francisco: Lindesmith Center.

Rubonis, A. V., S. M. Colby, P. M. Monti, D. J. Rohsenow, S. B. Gulliver, and A. D. Sirota. 1994. "Alcohol Cue Reactivity and Mood Induction in Male and Female Alcoholics." *Journal of Studies on Alcohol* 55: 487–94.

Ryan, V., and J. Popour. 1983. *Five Year Women's Plan. Developed by the Capitol Area Substance Abuse Commission, for the Office of Substance Abuse* (OSAS Publication, IV, 4c, IV, 12c.). Michigan: Department of Health.

SAMHSA, U.S. Department of Health and Human Services Substance Abuse and Mental Health Services Administration. 2000. *1999 National Household Survey on Drug Abuse.* Rockville, MD: U.S. Department of Health and Human Services.

———. 2004, September. *Results from the 2003 National Survey on Drug Use and Health: Detailed Tables.* Retrieved November 8, 2005, <www.oas.samhsa.gov/nhsda/2k3tabs/toc.htm>.

Schur, E. 1984. *Labeling Women Deviant: Gender, Stigma, and Social control.* New York: Random House.

Smith, D. 1987. *The Everyday World as Problematic: A Feminist Sociology.* Toronto, ON: University of Toronto Press.

Underhill, B. 1991. "Recovery Needs of Lesbian Alcoholics in Treatment." Pp. 73–86 in N. Van Den Bergh, ed., *Feminist Perspectives on Addiction.* New York: Springer.

Ussher, J. 1998. "A Feminist Perspective." In R. Velleman, A. Copello, and J. Maslin, eds., *Living with Drink: Women Who Live with Problem Drinkers.* London: Longman.

Van Den Bergh, N. 1991. "Having Bitten the Apple: A Feminist Perspective on Addictions." Pp. 3–30 in N. Van Den Berg, ed., *Feminist Perspectives on Addiction.* New York: Springer.

Van Den Bergh, N., and L. Cooper. 1986. *Feminist Visions for Social Work.* Silver Spring, MD: National Association of Social Workers.

Weinberg, D. 1994. *Working a Program: The Social Construction of Personal Recovery in a Social Model Treatment Program.* Association Paper. University of California, Los Angeles, Department of Sociology.

Wilsnack, S., and L. Beckman, eds. 1984. *Alcohol Problems in Women: Antecedents, Consequences and Intervention.* New York: Guilford.

Woodward, A., J. Epstein, J. Gfroerer, D. Melnick, R. Thoreson, and D. Willson. 1997. "The Drug Abuse Treatment Gap: Recent Estimates." *Health Care Financing Review* 18, no. 3: 15.

9

Rural Crime, Poverty, and Community

Joseph F. Donnermeyer, Pat Jobes, and Elaine Barclay

In this chapter, we begin the development of a cross-community sociological perspective for the examination of crime among rural populations. We utilize "community" as the central concept linking broad change and the behaviors of individuals, both as possible perpetrators and victims of crime.

Throughout most of the twentieth century rural crime ranked among the least studied phenomena in criminology, especially in the U.S. If rural was considered at all, it was as a convenient "ideal type" contrasted with the criminogenic conditions assumed to exist exclusively in urban locations. Rural crime was rarely examined, either comparatively with urban crime or as a subject worthy of investigation in its own right. Occasional work by Clinard on rural criminal offenders (1942; 1944); Gibbons (1972) and Dinitz (1973) on victimization in rural communities; and Lentz (1956), Feldhusen, Thurston and Ager (1965) and Polk (1969) on rural juvenile delinquency were early exceptions to the dominant urban focus of the time.

The urban-exclusive orientation of criminology began to change in the early 1980s through pioneering work by Phillips and associates (see book of readings by Carter, Phillips, Donnermeyer and Wurschmidt 1982; Donnermeyer and Phillips 1984; Mullen and Donnermeyer 1985; Donnermeyer and Mullen 1987), Fischer's (1980) examination of the spread of violence to rural communities, Wilkinson's work on the combined effects of geographic isolation and poverty on rural crime (1984a; 1984b), and a series of agricultural crime studies, summaries of which can be found in Barclay and Donnermeyer (2002).

The 1990s and the first years of this new century have witnessed a continued expansion of rural crime research. Of special note is:

1) extensive scholarship focused on rural substance use and drug production (Clayton 1995; Donnermeyer 1993; Donnermeyer and Park 1995; Donnermeyer and Scheer 2001; Edwards 1992; Edwards and Donnermeyer 2002; O'Dea, Murphy and Balzer 1997; Robertson, Sloboda, Boyd, Beatty and Kozel 1997; Robertson and Donnermeyer 1997; 1998; Scheer, Borden and Donnermeyer 2000; Weisheit 1992);
2) a special issue on rural violence and substance use (Blaser 1994);
3) a focus on victimization and fear of crime among rural populations (Bachman 1992; Ball 2001; Saltiel, Gilchrist and Harvie 1992);
4) a thorough synthesis of scholarly work on rural crime by Weisheit, Falcone and Wells (2005);
5) a rich series of studies examining the relationship between rural community characteristics and crime (Arthur 1991; Barnett and Mencken 2002; Freudenburg and Jones 1991; Jobes 1999a; Kowalski and Duffield 1990; Lee, Maume and Ousey 2003; Nisbett 1993; Nolan 2004; Osgood and Chambers 2000; Petee and Kowalski 1993; Reisig and Cancino 2004; Rephann 1999; Wells and Weisheit 2004);
6) the examination of policing within the context of rural communities (Bass 1995; Falcone, Wells and Weisheit 2002; O'Shea 1999; Payne, Berg and Sun 2005; Thurman and McGarrell 1997) and rural criminal justice agencies (McDonald, Wood and Pflüg 1996); and
7) studies on domestic violence in the rural context (DeKeseredy and Joseph 2005; Gagne 1992; Krishnan, Hilbert and Van Leeuwen 2001; Miller and Veltkamp 1989; Navin, Stockum and Campbell-Ruggaard 1993; Websdale, 1995; 1997).

All of the work cited above focuses on rural crime in the United States, although the Edwards and Donnermeyer (2002) edited volume examines substance use from an international perspective. Also, recent work in Australia (Barclay and Donnermeyer 2002; Barclay, Donnermeyer and Jobes 2004; Donnermeyer and Barclay 2005; Hogg and Carrington 1998; 2003; Jobes 2004; Jobes, Barclay, Weinand and Donnermeyer 2004; Jobes, Donnermeyer and Barclay 2005), Canada (Wood and Griffiths 1996), Great Britain (Aust and Simmons 2002; Dingwall and Moody 1999) and several other nations (Åsling-Monemi, Peña, Ellsberg and Persson 2003; Fafchamps and Moser 2003; Greenberg 1989; Jobes 1999b; 2004; Koenig et al. 2003; Panda and Agarwal 2005; Sanon, Sadowski and Hunter 2004) has served to broaden the focus of rural crime theory and research.

These references demonstrate that rural crime is of interest to a growing number of scholars. However, at this point there is one major shortcoming which severely limits the burgeoning body of scholarly work on rural crime. Simply put, rural crime research has yet to develop a critical conceptual framework that can synthesize current scholarship and point the way toward future theoretical and research developments that are able to advance both theory and research. We propose a "preliminary" solution to the problem by utilizing the sociological concept of community, although not in a strictly functionalist sense. Rather, we propose that the concept of community, when considered as a vehicle for the application of C. W. Mills's (1959) "Sociological Imagination," will allow for a simultaneous consideration of local context and broad structural factors, including poverty, towards greater understanding of rural crime.

Community, Change and Rural Crime: "Public Issues—Personal Troubles"

Nearly fifty years ago, C. Wright Mills (1959) identified a fundamental relationship between macro-level change and what happens to people at the micro level. He referred to it as the link between "public issues" (i.e., macro level) and "personal troubles" (i.e., micro level). Mills observed that personal troubles cannot be understood without knowing something about what is happening at the macro level. A shopkeeper in Mars Hill, Maine, whose storefront is vandalized frequently, a rancher near Melstone, Montana, who now grows marijuana in place of beef cattle as his primary source of income, and a teenager from near Magee, Mississippi, whose underprivileged schooling and limited job opportunities leads to involvement in drug trafficking, are examples of an individual's personal experience being part of a larger set of economic and social structural factors related to a globalizing economy, the ubiquitous influence of mass media, and the growing interdependence of rural and urban areas.

Sociologists examine more than change; they study issues as well, such as crime. Issues are reflective of differences among groups and individuals within a society and are brought on or instigated by long-term change. Issues, including crime, are not constructed outside accepted definitions of what is problematic and what is deviant within the context of various cultures and societies of the world (Kitsuse and Spector 1973). Further, these definitions are indicative of the norms, mores and ideologies of superordinate groups who seek to maintain dominance over other groups with less economic and political power (Greenberg 1981).

Undoubtedly, the concept of community can be criticized because of a singular lack of agreement among sociologists regarding a standard definition, which implies there is difficulty in establishing valid and reliable measures (Bell and Newby 1978; Liepins 2000). However, we contend that community is an indispensable generalizing concept because no other concept can replace it. Whatever community's conceptual faults may be, three things are certain about most, but not all, rural places. First, rural communities have, by definition, smaller populations and lower population densities. Also, the comparative variety of day to day activities are generally more limited in rural than in urban communities, and involve a greater share of persistent personal face-to-face interactions among residents who know each other. Furthermore, rural communities in postmodern times are much less autonomous. They are greatly influenced by external cultural, economic and social forces, depending on their proximity to cities, industries with absentee ownership, tourism, and development policies of nation-states.

Community is the generalizing concept that links the personal problems of people (i.e., crime) and broad, national level and cross-national change (Arensberg 1981; Liepens 2000). Community is both a geographic place and a network of actors. Communities may function as a buffer from larger, global forces, that is, protecting members of a rural community from factors that promote criminal and deviant behavior. Alternatively, community may facilitate or enable these forces in ways that influence the development of crime.

Second, a community is an interaction system where members and groups both cooperate and compete on a daily basis. Sometimes the processes of cooperation and competition are in the political arena. Other times, these interactions are mostly economic, social or cultural in character, or a mix of types. Further, aspects of cooperation and conflict at the local level are often reflective of similar processes at the national level, or the manifestation of influences from the outside.

Third, community is a place where residents experience their society and culture, plus world events and globalizing influences. This occurs in two ways. First, most rural places possess their own array of local media, but this media relies heavily on national and international sources for many of their stories. However, news and other media-based information are not disseminated in a homogeneous fashion. Each transfer of a story is subject to reinterpretation. Local newspaper editors may rewrite the headline of a syndicated news story, but not the story itself. Local radio stations select which news items are read on the air, and to which political commentators they subscribe. In addition, regardless of whether information obtained through the media is locally processed or not, it is through a local web of interpersonal communications with neighbors, acquaintances and family that the information is discussed and reinterpreted.

Fourth, communities provide the specific geographic and social context in which people express behaviors, including criminal behavior, and the behavior of victims as well. Specific places provide different kinds of opportunities for criminal behavior. U.S. rural communities near the borders with Canada and Mexico are places where illegal smuggling of drugs and other commodities occurs. Marijuana is the staple crop of many rural Appalachian counties (Clayton 1995; Weisheit, Falcone and Wells 2005). Tolerance of domestic violence by local law enforcement varies greatly within different rural regions of the U.S. (DeKeseredy and Joseph 2005; Gagne 1992; Websdale 1997).

Fifth, a community functions to socialize its members into values, beliefs and norms of society. A community controls the attitudes and behaviors of individuals, mostly through such primary groups as family, school and peers, but also through formal agencies, such as the police and courts (Oetting, Donnermeyer and Deffenbacher 1998). Further, through their interactions, residents create the specific context in which a sense of community is expressed, which in turn influences their attitudes and behaviors (Liepins 2000). Warren (1978) described this common identity with place as "***weness.***" These characteristics of rural communities collectively facilitate and constrain the development of crime. It is within the local context that social class, race/ethnic and other differences create both a class of local elites and a class of marginalized residents. It is at the local level that the "haves" and the "have nots" learn their relative positions within the greater society.

The characteristics that are described in the above paragraphs reiterate those that Tönnies (1957) used to conceptualize *Gemeinschaft* as the antithesis of *Gesellschaft.* Community is a unit of analysis that connotes a set of structures and processes that are crucial for analysis and interpretation of behavior. Bell and Newby (1978) were among the first scholars to warn against any use of the concept that implies historical nostalgia or advocacy for a traditional life. The universal and holistic character of the concept made it a foundation among the theories of Weber, Marx, Durkheim and Simmel. Because the social structure was evolving to society, analyses of community were often couched in terms of a null concept, of a system that was passing.

The essential utility of the concept was recognized in major research centers throughout the first half of the twentieth century. The Chicago School expanded community concepts in the development of social disorganization theory for urban settings. The paucity of sociological texts and scholars in Europe following World War II led Bourdieu, Chamboredon, and Passeron (1991) to develop their own epistemology through a synthesis of classic European texts and more recent American sociology. A scholarly German émigré in England wrote *The Civilising Process* drawing upon similar materials (Elias 1982). Holistic notions of community are fundamental to each, and indicate the fundamental essentialism of the concept. Bourdieu recognizes the importance of structural influences for shaping human action and shared values and norms (Bourdieu and Passeron 1977). *Habitus* occupies the slippery boundary between objective structure and subjective interpretation. The agent is always present, but is under the constant influence of structure in habitus. Elias emphasizes the sociological importance for reflecting on historical origins of social structure in order to understand the evolution toward modern society. More recently, sociologists have embraced social capital theory to examine the web of interaction within communities and to examine power and decision-making at the local level (Flora 1998; Liepins 2000; Sharp 2001).

Community in its varying metamorphoses indicates not only the persistence, but also the need for the concept. Whether interpreting a traditional, modern or postmodern world, the need for incorporating location, personal interaction, normative presence and shared identity around a single concept is apparent (Liepins 2000).

The development of place-based theory has an established utility in criminology as a subfield of sociology for the development of cross-cultural perspectives on rural community characteristics that can encompass a more critical approach to the study of crime. Referred to as "social disorganization" theory (Tittle 2000), it provides a view of crime which assumes that behavior occurs in a geographic location because of local social structures and their influences. Local structural factors influence whether people become criminal or engage in other behaviors that are considered criminal and deviant, as well as the probability that they will be victimized by crime. Local community structures also provide the context in which criminal behavior is expressed. Types of actions engaged in by individuals are strongly influenced by their position in the local structure of a community and the nature of that particular community's norms, values, and beliefs.

Social disorganization theory, both in its historic form and its more recent contemporary application, however, is not very critical in its orientation. It merely assumes that there are differences between various places based on cultural, demographic, economic and social characteristics (Jobes et al. 2004; Sampson 1986; Tittle 2000) and that these differences are correlated with differing rates of crime and other social phenomena. However, when C. W. Mills' (1959) concept of "public issues-personal troubles" is combined with Bourdieu's conception of habitus and the sociological definition of social capital, social disorganization theory takes on a more critical stance in its view of crime. Now, in reference to both rural and urban places, community characteristics become expressions of the relationship of places to broad social structural and economics forces, that is, the local political economy. Yet, it avoids a deterministic orientation by recognizing that specific expressions of crime are dependent on the local context, and furthermore, reactions to crime are conditioned by the local milieu of community norms and the structure of relationships between people within specific places. Further, we argue that this conceptual approach allows scholars who conduct cross-sectional, statistical studies of rural crime as well as those who prefer qualitative and case study methodologies to compare and contrast their findings.

Applied to rural crime, this reconceptualization of social disorganization theory allows for the consideration of broad rural-urban differences without treating "rural" areas as a type of homogeneous residual, which implies the dualistic myths that rural areas are mostly the same and most rural places have little crime. Hence, it is not a matter of aligning rural places on a continuum of increasing urbanity in order to explain crime. In fact, some of the most isolated rural areas display unusually high levels of crime in general, or specific kinds of crime syndromes (Gagne 1992; Jobes et al. 2004; Wilkinson 1984b). Rural places are incredibly diverse, as each represents a differing mix of exogenous and endogenous cultural, demographic, economic and social forces, which in turn create diverse patterns of crime. Indeed, criminology would be better served by discarding wholesale its urban bias and conducting research in rural communities instead, as they provide a better laboratory for the conduct of both quantitative and qualitative research on crime.

Historically, in U.S. criminology and the criminological traditions of other advanced capitalist countries, such as Australia, Canada and Greater Britain, rural communities were assumed to have less crime because their social structures were more homogeneous, cohesive and integrated than those in urban places. In short, rural places manifested less social disorganization. It is evident from recent research that rural communities are not crime free. In fact, rural rates may be higher than urban rates at particular types of rural places and for specific kinds of crime (Carter et al. 1982; Jobes et al. 2004; Weisheit and Donnermeyer 2000). Rurality does not imply the sociological equivalent of immunity from crime.

Previous analyses of rural crime and community characteristics suggest an interesting conclusion about the interrelationship of local structural factors and rural crime. Research by Rephann (1999), Osgood and Chambers (2000), Jobes et al. (2004), and Wells and Weisheit (2004) have consistently found that social and cultural factors account for more crime in rural areas than in metropolitan areas. Conversely, economic factors directly explain comparatively more crime in urban areas. The findings indicate that cohesive and integrating social factors are associated with lower crime in both rural and urban locations. However, social factors have much more direct effects in rural areas because their disintegration implies the loss of community. This is because rural places have smaller population size and consequently, they are more vulnerable to disruptions to their established social order. There is no social condition that prevents crime as effectively as personal, face-to-face, stable interaction around a familiar and accepted set of norms.

Focusing on rural-related crime in modern societies requires explicit acknowledgment of urban settings and the growing interdependence of rural and urban areas, as well as recognition that rural areas are in a relationship of dependency, to some extent, on urban areas (Clayton 1995). As part of the larger *Gesellschaft*, people in rural areas are subject to urban influences, especially through economics relations, the mass media and the distribution of various consumer products (Mamman, Brieger and Oshiname 2002; Wagner, Diaz, López, Collado and Aldaz 2002). Fischer (1980) maintains that rural areas generally evolve toward and follow urban trends in both social organization and the types of social problems expressed by people. Core-to-periphery relationships exist for many kinds of sociological phenomena. There is no absolute and definitive distinction between either the conceptual or real geographic boundaries of urban and rural areas. Depending upon the society under consideration, there may be abrupt differences, either geographically, culturally, or both; or, there may be a rural to urban continuum with many types of places exhibiting varying characteristics of both "rural-ness" and "urban-ness."

Social Disorganization, Crime and Rural Communities

A social disorganization orientation provides a versatile starting point for developing conceptual models that encourage rural crime research because it is a placed-based theory that can incorporate both macro change and local context. Ironically, social disorganization theory was first developed by the "Chicago School of Sociology" in the U.S. during the 1920s and 1930s as a way to examine a variety of social phenomena in the city's neighborhoods, which were distinctive in their racial and ethnic composition. After a gradual decline in use as an explanation of crime, social disorganization has again become a central theory in criminology, thanks mainly to the work of Reiss (1986), Bursik and Gransmick (1999), Sampson and associates (Sampson 1986; Sampson and Groves 1989; Sampson et al. 1997) and others, and is further reinforced by the work of Braithwaite (1989) and others on restorative justice in post-modern times.

Social disorganization theory applies an ecological approach to the study of crime problems by analyzing how the spatial distributions of various behaviors are reflective of structural and cultural features that distinguish places (Osgood and Chambers 2000). Rural areas typically have less evidence of disorganization than metropolitan communities (Freudenburg 1986) because they display more *Gemainschaft* type qualities that supposedly produce less crime, although there are many exceptions to the rule. Systematic social organization occurs in three specific ways. First, strong informal relations among primary groups such as neighbors, friendship groups, cliques, and extended family create a density of acquaintanceship (Freudenburg 1986) that controls the behavior of members. Punishments can include negative gossip, ostracism and intolerance from other community members. Second, community membership within these various primary groups overlaps to a considerable extent. Residents exhibit an extended (Freudenburg 1986) acquaintanceship or networks that reinforce conformity across demographic and social class (or caste) characteristics, within the geographic boundaries of rural neighborhoods and the community as a whole. Further, internal cohesion is reinforced by external controls, which establishes a third dimension of rural community structure. The ability of communities to maintain external relationships through which outside resources can be gained and through which undesirable influences can be reduced helps to maintain the established structure of conformity (Gilchrist 2000). Hence, compared to urban places, rural communities are assumed to manifest more intact families, more stable populations, greater homogeneity and more social bonding among members. They have more meaningful personal interaction, what Freudenburg (1986) terms "density of acquaintanceship." Although these basic urban-rural distinctions persist, it is also true that rural communities themselves are quite diverse. Crime and deviance rates will vary according to the levels of disorganization characterized by different types of rural places (Jobes et al. 2004).

Before identifying specific types of social disorganization, two caveats are in order. We discard the traditional functionalist notion that social disorganization is atypical, and that all social systems, rather rural or urban, adjust to disruptions in their social structure and return to a mythical state of social organization. We reject this notion, not because it is theoretically false, but because it is empirically untrue given the major trends and issues which continuously influence rural communities (Donnermeyer and Jobes 2000).

A second caveat is that there is some evidence, although sociologists have rarely focused on it, that social organization itself may facilitate some types of crime, even as it constrains other types (Barclay and Jobes 2004). This pattern occurs through the reluctance of citizens to report crime, the disinclination of local police to investigate crimes committed by individuals who possess higher social status than those they victimized (which include aspects of bribery and corruption), and the selective blaming of victims who are marginalized within the community in some fashion. This is an area that clearly needs much more research, as it identifies more fully how social class divisions at the local level influence crime and how the police and criminal justice agencies respond to local expressions of crime.

Furthermore, it could be the case that aspects of organization and disorganization operate simultaneously in most rural localities, creating unique conditions for the expression of crime. Local elites may display all the conditions associated with stereotypical forms of *Gemeinschaft*, that is, a high density of acquaintanceship, while marginalized groups at the same locations may exhibit all the characteristics traditionally identified by social disorganization theory. Although statistical studies which rely on census data will continue to be useful for the study of rural crime, it is also true that many of the dynamics of rural crime's expression at specific places cannot be understood without resort to a more qualitative, case-study approach (Jobes et al. 2005).

Aspects of Social Disorganization and Rural Communities

Social disorganization emerges because of several interacting factors. In this section, five sources of social disorganization are reviewed. The first source of social disorganization is poverty. Both rural and urban communities who manifest higher than average rates of poverty also possess fewer resources to support institutions, such as schools, which promote prosocial (i.e., less criminal, less deviant) behavior (Oetting et al. 1998). In some situations, poverty may act as a protective factor against the development of crime if it serves to reinforce cohesion among the members of a rural community where class differences are minimal because the community itself is both economically and politically marginalized. However, it is equally true that poverty is also an indicator of deeper cleavages within a community, such as social class divisions and large gaps between a few "haves" and many "have-nots" (Greenberg 1981). With economic inequality comes social and political inequality, representing a kind of social disorganization that reduces the overall cohesion of communities, dividing many rural communities into subgroups with divergent values and loyalties (Nisbett 1993). Racial and ethnic heterogeneity of populations, combined with poverty and economic inequality, can dramatically affect social integration and cohesion as well. Further, inequality among populations living in rural places may be local manifestations of larger social, cultural and economic forces that represent connections between rural places and urban centers, which can influence local decision-making processes and reducing local autonomy (Lee, Maume and Ousey 2003).

A second variation on the relationship between poverty and crime can be found in rural places with persisting poverty, that is, conditions that continue from one generation to the next. Rural people begin to develop alternative means of sustenance, some of which may include involvement in illegal activities, especially drug production (Weisheit 1992; O'Dea, Murphy and Balzer 1997; Rojas 2002). Also, communities with persistent poverty can create "retreatist" and "rebellious" subcultures in Merton's (1968) classic sense of these terms. Often, their norms are in conflict with those of the broader society vis-à-vis the national government. Examples include violence against women and children (i.e., domestic violence) and violations of laws restricting hunting and use of both endangered flora and fauna in ceremonies and community traditions (Polk 1969; Miller and Veltkamp 1989; Gagne 1992).

The second is population. In general, rural communities have smaller populations and lower population densities; characteristics presumed to protect rural people from the influences that create higher levels of social problems in urban communities. The idea that urbanism (Wirth 1938) primarily causes crime and that crime diffuses, after a period of lag, to rural communities (Fischer 1980) needs to be revisited and revised to reflect contemporary postmodern contexts. Local social structures and cultural contexts are critical for understanding how these external social forces are expressed at the local level.

Wilkinson (1984b) was among the first authors to suggest that rural communities may exhibit more variability in rates of crime by the very nature of their smaller populations. In other words, it is not size itself which counts, but size along with a degree of geographic isolation that helps buffer some rural communities from disruptive society-wide trends and issues, or conversely, increases vulnerability to these same forces. Rural communities proximate to large urban areas or rural communities that experience rapid economic, population and other forms of change may be particularly vulnerable to a disruption of their established social structures. The specific source of disequilibrium may be the relocation of factories, military bases, energy development, tourism, and other kinds of new economic activities (Freudenburg and Jones 1991; Petee and Kowalski 1993; Wilkinson 1984a). Further, many of these economic activities are exploitative of rural people, that is, ownership and control is nonlocal, with directives emanating from urban-located headquarters. These rural communities become more vulnerable to economic dislocations that put severe stress on community life. Cooperation among neighbors may turn to competition, and the *Gemeinschaft* qualities of these places are lost. Further, in many societies, police, courts and other criminal justice services have centralized, consolidated, and become increasingly bureaucratized and vertically integrated with national systems of justice, leaving rural communities with more limited and less flexible infrastructures to deal with specific expressions of crime. The evidence is compelling that under certain conditions, small population size enhances the vulnerability of rural communities to macro-level forces that create crime (Weisheit et al. 2005; Wilkinson 1984b).

A third factor related to the social disorganization of rural communities is population mobility, especially when it is associated with economic and cultural change. One aspect of population mobility is the case of rural "boom towns" that suddenly experience an influx of new residents because of rapid economic development (Freudenburg and Jones 1991). Less dramatic changes that have been sought by residents, such as the introduction of tourism and the location of new industry to exploit cheap rural labor can be disruptive and can also increase crime (Jobes 1999a). Equally disruptive in many societies is the kind of population transience caused by the need for men (and women) to seek jobs in distant urban areas (United Nations 1994). Families are left behind, often to fend for themselves. Rural workers in cities may send money to their families to improve economic conditions, but the pattern itself is disruptive. One especially virulent form is the cross-migration between particular rural and urban slums involving streams and counter-streams of highly disenfranchised people with high rates of crime. Following a recent riot in the "Redfern" district of Sydney, Australia, reference was made to cross-migration with the rural town of Walgett. Both locations have high proportions of unemployed Aboriginal People, and have extremely high levels of crime and other indicators of social disorganization (Nation Master Encyclopedia: Redfern 2004).

A fourth factor is racial and ethnic disorganization. As Thomas and Znaniecki (1918) first indicated, ethnic diversity within a population presents problems of social disorganization. Differences in customs and a lack of shared experiences lead to a breakdown in communication and may breed fear and distrust (Sampson and Groves 1989), especially when combined with poverty and various forms of economic, social and political inequality along race/ethnic lines.

Even remote locations occupied by a single race/ethnic group that has relatively little contact with outsiders can manifest social disorganization. In Australia, some of the communities with persistently high levels of crime are small remote places with high proportions of poor unemployed Aboriginal people (Jobes et al. 2004). When indigenous cultures are disturbed, increased crime and other deviance often follow, demonstrating that residual patterns of disorganization can develop and persist even in small remote communities. When indigenous cultures remain intact, or are somehow reorganized, and/or integrated into the local mainstream, crime is less problematic (Jobes et al. 2005).

Finally, much of the time, family is a primary source that communicates the values, beliefs and norms of a culture (Oetting et al. 1998). Extended families remain relatively important in many rural communities. Sampson (1986) argues that single parents are strained for time and money to effectively supervise their children and to interact with other adults. When established structures of families (and extended family systems) in rural locations are disrupted by broader, society-wide trends and issues, the social organization of smaller communities becomes more disorganized. Family disruption may be due to the search for gainful employment, as mentioned previously. Whatever the reason, alternative structures for socialization develop, including gangs, further weakening the influence of family (Donnermeyer 1994). Although juvenile delinquency perhaps receives the most attention, suicide, alcoholism, and family violence also are serious consequences of rural disorganization (Pitman, Herbert, Land and O'Neill 2003).

Conclusion

There is increasing recognition that rural crime is a phenomenon that merits serious criminological analysis. There is a need for a framework that will permit the integration and synthesis of findings from studies focused on specific places, and there is a need for more localized research on rural crime in order to uncover the relationship between the broad societal and global forces at the top of the hourglass and specific expressions of crime. More importantly, incorporating a theoretically grounded approach to studies of rural crime will facilitate innovative and fertile discourse among scholars, whether their approach is qualitative or quantitative, and whether their research is a single case study or includes multiple rural locations.

The authors fully recognize that we begin this discourse leaning heavily on ideas and principles from place-based criminological theory and research in the U.S., and from Australia, Canada, and Great Britain, all of which are advanced capitalist societies. However, we argue that when the concept of community and social disorganization theory are reformulated to shed their functionalist presumptions, they become powerful starting points for the kind of theoretical development that can encompass rural places from societies around the world. As a generalizing concept that is seen as mediating "public issues" and "personal troubles" (Mills 1959), community can accommodate variations in culture and society. Community structure provides a foundation for comparative analyses across the full spectrum of social structures from traditional to postmodern. Equally important, community structure is a crucial causal force behind crime in rural areas, which is why it can be combined with social disorganization theory as the start of further empirical and theoretical work on rural crime.

The five factors delineated as key components of crime in rural areas do not occur in isolation. They converge in unique combinations, creating high variability in the specific contexts of rural communities in societies around the world. However, they do have one thing in common. The source of social disorganization is frequently nonlocal, that is, rural communities which exhibit high rates of crime often display aspects of structural disruption based on relationships of dependency. Although unique and isolated cultural patterns may explain some types of rural crime, it is the position of the authors that rural crime can be most effectively compared and understood through the organizing concept of community and sociological theories that either implicitly or explicitly accommodate place-based factors. Social disorganization provides a particularly applicable perspective for analyzing how global cultural, economic, and social forces affect the unique contexts in which rural people live, analyses of what C. W. Mills (1959) referred to as "public issues" and "personal troubles."

References

Arensberg, C. 1981. "Cultural Holism through Interaction Systems." *American Anthropologist* 83: 562–81.

Arthur, J. 1991. "Socioeconomic Predictors of Crime in Rural Georgia." *Criminal Justice Review* 16: 29–41.

Åsling-Monemi, K., R. Peña, M. C. Ellsberg, and L. Å. Persson. 2003. "Violence against Women Increases Risk of Infant and Child Mortality: A Case-referent Study in Nicaragua." *Bulletin of the World Health Organization* 81: 10–19.

Aust, R., and J. Simmons. 2002. *Rural Crime in England and Wales.* London: Home Office.

Bachman, R. 1992. "Crime in Nonmetropolitan America: A National Accounting of Trends, Incidence Rates, and Idiosyncratic Vulnerabilities." *Rural Sociology* 57: 546–60.

Ball, C. 2001. "Rural Perceptions of Crime." *Journal of Contemporary Criminal Justice* 17: 37–48.

Barclay, E., and J. F. Donnermeyer. 2002. "Property Crime and Crime Prevention on Farms in Australia." *Crime Prevention and Community Safety: An International Journal* 4: 47–61.

Barclay, E., and P. C. Jobes. 2004. "The Dark Side of *Gemeinschaft*." *Crime Prevention and Community Safety: An International Journal* 6: 7–22.

Barnett, C., and F. C. Mencken. 2002. "Social Disorganization Theory and the Contextual Nature of Crime in Nonmetropolitan Counties." *Rural Sociology* 67: 372–93.

Bass, J. 1995. "Rural Policing: Patterns and Problems of Micro Departments." *Justice Professional* 9: 59–74.

Bell, C., and H. Newby. 1978. *Community Studies*. London: George Allen & Unwin.

Blaser, J., ed. 1994. *Perspectives on Violence and Substance Use in Rural America*. Chicago: North Central Regional Educational Laboratory.

Bourdieu, P., J.-C. Chamboredon, and J.-C. Passeron. 1991. *The Craft of Sociology: Epistemological Preliminaries*. Ed. B. Krais. Trans. R. Nice. Berlin: Walter de Gruyter.

Bourdieu, P., and J.-C. Passeron. 1977. *Reproduction: In Education, Society and Culture*. Trans. R. Nice. Beverly Hills, CA: Sage.

Braithwaite, J. 1989. *Crime, Shame, and Reintegration*. New York: Cambridge University Press.

Bursik, R. J., Jr., and H. G. Gransmick. 1999. "Neighborhoods and Crime: The Dimensions of Effective Community Control." New York: Lexington Books.

Carter, T. J., H. G. Phillips, J. F. Donnermeyer, and T. N. Wurschmidt, eds. 1982. *Rural Crime: Integrating Research and Prevention*. Totowa, NJ: Allanheld, Osmun.

Clayton, R. R. 1995. *Marijuana in the "Third World": Appalachia, U.S.A.* Boulder, CO: Lynne Reinner.

Clinard, M. 1942. "The Process of Urbanization and Criminal Behavior: A Study of Culture Conflict." *American Journal of Sociology* 48: 202–13.

———. 1944. "Rural Criminal Offenders." *American Journal of Sociology* 50: 38–45.

DeKeseredy, W. S., and C. Joseph. 2005. "Separation and/or Divorce Sexual Assault in Rural Ohio: Preliminary Results of an Exploratory Study." *Violence Against Women* 11: 1–13.

Dingwall, G., and S. R. Moody. 1999. *Crime and Conflict in the Countryside*. Cardiff: University of Wales Press.

Dinitz, S. 1973. "Progress, Crime and the Folk Ethic: Portrait of a Small Town." *Criminology* 11: 3–21.

Donnermeyer, J. F. 1993. "Rural Youth Usage of Alcohol, Marijuana, and 'Hard' Drugs." *The International Journal of the Addictions* 28: 249–55.

———. 1994. "Crime and Violence in Rural Communities." Pp. 27–64 in J. Blaser, ed., *Perspectives on Violence and Substance Use in Rural America*. Chicago: North Central Regional Educational Laboratory.

Donnermeyer, J. F., and E. Barclay. 2005. "The Policing of Farm Crime." *Police Practice and Research* 6: 3–17.

Donnermeyer, J. F., and P. C. Jobes. 2000. "Rural Crime." Pp. 461–64 in C. D. Bryant, ed., *Encyclopedia of Criminology and Deviant Behavior*. Philadelphia: Running Press/Routledge.

Donnermeyer, J. F., and R. E. Mullen. 1987. "Use of Neighbors for Crime Prevention: Evidence from a State-wide Rural Victim Study." *Journal of the Commmunity Development Society* 18: 15–29.

Donnermeyer, J. F., and D. S. Park. 1995. "Alcohol Use among Rural Adolescents: Predictive and Situational Factors." *The International Journal of the Addictions* 30: 459–79.

Donnermeyer, J. F., and G. H. Phillips. 1984. "Vandals and Vandalism in the USA: A Rural Perspective." Pp. 133–49 in C. Lévy-Leboyer, ed., *Vandalism: Behaviour and Motivations.* Amsterdam: North-Holland.

Donnermeyer, J. F., and S. D. Scheer. 2001. "An Analysis of Substance Use among Adolescents from Smaller Places." *Journal of Rural Health* 17: 105–13.

Edwards, R. W., ed. 1992. *Drug Use in Rural American Communities.* New York: Harrington Park Press.

Edwards, R. W., and Donnermeyer, J. F., eds. 2002. "Introduction: Substance Use in Rural Communities around the World." *Substance Use and Misuse* 37: vii–xii.

Elias N. 1982. *The Civilizing Process. State Formation and Civilization.* Oxford: Basil Blackwell.

Fafchamps, M., and C. Moser. 2003. "Crime, Isolation and Law Enforcement." *Journal of African Economics* 12: 625–71.

Falcone, D., E. Wells, and R. Weisheit. 2002. "The Small-town Police Department." *Policing: An International Journal of Police Strategies and Management* 25: 371–84.

Feldhusen, J. F., J. R. Thurston, and E. Ager. 1965. "Delinquency Proneness of Urban and Rural Youth." *Journal of Research in Crime and Delinquency* 2: 32–44.

Fischer, C. 1980. "The Spread of Violent Crime from City to Countryside, 1955 to 1975." *Rural Sociology 44*: 416–34.

Flora, J. L. 1998. "Social Capital and Communities of Place." *Rural Sociology* 63: 481–506.

Freudenburg, W. R. 1986. "The Density of Acquaintanceship: An Overlooked Variable in Community Research." *American Journal of Sociology* 92: 27–63.

Freudenburg, W. R., and R. M. Jones. 1991. "Criminal Behavior and Rapid Community Growth: Examining the Evidence." *Rural Sociology* 56: 619–45.

Gagne, P. L. 1992. "Appalachian Women: Violence and Social Control." *Journal of Contemporary Ethnography* 20: 387–415.

Gibbons, D. C. 1972. "Crime in the Hinterlands." *Criminology* 10: 117–91.

Gilchrist, A. 2000. "The Well-connected Community: Networking to the 'Edge of Chaos.'" *Community Development Journal* 35: 264–75.

Greenburg, D. F, ed. 1981. *Crime and Capitalism: Readings in Marxist Criminology.* Palo Alto, CA: Mayfield.

Greenburg, J. B. 1989. *Blood Ties: Life and Violence in Rural Mexico.* Tuscon: University of Arizona Press.

Hogg, R., and K. Carrington. 1998. "Crime, Rurality and Community." *The Australian and New Zealand Journal of Criminology* 31: 160–81.

———. 2003. "Violence, Spatiality and Other Rurals." *The Australian and New Zealand Journal of Criminology* 36: 293–319.

Jobes, P. C. 1999a. "Residential Stability and Crime in Small Rural Agricultural and Recreational Towns." *Sociological Perspectives* 42: 499–524.

———. 1999b. "Poverty, Gender and Social Justice and Social Problems in Rural Pakistan." Pp. 89–122 in Dan A. Chekki, ed., *Research in Community Sociology,* vol. 9. Greenwich, CT: JAI Press.

———. 2004. "Colonialization and Crime: Contemporary Consequences of Invasion on Indigenous Peoples in Rural Places." *International Review of Sociology* 14: 51–71.

Jobes, P. C., E. Barclay, H. Weinand, and J. F. Donnermeyer. 2004. "A Structural Analysis of Social Disorganization and Crime in Rural Communities in Australia." *The Australian and New Zealand Journal of Criminology* 37: 114–40.

Jobes, P. C., J. F. Donnermeyer, and E. Barclay. 2005. "A Tale of Two Towns: Social Structure, Integration and Crime in Rural New South Wales." *Sociologia Ruralis* 45: 224–44.

Kitsuse, J. I., and M. Spector. 1973. "Toward a Sociology of Social Problems: Social Conditions, Value Judgments and Social Problems." *Social Problems* 20: 407–19.

Koenig, M. A., T. Lutalo, F. Zhao, F. Nalugoda, F. Wabwire-Mangen, N. Kiwanuka, J. Wagman, D. Serwadda, M. Wawer, and R. Gray. 2003. "Domestic Violence in Rural Uganda: Evidence from a Community-based Study." *Bulletin of the World Health Organization* 81: 53–60.

Kowalski, G. S., and D. Duffield. 1990. "The Impact of the Rural Population Component on Homicide Rates in the United States: A County-level Analysis." *Rural Sociology* 54: 76–90.

Krishnan, S. P., J. C. Hilbert, and D. Van Leeuwen. 2001. "Domestic Violence and Help-seeking Behaviors among Rural Women: Results from a Shelter-based Study." *Family Community Health* 24: 28–38.

Lee, M. R., M. O. Maume, and G. C. Ousey. 2003. "Social Isolation and Lethal Violence across the Metro/nonmetro Divide: The Effects of Socioeconomic Disadvantage and Poverty Concentration on Homicide." *Rural Sociology* 68: 107–31.

Lentz, W. P. 1956. "Rural-urban Differentials and Juvenile Delinquency." *Journal of Criminal Law, Criminology and Police Science* 47: 331–39.

Liepins, R. 2000. "New Energies for an Old Idea: Reworking Approaches to 'Community' in Contemporary Rural Studies." *Journal of Rural Studies* 16: 23–35.

Mamman, L. S., W. R. Brieger, and F. O. Oshiname. 2002. "Alcohol Consumption Pattern among Women in a Rural Yoruba Community in Nigeria." *Substance Use and Misuse* 37: 579–98.

McDonald, T. D., R. A. Wood, and M. A. Pflüg, eds. 1996. *Rural Criminal Justice.* Salem, WI: Sheffield Publishing Company.

Merton, R. K. 1968. *Social Theory and Social Structure.* New York: The Free Press.

Miller, T. W., and L. J. Veltkamp. 1989. "Child Sexual Abuse: The Abusing Family in Rural America." *International Journal of Family Psychiatry* 9: 259–75.

Mills, C. W. 1959. *The Sociological Imagination.* New York: Oxford University Press.

Mullen, R. E., and J. F. Donnermeyer. 1984. "Age, Trust, and Perceived Safety from Crime in Rural Areas." *The Gerontologist* 25: 237–42.

Nation Master: Encyclopedia. 2004. New South Wales. Retrieved November 18, 2005, <www.nationmaster.com/encyclopedia/2004-Redfern-riots>.

Navin, S., R. Stockum, and J. Campbell-Ruggaard. 1993. "Battered Women in Rural America." *Journal of Human Educational Development* 32: 9–16.

Nisbett, R. E. 1993. "Violence and U.S. Regional Culture." *The American Psychologist* 48: 441–49.

Nolan III, J. J. 2004. "Establishing the Statistical Relationship between Population

Size and UCR Crime Rate: Its Impact and Implications." *Journal of Criminal Justice* 32: 547–55.

O'Dea, P., B. Murphy, and C. Balzer. 1997. "Traffic and Illegal Production of Drugs in Rural America." Pp. 79–89 in E. B. Robertson, Z. Sloboda, G. M. Boyd, K. L. Beatty and N. J. Kozel, eds., *Rural Substance Abuse: State of Knowledge and Issues.* NIDA Research Monograph 168. Rockville, MD: National Institute of Drug Abuse, U.S. Department of Health and Human Services.

Oetting, E. R., J. F. Donnermeyer, and J. L. Deffenbacher. 1998. "Primary Socialization Theory: The Influence of the Community on Drug Use and Deviance." *Substance Use and Misuse* 33: 1629–65.

Osgood, D. W., and J. M. Chambers. 2000. "Social Disorganization outside the Metropolis: An Analysis of Rural Youth Violence." *Criminology* 38: 81–116.

O'Shea, T. 1999. "Community Policing in Small Town Rural America." *Policing and Society* 9: 59–76.

Panda, P., and B. Agarwal. 2005. "Marital Violence, Human Development and Women's Property Status in India." *World Development* 33: 823–50.

Payne, B. K., B. L. Berg, and I. Y. Sun. 2005. "Policing in Small Town America: Dogs, Drunks, Disorder, and Dysfunction." *Journal of Criminal Justice* 33: 31–41.

Petee, T. A., and G. S. Kowalski. 1993. "Modeling Rural Violent Crime Rates: A Test of Social Disorganization Theory." *Sociological Focus* 26: 77–89.

Pitman, S., T. Herbert, C. Land, and C. O'Neill. 2003. *Profile of Young Australians: Facts, Figures and Issues.* Melbourne: The Foundation for Young Australians.

Polk, K. 1969. "Delinquency and Community Action in Nonmetropolitan Areas." In R. R. Cressey and D. A. Ward, eds., *Delinquency, Crime and Social Process.* New York: Harper and Row, Publishers.

Reisig, M. D., and J. M. Cancino. 2004. "Incivilities in Nonmetropolitan Communities: The Effects of Structural Constraints, Social Conditions, and Crime." *Journal of Criminal Justice* 32: 15–29.

Reiss, A. J., Jr. 1986. "Why Are Communities Important in Understanding Crime?" Pp. 1–34 in A. J. Reiss Jr. and M. Tonry, eds., *Communities and Crime.* Chicago: University of Chicago Press.

Rephann, W. S. 1999. "Links between Rural Development and Crime." *Papers in Regional Science* 78: 365–86.

Robertson, E., and J. F. Donnermeyer. 1997. "Illegal Drug Use among Rural Adults: Mental Health Consequences and Treatment Utilization." *American Journal of Drug and Alcohol Abuse* 23: 467–84.

———. 1998. "Patterns of Drug Use among Nonmetropolitan and Rural Adults." *Substance Use and Misuse* 33: 2109–29.

Robertson, E., Z. Sloboda, G. M. Boyd, L. Beatty, and N. J. Kozel, eds. 1997. *Rural Substance Abuse: State of Knowledge and Issues.* NIDA Research Monograph 168. Rockville, MD: National Institute of Drug Abuse, U.S. Department of Health and Human Services.

Rojas, M. R. 2002. "Attitudes and Values of Peruvian Coca Growers." *Substance Use and Misuse* 37: 687–714.

Saltiel, J., J. Gilchrist, and R. Harvie. 1992. "Concern about Crime among Montana Farmers and Ranchers." *Rural Sociology* 57: 535–45.

Sampson, R. J. 1986. "Crime in Cities: The Effects of Formal and Informal Social Control. Pp. 271–312 in A. J. Reiss Jr. and M. Tonry, eds., *Communities and Crime.* Chicago: University of Chicago Press.

Sampson, R. J., and W. B. Groves. 1989. "Community Structure and Crime: Testing Social-disorganization Theory." *American Journal of Sociology* 94: 774–802.

Sampson, R. J., S. W. Raudenbush, and F. Earls. 1997. "Neighborhoods and Violent Crime: A Multilevel Study of Collective Efficacy." *Science* 277: 918–24.

Sanon, J., L. Sadowski, and W. Hunter. 2004. "Violence against Women in India: Evidence from Rural Maharashtra." *Rural and Remote Health* 4: 304. Retrieved August 2, 2005, <http://rrh.deakin.edu.au>.

Scheer, S. D., L. M. Borden, and J. F. Donnermeyer. 2000. "The Relationship between Family Factors and Adolescent Substance Use in Rural, Suburban and Urban Settings." *Journal of Child and Family Studies* 9: 105–15.

Sharp, J. S. 2001. "Locating the Community Field: A Study of Interorganizational Network Structure and Capacity for Community Action." *Rural Sociology* 66, no. 3: 403–24.

Thomas, W. I., and F. Znaniecki. 1918. *The Polish Peasant in Europe and America.* New York: Alfred A. Knopf.

Thurman, Q. C., and E. F. McGarrell, eds. 1997. *Community Policing in a Rural Setting.* Cincinnati: Anderson Publishing Company.

Tittle, C. R. 2000. "Theoretical Development in Criminology." Pp. 51–101 in G. LaFree, J. F. Short, R. J. Bursik Sr., and R. B. Taylor, eds., *Criminal Justice 2000. Volume 1: The Nature of Crime.* Washington, DC: U.S. Department of Justice, National Institute of Justice.

Tönnies, F. 1957. *Community and Society.* Trans. C. P. Loomis. East Lansing: Michigan State University Press.

United Nations. 1994. *National Perspectives on Population and Development: Synthesis of 168 National Reports Prepared for the International Conference on Population and Development.* New York: United Nations Population Fund.

Wagner, F., D. B. Diaz, A. L. López, M. E. Collado, and E. Aldaz. 2002. "Social Cohesion, Cultural Identity, and Drug Use in Mexican Rural Communities." *Substance Use and Misuse* 37: 715–48.

Warren, R. 1978. *The Community in America.* 3rd edition. Chicago: Rand McNally.

Websdale, N. 1995. "Rural Woman Abuse: The Voices of Kentucky Women." *Violence Against Women* 1: 309–38.

———. 1997. *Rural Women Battering and the Justice System.* Thousand Oaks, CA: Sage Publications.

Weisheit, R. A. 1992. *Domestic Marijuana: A Neglected Industry.* Westport, CT: Greenwood.

Weisheit, R. A., and J. F. Donnermeyer. 2000. "Change and Continuity in Crime in Rural America." Pp. 309–58 in G. LaFree, J. F. Short, R. J. Bursik Sr., and R. B. Taylor, eds., *Criminal Justice 2000. Volume 1: The Nature of Crime.* Washington, DC: U.S. Department of Justice, National Institute of Justice.

Weisheit, R. A., D. N. Falcone, and L. E. Wells. 2005. Crime and Policing in Rural and Small-town America. 3rd ed. Prospect Heights, IL: Waveland Press.

Wells, E., and R. A. Weisheit. 2004. "Patterns of Rural and Urban Crime: A County Level Comparison." *Criminal Justice Review* 29: 1–22.

Wilkinson, K. P. 1984a. "A Research Note on Homicide and Rurality." *Social Forces* 63: 445–52.

———. 1984b. "Rurality and Patterns of Social Disruption." *Rural Sociology* 49: 23–36.

Wirth, L. 1938. "Urbanism as a Way of Life." *American Journal of Sociology* 40: 1–24.

Wood, D. S., and C. T. Griffiths. 1996. "Patterns of Aboriginal Crime." Pp. 222–33 in R. A. Silverman, J. J. Teevan, and V. F. Sacco, eds., *Crime in Canadian Society*. Toronto: Harcourt Brace & Company, Canada.

10

Toward a Critical Penology of the Mentally Ill Offender: On Law, Ideology, and the Logic of "Competency"

Bruce A. Arrigo

THE STATUS OF PERSONS with psychiatric disorders is an area of ongoing debate and deep-seated concern for various law and social science scholars. Questions persist about such contentious and complicated matters as the requisite qualifications for rights-claiming by persons with mental illness (Failer 2002); the court system's (inadequate) understanding of adolescence and the developmental needs of children (Grisso and Schwartz 2003); the role of "sanism" as a pretext underpinning much of mental disability law, policy, and practice (Perlin 2000); the ethics of advanced directives that contractually bind psychiatric citizens to self-imposed involuntary confinement mandates (Saks 2002); and the limits of psycholegal decision-making based on narrow and restrictive notions of health, illness, autonomy, and healing (Williams and Arrigo 2002). These and many other issues pervade the civil and criminal divide that constitutes mental health law.

One matter of considerable concern focuses on the dynamics of punishment and how legal and psychiatric authorities work in concert to affect these ends, mostly failing to realize that their interventions can (and do) produce marginalizing outcomes. Along these lines, critics draw attention to the disturbing "interpersonal and organizational contexts in which persons with mental disorders generally are cared for and treated . . . often resulting in routine practices and social policies that punish psychiatric citizens for thinking, acting, and being different" (Shon and Arrigo 2006, 60). Although contemporary investigators have examined this level of harm from an array of perspectives (Isaac and Armat 2000; LaFond and Durham 1992; Newnes, Holmes and Dunn 2001; Torrey 1997), it is the postmodern approach that offers the most promise for purposes of the present inquiry (Arrigo 2002).

Postmodern thought addresses the linguistic and symbolic forces that positionally, relationally, and provisionally encode reality and invite action (e.g., Arrigo, Milovanovic and Schehr 2005; Best and Kellner 1997). In this schema, both human subjects and the organizational forces of which humans are a part (e.g., the legal and psychiatric systems) co-shape the world they inhabit and are defined by its logic (Henry and Milovanovic 1996; 1999). More specifically, postmodern criminology identifies the value-laden, non-neutral, and ideological dimensions of discourse, the unique and unexamined sense of identity embodied in all communication, and the circumscribed knowledge that results given the overlapping effects of what is said (i.e., discourse) and the person/group who speaks (i.e., identity) (Milovanovic 1997; 2003). Thus, in the process of naming phenomena (e.g., what is a crime? who is a criminal?), punishment is an artifact of implicit assumptions, covert messages, and hidden values that privilege a certain version of truth and reality while dismissing, ignoring, or quashing all other accounts (e.g., Bosworth 1999; Howe 1994).

Efforts to apply the heterodox principles of postmodernism to the phenomenon of mental illness are discernible, especially as a critical basis by which to understand the manifestation and maintenance of punishment. For example, in my own work, I have described how definitions of mental illness and interpretations of civil commitment are reduced to a logic that esteems science and fact as stand-ins for citizen justice and structural reform (Arrigo 1993); how determinations of mental illness and criminal insanity are based on an appeal to those very tribunals and decision brokers that pathologize difference (Arrigo 1996); and how the tight, rigid control of positivism seeks only to quantify, reduce, and correct disease, as legitimized by the law, thereby negating more organic and humanistic prospects for self-organization, adaptation, and orderly disorder (Williams and Arrigo 2002).

Most recently, I have examined the unconscious forces at work that encode reality in various civil and criminal mental health law contexts, resulting in linguistic and symbolic punishment for persons with psychiatric illness (Arrigo 2002). The insights of constitutive thought (Giddens 1984), psychoanalytic semiotics (Lacan 1977), chaos theory (Porter and Gleick 1990; Prigogine and Stengers 1984), and deconstructive practice (Derrida 1978) have informed my analysis. To a significant degree, the framework appropriated here disturbingly suggests that

> definitions of mental illness, descriptions of psychiatric services, and organizational practices impacting both are mobilized and activated in the psychic appa-

ratus, assume expressive form and narrative coherence by way of a bounded discourse that privileges shared meaning over intrinsic being, and subsequently undergo a process of legitimacy enacted through various institutional policies, procedures, and laws. As a result, dominant interpretations of reality (e.g., identity and difference) are reinforced, while multiple, discordant, and fuller expressions of the same are dismissed. (Shon and Arrigo 2006, 60)

One underexamined facet to this postmodern theory of punishment for persons with psychiatric disorders is found in the concept of "competency." The competency construct assumes a prominent role in an array of mental health law determinations (Perlin 2001). Two particularly troublesome areas include criminal competency to stand trial (Bardwell and Arrigo 2002; Bonnie 1992; Zapf, Hubbard, Cooper, Wheeles and Ronan 2004) and competency to be executed (Brodsky, Zapf and Boccacini 2001; Hensl 2004; Miller and Radalet 1993). The former is considered by many to be "the most significant mental health inquiry pursued in the system of criminal law" (Winick 1985, 921): the point at which the psychiatric citizen first invokes an array of treatment rights (Bardwell and Arrigo 2002). The latter is acknowledged as the "last" competency (Brodsky et al. 2001, 1): the point at which a mentally disordered offender exercises his or her final treatment rights (Arrigo and Tasca 1999). In both instances, the legal apparatus cannot assert its dominion over the psychiatrically ill citizen (i.e., to stand trial, to be executed), until such time as the person's competence is restored. Although some critical and postmodern efforts to address the limits of this doctrine as applied to trial fitness (Arrigo 2003) and death row executions (Arrigo and Williams 1999) have been undertaken, the overall ideological significance of the competency construct in relation to the mentally ill offender has not been investigated.

Accordingly, in this chapter, the psycholegal doctrine of "competency" is subjected to careful textual and postmodern exegeses. In particular, how this construct linguistically (and socially) operates to punish psychiatrically ill offenders is systematically examined. The position taken here is that, consistent with much of mental disability law policy, and practice, the values and assumptions of psychiatric justice are anchored in a specialized discourse whose linguistic parameters are narrowly defined. The coordinates of this grammar self-referentially signify that which is acceptable, normative, and healthy. As such, this specialized discourse privileges certain ways of thinking, acting, and knowing in which alternative renderings of reality are discounted and replacement versions of truth are delegitimized. Consequently, difference in identity, in reasoning, and in being, mobilized unconsciously and activated in speech, is pathologized (Arrigo 2002). The pathology of difference is an ideologically driven and covertly communicated stand-in for the sign of punishment, especially in relation to persons with psychiatric disorders (Arrigo 1995).

To address these matters, the law and social science literature on competency to stand trial and competency to be executed is summarily described. Of particular concern is the U.S. Supreme Court position on both of these matters. In addition, the essential theoretical components of my postmodern and critical theory of punishment for persons with mental illness are delineated. In this presentation, emphasis is placed on the unconscious forces operating to encode reality in a circumscribed fashion. Finally, the application of the conceptual model to the phenomenon of competency is outlined. At issue here is how the logic and language of competency punishes the mentally ill offender first through discourse, subsequently legitimized through social effect.

Competency to Stand Trial and to Be Executed: A Review of the Law and Social Science Literature

Competency to Stand Trial

The current standard regarding trial fitness is derived from the case of *United States vs. Dusky* (1960). Although the decision itself represents a rather brief articulation of the Court's position on the matter, the logic of *Dusky* is used in federal court, and many state jurisdictions follow the opinion in substance or adopt variations of it (Bardwell and Arrigo 2002). As such, the succinct rationale outlined in *Dusky* represents the customary basis by which lower court judges in the United States assess a criminal defendant's competence to stand trial. The test established in *Dusky* stipulated:

> It is not enough for the district judge to find that the defendant [is] oriented to time and place and [has] some recollection of events. . . . [T]he test must be whether [one] has sufficient present ability to consult with [one's] lawyer with a reasonable degree of rational understanding and whether [one] has a rational as well as a factual understanding of the charges against [oneself]. (*United States vs. Dusky* 1960, 402)

Given the Court's limited exposition concerning trial fitness and its meaning, legal analysts and social science scholars have examined both the criminal law logic of *Dusky* (Melton, Petrila, Poythress and Slobogin 1997), as well as its underlying jurisprudential intent (Bardwell and Arrigo 2002, 36–40). Overall, investigators note that while the *Dusky* standard establishes some flexibility for ascertaining the defendant's psychological state with respect to participating in and understanding the criminal trial, "the 'openness' of the competency [construct] is a source of considerable confusion among mental health and legal professionals" (Golding, Roesch and Schreiber 1984, 323). This is especially the case given that the opinion utilizes "legal constructions such as 'sufficient present ability,' 'reasonable degree of understanding,' and 'rational and factual understanding' . . . [expressions that] represent difficult interpretive challenges for lower court judges and forensic experts" (Arrigo 2003, 59).

Endeavoring to address some of the shortcomings found in *Dusky*, the United States Supreme Court revisited the matter of criminal competency to stand trial in two subsequent opinions. The first of these was *Faretta vs. California* (1975). The *Faretta* case considered whether a competent defendant possessed a federal constitutional right to waive the assistance of counsel such that the accused could then elect to *pro se* at trial. In pertinent part, the *Faretta* Court noted that:

> a defendant in a state criminal trial has a right to proceed without counsel when [one] voluntarily and intelligently elects to do so, and that the state may not force a lawyer upon [an individual] when [the defendant] insists that he [or she] wants to conduct [his or her] own defense. (1975, 806)

Although competent defendants can (and should) assess the various defense strategies at their disposal (including self-representation), the decision in *Faretta* left unresolved the issue of whether a mentally ill, though competent to stand trial, defendant expressly benefited from a similar guarantee. Indeed, following *Faretta*, "the absence of differentiation among possible litigants meant that . . . persons found competent to stand trial were held to the same standard as those whose trial fitness was not at issue" (Arrigo 2003, 60; see also Corinis 2000). However, what makes this logic so troubling is the Court's implied reasoning that as long as a defendant "voluntarily and intelligently" relinquishes counsel, the waiver would be deemed constitutionally permissible. Here, too, the Court's choice of language obfuscated more than clarified, especially since the defendant in question was, *ipso facto*, defined as psychiatrically ill (Bonnie 1992; Decker 1996).

In an effort to remedy the confusion surrounding the decision in *Faretta* and its relationship to mentally disordered defendants, the United States Supreme Court once again reviewed the competency to stand trial issue in the case of *Godinez v. Moran* (1993). In particular, the Court determined whether, following a trial fitness finding, the competency standard for pleading guilty or relinquishing counsel exceeded or was otherwise different than the competency standard used to determine trial fitness itself. The Court reasoned that:

> there is no reason to believe that the decision to waive counsel requires an appreciably higher level of mental functioning than the decision to waive other constitutional rights. . . . It [is] clear that the defendant's legal knowledge is not relevant to the determination [of] whether [he or she] is competent to waive the right to counsel. (*Godinez v. Moran* 1993, 397)

In effect, then, the *Godinez* Court held that the threshold requirements for the two competency standards (i.e., to stand trial and to waive counsel) were identical. However, of particular importance was the language invoked by the Court to substantiate its position and to situate the overall decision within the competency legal doctrine built around prior rulings on the matter of trial fitness. In short, following such a finding, "the competency standard for a mentally ill defendant who relinquishes intelligently and voluntarily his or her right to counsel means that the waiver must be based on the [same] 'rational understanding' test developed in *Dusky*" (Arrigo 2003, 61). Thus, the logic of competency to stand trial is based on the discourse of rationality and its specific meanings (i.e., voluntarily and intelligently) as defined within the realm of psychiatric justice.

Competency to Be Executed

The current United States Supreme Court position regarding the execution of competent, though mentally ill, persons was first articulated in the case of *Ford vs. Wainwright* (1986). The pivotal question reviewed in *Ford* was "whether intrusive treatment administered essentially for reasons of punishment (to enable the state to carry out the death penalty) would offend contemporary standards of decency and therefore constitute cruel and unusual punishment in violation of the Eighth Amendment" (408; see also Winick 1997, 299). Of particular concern was the administration of drug therapy as a form of medical treatment and the likely competency restoration that would follow, resulting in inmate Ford's death row execution (Hensl 2004). "Thus, the Court considered whether said treatment amounted to 'medical punishment'" (Arrigo and Williams 1999, 373). In pertinent part, the Court concluded the following:

> the various reasons put forth in support of the common-law restriction [regarding the execution of the mentally ill] have no less logical, moral, and practical force than they did when first voiced. For today, no less than before, we may seriously question the retributive value of executing a person who has no comprehension of why he has been singled out and stripped of his fundamental right to life. (*Ford vs. Wainwright* 1986, 421)

As a practical matter, the *Ford* decision acknowledged that the only conditions under which a mentally ill inmate could be subjected to capital punishment was if the person "was aware of the punishment [he or she] was about to suffer and why [he or she] was about to suffer it" (*Ford vs. Wainwright* 1986, 422). Interestingly, however, critics of this competency standard note that it is flawed on several grounds. First, it is too all-inclusive and ambiguous, resulting in the execution of psycho-diagnostically incompetent death row inmates (Jenkins 1995). Second, the standard fails to recognize the inherent unpredictability associated with the administration of antipsychotic medications, leaving unresolved a host of concerns about "the duration, maintenance, and relapse of competency . . . when determining whether a person should be executed" (Hensl 2004, 301). Third, questions persist about whether chemically induced and maintained competency restoration hurdles the Eighth Amendment prohibition on the execution of psychiatrically disordered and incompetent death row inmates (Brodsky et al. 2001).

Notwithstanding these weighty and contentious matters, the United States Supreme Court further addressed the issue of competency to be executed in the case of *Washington vs. Harper* (1990). The decision in *Harper* examined the constitutional basis of forced or involuntary drug treatment (i.e., therapy) in relation to competency restoration for mentally ill death row inmates (Arrigo and Tasca 1999). The Court balanced inmate Harper's privacy interests in remaining free from unwanted and invasive medication against the state's interest in maintaining prison security, as well as correctional staff (and other inmate) safety (Arrigo and Williams 1999). With these competing interests in mind, the Court concluded that a state "may treat a prison inmate who has a serious mental illness with antipsychotic drugs against his [or her] will if the inmate is dangerous to self or others and the treatment is in the inmate's [best] medical interest" (*Washington vs. Harper* 1990, 227). Moreover, the Court noted that said treatment "must be medically appropriate and the least intrusive means available" to assist the mentally ill and incompetent inmate awaiting execution (Hensl 2004, 307).

Although the United States Supreme Court has yet to rule on whether there is a federal constitutional right to refuse treatment that restores competency resulting in execution for persons on death row, two appellate decisions are worth noting. In *State vs. Perry* (1992), the Louisiana Supreme Court concluded that the administration of forced medication for the sole purpose of competency restoration and execution violated the Eighth Amendment ban on cruel and unusual punishment when the drug treatment merely served as a "tool for punishment" (751). In this instance, the restoration of competency was synonymous with medicate-to-execute, despite concerns for prison safety or the inmate's best medical interests.

In *Singleton vs. Norris* (2003), the Eighth Circuit considered whether a state could execute a condemned convict who was involuntarily given antipsychotic medication and rendered competent, consistent with the decision in *Harper*. In brief, "the court upheld the constitutionality of the forcible administration of medication, despite . . . the inmate [having been involuntarily] restored to competence under the Eighth Amendment" (Hensl 2004, 317). In this instance, the Eighth Circuit found that the psychotropic medication was in the inmate's best medical interest (and therefore appropriate), especially since it produced minimal side effects. Moreover, because Singleton became psychotic and potentially incompetent without the medication, the court reasoned that the forcible administration of psychotropic drug therapy was the least invasive means available that provided efficacious medical treatment.

Given the relevant law on competency to be executed, the cases of *Ford*, *Harper*, *Perry*, and *Singleton* are significant for what they suggest about psychiatric disorder and one's psychological fitness to be put to death. Ostensibly, this notion of fitness is consistent with the underlying rationale governing criminal competency to stand trial determinations. Simply stated, the logic of competency in both instances implicates a unique (and unspoken) understanding of mental health vs. mental illness anchored in implicit psycholegal values about the same. As such, the logic of competency for purposes of execution is built on a discourse of reason, intelligence, and volition consistent with the meanings assigned to these constructs as developed within the domain of psychiatric justice.

Outline of a Critical and Postmodern Theory of Punishment for Persons with Mental Illness

Figure 10.1 visually depicts the most salient features of a critical theory of punishment for persons identified as psychiatrically ill. At the outset, it is noted that the ensuing theory does not dismiss or ignore the structural, institutional, and interpersonal dynamics that foster or sustain the manifestation of punishment and/or various punitive practices for persons labeled mentally ill. Instead, the position outlined here draws specific attention to the intrapsychic, linguistically mediated, and discursively constructed dynamics that underpin these forces. Consequently, the proposed theory elucidates how "human subjects progressively lose sight of their productive contribution [to harm others], and increasingly in that which they produce to the point of some becoming excessive investors and others victims of denial, reduction,

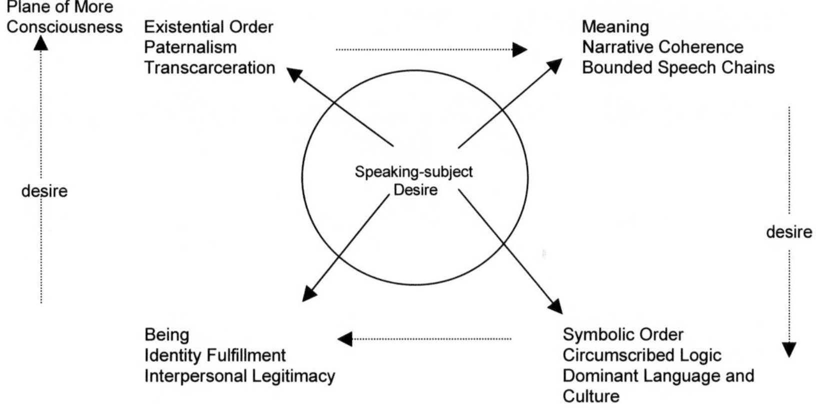

FIGURE 10.1.
A Critical Theory of Punishment for the Mentally Ill[1]

1. Adapted from Arrigo 2002, 185.

repression" (Henry and Milovanovic 1996, 170; Milovanovic and Henry 1991).

Located at the upper left and lower right hand portions of figure 10.1 are the planes of more and less consciousness. Consciousness refers to the level and type of awareness one experiences about a phenomenon, person, or situation, as well as some combination of these (Freud 1914). Jointly, these domains constitute the pivotal divide by and through which one's desire (Lacan 1977) is spoken or unspoken, present or concealed, mobilized or repressed. The significance of desire stems from its capacity to represent a circumscribed knowledge informed by what one says (the role of discourse) and who one is (the role of identity). Thus, we understand that desire "speaks the subject" or is a coded word for the "speaking-subject."

Depending on the social capital of the speaking-subject (e.g., as disabled citizen, as attending psychiatrist, as courtroom advocate) the frequency, duration, and intensity of the person's desire is embodied in and consistent with clinicolegal speech. Clinicolegal speech is the accepted and normative argot of mental illness steeped in and governed by a grammar that privileges disciplinary systems (e.g., psychiatry and law, criminal justice) (Foucault 1965; 1977) and their interdependent and overlapping operation (Arrigo 1993). However, regardless of one's social standing, desire anchors how the other elements of figure 10.1 interactively function. Accordingly, the speaking-subject is the locus of all thought, discourse, agency, and action.

There are two intersecting axes that pass through the speaking-subject. These axes include the plane of meaning and being, and the plane of the existential and the symbolic. The plane of meaning and being reflects the struggle the psychiatric citizen encounters when seeking identity fulfillment and interpersonal legitimacy through an established, though limiting, system of communication (e.g., the discourse on competency to stand trial or to be executed). The plane of the existential and the symbolic specifies the dilemma disciplinary systems and, by extension, their agents (lawyers, correctional administrators, psychologists) confront when circulating and reproducing only certain meanings and particularized values about mental illness, consistent with their own internal, self-referential, and pre-thematic logic. This is the realm in which dominant culture and language is valorized (the Symbolic Order) (Lacan 1977), and assumes expressive form through tangible social effects (the Existential Order). Both of these axes interactively extend from the sphere of the unconscious to the sphere of the conscious.

The plane of meaning and being, as well as and the plane of the existential and the symbolic, pass through the speaking-subject. This occurs because both axes are mediated by this person's desire. In addition, these two axes intersect and cross over at the point of the speaking-subject. This dynamic draws attention to the psychic and ideological forces that always and already encode reality for the individual defined as mentally ill. These forces include, but are not limited to, the influence of law and science, as well as political, economic, religious, and educational factors that co-shape reality.

There are two horizontal arrows identified in the figure. The arrows represent movement. The arrow crossing from the upper left to the upper right conveys conscious activity. This is the behavior of disciplinary systems (Foucault 1977) or steering mechanisms (Habermas 1975) such as law, penology, and psychiatry embodying values (e.g., paternalism, identity politics) and locating them in narratively coherent speech chains (e.g., the discourse of competency). The arrow crossing from the lower right to the lower left signifies unconscious activity. What the conscious movement affirms are certain phenomenal forms (e.g., the therapeutic as just, the normalization of identities), situated in a conventional, taken-for-granted system of communication (the Symbolic Order) (Lacan 1977). As both source and product of institutional decision-making, these phenomenal forms repress, reduce, or otherwise silence the humanity of psychiatric citizens. Indeed, persons with mental illness are pathologized and homogenized, rendering as absent (i.e., denied) the difference that they would otherwise embody in speech and action. This, then, is the manifestation of punishment assuming a discursive linguistic form. The subsequent section of this chapter demonstrates how the logic of competency, especially with respect to determinations of trial fitness and death row executions, confirms and amplifies this process.

However, notwithstanding their felt victimization, psychiatric citizens legitimize the language of disciplinary systems (the prevailing discourse about mental illness) through their engagement with transcarceration. Transcarceration is the ideological mechanism in which the pathology of difference is reified and sanctioned (Arrigo 2002). It is that activity in which persons labeled psychiatrically disabled routinely are funneled to and from confinement venues and treatment settings (e.g., the hospital, the jail, the rehabilitation unit); a practice understood to be natural, inevitable, and healthy (Arrigo 1997; 2001). The identity of psychiatric citizens is defined through the habitual process of transcarceration. As such, their sustained and mostly uncritical involvement with this ritual gives rise to the spoken values of and traditional beliefs about paternalism, identity politics, and the like (i.e., protect society from seemingly dangerous, disordered, and diseased individuals). In this context, then, persons with mental illness contribute, knowingly or not, to the very marginalization and alienation they seek to renounce. Thus, the meaning of psychiatric illness is transformed into the sign of punishment where the cycle of harm repeats itself—from unconscious desire to articulated thought/action, from institutional decision-making to unreflective public endorsement. This process reoccurs over and over again much like a feedback loop.

The Logic of Competency, Postmodern Penology, and the Mentally Ill Offender

Figure 10.2 visually depicts how the notion of competency functions as a stand-in for punishment in relation to mentally ill offenders (i.e., persons whose trial fitness is psychologically assessed, persons whose readiness for execution is psychologically evaluated). Situated in the center of the figure is the speaking-subject. For purposes of this inquiry, the desiring subject is the psychiatric citizen. The desire of such citizens is mobilized and activated through their respective engagements with the psychiatric courtroom. These are interactions with legal and psychological decision brokers (e.g., mental health law advocates, testifying forensic experts) who provide the psychiatric citizen with a circumscribed context out of which to speak (the role of discourse) and to be (role of identity).

Two intersecting axes pass through the speaking-subject. One of these is the plane of meaning and being. This axis identifies the predicament the mentally ill offender confronts when endeavoring to express an intimate and

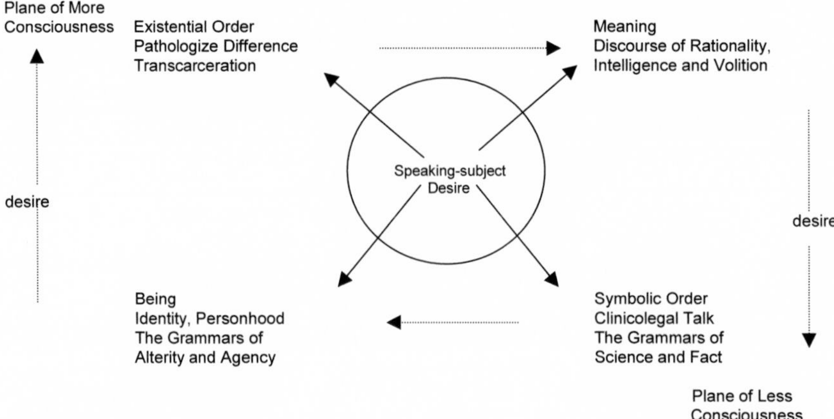

FIGURE 10.2.
The Logic and Language of Competency as Punishment for the Mentally Ill Offender

genuine sense of self to others within the psychiatric courtroom, notwithstanding the linguistic (and social) limits imposed by the conventional system of speaking. The customary system of communication in full operation during competency proceedings is clinicolegal speech. This grammar structures all such interactions.

At the unconscious level (the realm of being), the psychiatric citizen whose competency to stand trial or to be executed is called into question is confronted with a Hobson's choice. On the one hand, the mentally ill offender can embrace a non-normalizing discourse that affirms one's personhood and embodies one's identity (the grammars of alterity and agency). However, at the conscious level (the realm of meaning), these intimate and authentic articulations of self are interpreted only from within the logic and language of competency. This is a discourse built around conventional clinicolegal interpretations for "rationality," "intelligence," and "volition," as specified in the prevailing United States Supreme Court case law on such matters. If the psychiatric citizen communicates his or her being from within the grammar of alterity and agency, the person is subjected to protracted civil confinement until such time as one's competency to stand trial is restored or, alternatively, is subjected to forced medication (psychotropic drug therapy) over one's objection to it, resulting in execution. Both outcomes, situated in the language and logic of competency, pathologize difference.

On the other hand, returning to the level of being, the psychiatrically ill offender can appropriate (and thus reify) the standard argot of mental health/illness, endeavoring to comport him- or herself in speech, thought, and behavior as a "competent" citizen. At the unconscious level, what is compromised (indeed quashed) in this process is the person's unique sense of identity and intimate sense of personhood. However, at the conscious level (the realm of meaning), the discourse of rationality, intelligence, and volition prevails, consistent with the logic of competency as expressed through the United States Supreme Court case law on trial fitness and readiness for capital punishment. If the psychiatric citizen conveys her or his being from within the acceptable, normative parameters of clinicolegal argot, the trial proceeds as scheduled or the execution occurs as planned. Both outcomes, mediated by the language and logic of competency, pathologize difference. Indeed, the speaking-subject's identity is communicated in a way that supports the sense-making parameters of the governing discourse on competency and nothing more. Thus, in order to be heard, the psychiatric citizen produces a coherent narrative bounded by a specialized system of normalized communication that privileges shared meaning over intrinsic being (Arrigo 2002).

The second axis is the plane of the existential and the symbolic. It specifies the dilemma institutions (e.g., the system of criminal justice, the mental health apparatus) and their agents (e.g., lawyers, psychiatrists, judges) confront when circulating or reproducing only system-endorsing speech, along with their corresponding values and circumscribed logic. The language of competency in trial fitness determinations and death row executions fully demonstrates this predicament.

At the unconscious level, clinicolegal talk structures how participants in the psychiatric courtroom speak of and make decisions about competency issues. For those individuals who deal with mental health law controversies or concerns, this grammar is psychically encoded within the overlapping and interdependent domains of science and fact. Science privileges the quantification of knowing and, by extension, the preciseness of truth; fact privileges the certainty of experiencing and, by extension, the absoluteness of reality. Both symbolize a circumscribed logic regarding being and becoming, consistent with prevailing language and culture. In the realm of mental health law, this language and culture is defined as psychiatric justice (Arrigo 1993; 1996). Clinicolegal talk is mobilized and activated in the unconscious when questions concerning the application of psychiatric justice materialize (e.g., competency to stand trial determinations, competency to be executed findings).

At the conscious level, the existential effect of clinicolegal talk is the pathology of difference (Arrigo 2002). Difference here refers to what is interpreted as a non-normative articulation of identity, including speech that is inconsistent with the conventional meanings assigned to the competency construct. In particular, this includes interpretations of rationality, intelligence, and volition in relation to a mentally ill offender, as expressed through the relevant United States Supreme Court case law. For example, the absence of a criminal competency finding or the absence of a readiness for execution determination produces certain outcomes (coerced civil commitment and drug treatment respectively). These effects implicate the specialized logic of clinicolegal talk and how the unspoken parameters (and values) of science and fact narrowly and tightly encode reality in the psychiatric courtroom.

The existential and symbolic axis and the meaning and being axis pass through the center of the diagram (i.e., the speaking-subject). What this indicates is that the psychiatrically ill offender whose competency is at issue mediates the operation of these two planes. Moreover, both axes intersect and cross over at the point of the desiring subject, given the identified competency issue under review, the specific defendant/offender circumstances in dispute (including political, economic, cultural forces underpinning the matter), the unique narrative constructed by the attorneys, the distinct words appropriated and spoken by the various courtroom participants, and the particular message(s) received by the ultimate arbiter in the case. This dynamic amplifies the ideological forces at work in the drama that is a mental health proceeding such that the psychiatric citizen is constituted, hailed, named, or interpellated (Althusser 1971). More completely, given how the mentally ill offender mediates her or his own reality, the operation of both axes in relation to the psychiatric citizen delineates how the identity and humanity of the person in question is co-shaped.

The foregoing comments explain the various components and mechanics of figure 10.2 in relation to the competency construct and the mentally ill offender. Thus, these observations represent the necessary backdrop for developing a critical penology regarding the psychiatric citizen where questions of trial fitness and readiness for execution are evaluated. Of particular concern here is how the language and logic of competency linguistically functions as a stand-in for punishment in the case of persons labeled mentally ill.

Returning to the figure, the arrow crossing from the upper left (the existential plane) to the upper right (the plane of meaning) conveys conscious activity. Conscious activity refers to the discursive and rhetorical devices employed in the construction of a legal text (e.g., reliance on precedent, syllogistic reasoning, deductive logic, interest balancing), designed to establish a presumably impartial, value-neutral, and objective decision regarding the (competency) legal matter in contention. Because the issue investigated in this chapter deals expressly with mental health law, the disciplinary systems of law and psychiatry structure the dialogue. As such, the story that unfolds is built around the values of clinicolegal talk situated within a narratively coherent, though circumscribed, speech chain (e.g., the discourse of rationality, intelligence, volition). The texts on criminal competency to stand trial and competency to be executed explicitly convey this thematic and bounded logic as articulated within the United States Supreme Court case law on these respective matters.

The arrow crossing from the lower right (the realm of the symbolic) to the lower left (the realm of being) communicates unconscious activity. What the conscious movement affirms are certain phenomenal forms situated in an unexamined and mostly pre-thematic language system (i.e., clinicolegal talk). In the context of criminal competency to stand trial or competency to be executed determinations, these phenomenal forms include the control of disorder and the treatment of disease. As such, they "speak" the identity and agency of the person defined as mentally ill. Indeed, the jargon of controlling disorder and treating disease operates to disassemble and reassemble the reality of the mentally ill offender, consistent with the pathology of difference (the realm of the existential), as established deep within the psychic organization of science and fact, the circumscribed dimensions (and values) of clinicolegal talk (the realm of the symbolic).

However, lost in this process of reality construction, as communicated through the texts of criminal competency to stand trial and to be executed, is the possibility for alternative renderings of the speaking-subject (the criminal defendant, the death row prisoner). As the United States Supreme Court case law on these matters demonstrates, rationality, intelligence, and volition are the meanings by which one's competency is assessed within psychiatric justice where disorder (understood as potential violence or danger) and disease (understood as ongoing mental infirmity or defect) necessitate state mandated and system-sustaining intervention (a ruling by a mental health law tribunal). No other interpretations are verbally conveyed. This, then, *is* the manifestation of punishment assuming a discursive linguistic form.

Indeed, as both source and product of competency decision-making in the instances of trial fitness and death row executions, the notions of disorder and disease reconstitute the humanity of the individual defined as mentally ill. The notion of disorder functions to repress the person's humanity and the notion of disease functions to reduce it. As constitutive criminology explains, a harm (or crime) of repression occurs "when people experience a limit, or restriction, preventing them from achieving a desired position of standing" (Lanier and Henry 1998, 283). The person is prevented from being other or more than the ascription affixed to the individual by others. A harm (or crime) of reduction occurs "when offended parties experience a loss of some quality relative to their present standing" (283). The subject is denied in his or her attempts to be who the person is because of the behaviors and decisions of others. Jointly, harms of repression and reduction signify "the expression of some agency's energy to make a difference on others and it is the exclusion of those others who in the instant are rendered powerless to maintain their humanity. . . . [These] crimes, then, are the power to deny others their ability to make a difference" (Henry and Milovanovic 1996, 116). The consequence of these harms is profound. In short, persons are punished not simply for who they are (i.e., psychiatrically ill) or for how they interact interpersonally or socially (i.e., appropriating unconventional speech, articulating unusual thoughts, engaging in irregular behavior) but for the desire they embody when affirming and expressing their nonconforming ways of knowing and senses of being (Arrigo 2002)

In relation to competency to stand trial or to be executed, disorder defines and represses the identity of the psychiatric citizen, as communicated through the United States Supreme Court case law on these respective mental health law matters. When the person's speech-thought-behavior is equated with such descriptors as "suspicious," "rebellious," "oppositional," "defiant" or "menacing," disorder is contained and regulated. This is especially the case as these words stand in stark contrast to the clinicolegal values of "rational," "intelligent," and "knowing"; the requisite bases on which the psychiatric citizen's decisions (e.g., to relinquish counsel, to refuse treatment) are evaluated. In the case of criminal competency to stand trial, the control of disorder is guaranteed through involuntary civil confinement. In the case of competency to be executed, the control of disorder is assured through the administration of forced psychotropic medication. In both instances, authorities in the psychiatric courtroom interpret the subject's resistance to the discourse and practice of institutional decision-making as non-normative, unacceptable, and unhealthy. Thus, the standing denied to the individual inserted within this circumscribed logic is that of a citizen (a more complete person) beyond or in addition to the systemically imposed definition of a recalcitrant, noncompliant, or (potentially) dangerous defendant/offender.

When the speech-thought-behavior of the individual labeled mentally ill is equated with such descriptors as "infirmed," "impaired," "afflicted," or "defective," disease is arrested or corrected. This is particularly the case as these expressions are quite distinct from the clinicolegal values of "rational," "intelligent," and "knowing"; the necessary conditions under which a mentally ill citizen's choice making (e.g., to waive counsel, to proceed *pro se* to trial) is assessed. Once again, in the matter of trial fitness, the treatment of disease is linked to forced hospitalization. In the matter of readiness for execution, the treatment of disease is coupled with coercive medication. In both instances, the keepers of the kept define the subject's identity in discourse and action as non-normative, unacceptable, and unhealthy. Interestingly, rather than searching around and through the desiring subject's disorganized and non-normative speech (the plane of meaning) to locate the psychiatric citizen's uniquely felt and intimately lived reality (the plane of being), the mentally ill person whose competency is in dis(re)pute is summarily assigned the status of being deficient, deviant, or otherwise lacking. Thus, the loss suffered goes to the fullness of one's humanity and the richness of one's personhood.

Jointly, the discourse on the control of disorder and the treatment of disease, as discursively embedded within the U.S. Supreme Court case law narratives regarding competency to stand trial and to be executed, reveals how the mentally ill offender is first linguistically and then socially punished. The alterity psychiatric citizens typify through expressions of dissent or incoherence are relegated as absences; the knowledge they seek to affirm—fragmented, disconnected, and imprecise—is pathologized; the non-normalizing identities they constitute in speech, thought, and action, are homogenized (forcibly, if necessary). As such, the phenomenal forms of controlling disorder and treating disease, so fundamental to the deconstruction and reconstruction of the competency construct for persons defined as mentally ill, make possible the pathology of difference.

However, as co-architect of the text on competency to stand trial or to be executed, the desiring subject linguistically co-shapes his or her reality. Having experienced harms of repression and reduction and still in search of identity fulfillment and interpersonal legitimacy, the person now labeled incompetent (i.e., disordered and/or diseased) affirms the power of clinicolegal talk (the circumscribed discourse through which the logic of competency is fashioned and routine interaction in the psychiatric courtroom unfolds) to embody the person's desire, albeit incompletely and falsely. Indeed, faced with a loss in social standing in relation to other participants in the psychiatric courtroom, the unspoken but felt reconstitution of one's identity (as "unfit," "impaired," "ill"), and the psychic longing for something more, the psychiatric citizen pursues the system-maintaining process of appellate review. If the individual insists on this course of action and if sufficiently compelling justifications are noted, the case may eventually be reviewed by a higher court or tribunal.

In doing so, however, the mentally ill offender unconsciously contributes to the discourse of psychiatric justice (including its values and its logic) to define the person's reality; that is, to "speak" the subject. In this process, mobilized deep in the unconscious and activated unreflectively in speech, the desiring subject unknowingly affirms the performative power of clinicolegal talk, the domains of science and fact, and the prevailing logic of competency. This is because the linguistic coordinates that define psychiatric justice do not permit and do not make room for any other interpretations. As such, the systems that oppress are reified; the harm that originates in the unconscious, expressed through speech, is perpetuated; the pathology of difference is reenacted. Although the court may render a decision consistent with the mentally ill offender's articulated viewpoint, the subject must still insert him- or herself and be situated within the circumscribed parameters of meaning that define the competency construct. Thus, civil commitment following a finding of incompetency to stand trial remains legitimate; the administration of forced mind-altering drugs that restores competency for purposes of execution remains justified; transcarceration for the mentally ill offender remains acceptable. In the end, the assignment of punishment for the psychiatric citizen, through the language and logic of competency, is guaranteed. Consent by the public—unconscious, unintended, and devastating—transforms official sanction into hegemonic rule.

Conclusion

What the preceding commentary demonstrates is how the language and logic of competency in relation to the mentally ill offender functions as a stand-in for punishment. This is a cycle that establishes a circumscribed reality and an alienating identity for the psychiatric citizen, especially on matters of trial fitness and readiness for execution. Harms of repression (the grammar of disorder) and reduction (the grammar of disease), expressed through the United States Supreme Court case law on competency, support and make possible the pathology of difference. The person's identity is disassembled and reassembled through the narrative, consistent with clinicolegal talk. In the process, the individual is recognized as less than or other than rational, intelligent, and volitional. These outcomes, emblematic of psychiatric justice, prevail. The disciplinary systems of law and psychiatry (and their agents) enact and sustain this grammar; mentally ill offenders unwittingly endorse it. What struggles to be heard, what awaits validation, is the alterity of the desiring subject. This intimately lived sense of being more fully expresses the citizen's identity and more completely embodies the person's humanity.

References

Althusser, L. 1971. *Lenin and Philosophy and Other Essays.* Trans. B. Brewster. London: New Left Books.

Arrigo, B. A. 1993. *Madness, Language, and Law.* Albany, NY: Harrow and Heston.

———. 1995. Pp. 69–92 in "Subjectivity in Law, Medicine, and Science: A Semiotic Perspective on Punishment." In C. Sistare, ed., *Punishment: Social Control and Coercion*. New York: P. Lang.

———. 1996. *The Contours of Psychiatric Justice: A Postmodern Critique of Mental Illness, Criminal Insanity, and the Law*. New York: Garland.

———. 1997. "Transcarceration: Notes on a Psychoanalytically-informed Theory of Social Practice in the Criminal Justice and Mental Health Systems." *Crime, Law, and Social Change: An International Journal* 27, no. 1: 31–48.

———. 2001. "Transcarceration: A Constitutive Ethnography of Mentally Ill Offenders." *The Prison Journal* 81, no. 2: 162–86.

———. 2002. *Punishing the Mentally Ill: A Critical Analysis of Law and Psychiatry*. Albany: State University of New York Press.

———. 2003. "Justice and the Deconstruction of Psychological Jurisprudence: The Case of Competency to Stand Trial." *Theoretical Criminology: An International Journal* 7, no. 1: 55–88.

Arrigo, B. A., D. Milovanovic, and R. C. Schehr. 2005. *The French Connection in Criminology: Rediscovering Crime, Law, and Social Change*. Albany: State University of New York Press.

Arrigo, B. A., and J. J. Tasca. 1999. "Right to Refuse Treatment, Competency to Be Executed, and Therapeutic Jurisprudence: Towards a Systematic Analysis." *Law and Psychology Review* 23: 1–47.

Arrigo, B. A., and C. R. Williams. 1999. "Law, Ideology, and Critical Inquiry: The Case of Treatment Refusal for Incompetent Prisoners Awaiting Execution." *New England Journal on Criminal and Civil Confinement* 25, no. 2: 367–412.

Bardwell, M. C., and B. A. Arrigo. 2002. *Criminal Competency on Trial: The Case of Colin Ferguson*. Durham, NC: Carolina Academic Press.

Best, S., and D. Kellner. 1997. *The Postmodern Turn*. New York: Guilford.

Bonnie, R. J. 1992. "The Competence of Criminal Defendants: A Theoretical Reformulation." *Behavioral Sciences and the Law* 10: 291–316.

Bosworth, M. 1999. *Engendering Resistance: Agency and Power in Women's Prisons*. Sydney: Ashgate.

Brodsky, S. L., P. A. Zapf, and M. T. Boccaccini. 2001. "The Last Competency: An Examination of Legal, Ethical, and Professional Ambiguities Regarding Evaluations of Competence for Execution." *Journal of Forensic Psychology Practice* 1, no. 2: 1–25.

Corinis, J. 2000. "A Reasoned Standard for Competency to Waive Counsel after *Godinez vs. Moran*." *Boston University Law Review* 80, no. 2: 266–301.

Decker, S. 1996. "The Sixth Amendment Right to Shoot Oneself in the Foot: An Assessment of the Guarantee to Self-representation Twenty Years after *Faretta*." *Constitutional Law Journal* 6, no. 2: 483–98.

Derrida, J. 1978. *Writing and Difference*. Trans. A. Bass. Chicago: University of Chicago Press.

Failer, J. L. 2002. *Who Qualifies for Rights?: Homelessness, Mental Illness, and Civil Commitment*. Ithaca, NY: Cornell University Press.

Faretta vs. California, 422 U.S. 806. 1975.

Foucault, M. 1965. *Madness and Civilization: A History of Insanity in the Age of Reason*. Trans. R. Howard. New York: Pantheon Books.

———. 1977. *Discipline and Punish: The Birth of a Prison*. New York: Pantheon.
Ford vs. Wainwright, 477 U.S. 399. 1986.
Freud, S. 1914. *The Psychopathology of Everyday Life*. New York: MacMillan.
Giddens, A. 1984. *The Constitution of Society: Outline of a Theory of Structuration*. Oxford: Polity Press.
Godinez vs. Moran, 509 U.S. 389. 1993.
Golding, S., R. Roesch, and P. Schreiber. 1984. "Assessment and Conceptualization of Competence to Stand Trial." *Law and Human Behavior* 8, no. 3: 321–40.
Grisso, T., and R. G. Schwartz, eds. 2003. *Youth on Trial: A Developmental Perspective on Juvenile Justice*. Chicago: University of Chicago Press.
Habermas, J. 1975. *Legitimation Crises*. Boston: Beacon Press.
Henry, S. D., and D. Milovanovic. 1996. *Constitutive Criminology: Beyond Postmodernism*. London: Sage.
———, eds. 1999. *Constitutive Criminology at Work: Applications in Crime and Justice*. Albany: State University of New York Press.
Hensl, K. B. 2004. "Restored to Health to Be Put to Death: Reconciling the Legal and Ethical Dilemmas of Medicating to Execute in *Singleton v. Norris*." *Villanova University Law Review* 49: 291–328.
Howe, A. 1994. *Punish and Critique: Towards a Feminist Analysis of Penality*. London: Routledge.
Jenkins, R. K. 1995. "Comment, Fit to Die: Drug Induced Competency for the Purpose of Execution." *Southern Illinois University Law Journal* 20: 149–87.
Isaac, R. J., and V. C. Armat. 2000. *Madness in the Streets: How Psychiatry and the Law Abandoned the Mentally Ill*. New York: Trial Advocacy Center.
Lacan, J. 1977. *Ecrits: A Selection*. Trans. A. Sheridan. New York: W. W. Norton.
LaFond, J. Q., and M. L. Durham. 1992. *Back to the Asylum: The Future of Mental Health Law and Policy in the United States*. New York: Oxford University Press.
Lanier, M. M., and S. D. Henry. 1998. *Essential Criminology*. Boulder, CO: Westview Press.
Melton, G., J. Petrila, N. Poythress, and C. Slobogin. 1997. *Psychological Evaluation for the Courts: A Handbook for the Mental Health Professionals and Lawyers*. 2nd ed. New York: Guilford Press.
Miller, K. S., and M. L. Radalet. 1993. *Executing the Mentally Ill: The Criminal Justice System and the Case of Alvin Ford*. Newbury Park: Sage.
Milovanovic, D. 1997. *Postmodern Criminology*. New York: Garland.
———. 2003. *Critical Criminology at the Edge: Postmodern Perspectives, Integration, and Applications*. Westport, CT: Praeger.
Milovanovic, D., and S. D. Henry. 1991. "Constitutive Penology." *Social Justice* 18, no. 2: 204–24.
Newnes, C., G. Holmes, and C. Dunn. 2001. *This Is Madness Too: Critical Perspectives on Mental Health Services*. Llangarron, UK: PCCS.
Perlin, M. L. 2000. *The Hidden Prejudice: Mental Disability Law on Trial*. Washington, DC: American Psychological Association.
———. 2001. *Mental Disability Law 2001 Supplement*. Durham, NC: Carolina Academic Press.
Porter, E., and J. Gleick. 1990. *Nature's Chaos*. New York: Viking.

Prigogine, I., and I. Stengers. 1984. *Order out of Chaos*. New York: Bantam Books.

Saks, E. R. 2002. *Refusing Care: Forced Treatment and the Rights of the Mentally Ill*. Chicago: University of Chicago Press.

Shon, P. C. H., and B. A. Arrigo. 2006. "Reality-based TV and Police-citizen Encounters: The Intertextual Construction and Situated Meaning of Mental-illness-as-punishment." *Punishment and Society: The International Journal of Penology* 8, no. 1: 59–85.

Singleton vs. Norris, 319 F 3d 1018 (8th Cir.). 2003.

State vs. Perry, 610 So. 2d 746. 1992.

Torrey, E. F. 1997. *Out of the Shadows: Confronting America's Mental Illness Crisis*. New York: John Wiley & Sons.

United States vs. Dusky, 362 U.S. 402. 1960.

Washington vs. Harper, 494 U.S. 210. 1990.

Williams, C. R., and B. A. Arrigo. 2002. *Law, Psychology, and Justice: Chaos Theory and the New (Dis)order*. Albany: State University of New York Press.

Winick, B. J. 1985. "Restructuring Competency to Stand Trial." *UCLA Law Review* 32: 921–85.

———. 1997. *Right to Refuse Treatment*. Washington, DC: APA Press.

Zapf, P. A., K. L. Hubbard, V. G. Cooper, M. C. Wheeles, and K. A. Ronan. 2004. "Have the Courts Abdicated Their Responsibility for Determination of Competency to Stand Trial to Clinicians?" *Journal of Forensic Psychology Practice* 4: 27–44.

11

Constitutive Rhetoric and Constitutive Criminology: The Significance of *The Virtual Corpse*

Julie Borkin, Stuart Henry, and Dragan Milovanovic

THE LEGIBILITY OF THE "CRIMINAL" SEEMS ALWAYS ALREADY DECIDED AND DISMISSIBLE. BUT, ACCORDING TO CONSTITUTIVE CRIMINOLOGY[1] an affirmative holistic approach toward such "excessive investors" is not only possible but is productive for social transformation. Through the lens of a particular body donation case, we consider the potential for just such an affirmative redirection of justice and, in particular, the constitution of the human subject. Reading the recent HBO program *The Virtual Corpse*, we track the possibility of constitutive criminology's affirmative agenda by partnering its claims with those of constitutive rhetorical theory, a body of poststructural rhetorical work drawing from much of the same theoretical grounding. This documentary juxtaposes some of the personal and institutional machinations that facilitated an unprecedented project—the production of an intricately detailed set of 3-D images of the human anatomy overseen by the University of Colorado Medical School and sponsored by the National Library of Medicine, which claim to "recreate a virtual life." The donated cadaver was carved into over 1,800 thin cross-sectioned slices and recorded through the technology of MRI (Magnetic Resonance Imaging), CT (Computed Tomography) scans, and high-resolution digital color photography (Waldby 2000). The project facilitated a new level in on-screen maneuverability and rendition quality of a man and his parts creating, as one author boasts, a "sort of flight simulator for students of anatomy and surgery" (Roach 2003). The project also produced the first versions of the Visible

Human Project software, animations, and videos now licensed for institutional use.

Though subsequent similar projects continue to develop the medical utility of such technology,[2] here the status and legibility of the donor is uniquely complicated by the temporal discourses identifying the body. John Paul Jernigan, the project's selected "donor cadaver" and convicted death row criminal, authorized the donation of his body in conjunction with his execution by lethal injection for murder in 1981 in the state of Texas. In the program, a cacophony of testimony from the project director Dr. Victor Spitzer, the prison chaplain, attorneys, judge, and family members, seems aimed at qualifying the virtuous (or not) nature of Jernigan's donation. An emotional testimony by Jernigan's wife concludes: "he wasn't nobody but I guess he's somebody now" (Kasics n.d.). As one German documentary noted, "during his condemnation, no one suspected that he would rise again to be the "Visible One" of the internet, the first completely digitized human, a prototype of human anatomy . . . a unique interaction between law, science, family fate, and the American [social system]" (Kasics 2000).

Like constitutive criminology, the HBO presentation calls into question how Jernigan might be understood as a human subject. In this context it is useful to question how Jernigan is understood as subject prior to and after execution. Put differently, might the viewer come to read Jernigan's body donation as an act of restoration or redemption—that which proffers to take care of us rather than merely himself? The question, therefore, moves beyond one of act, agency, or even temporality. How the Jernigan case gets taken up, the donation as pedagogical technology, and how the viewer citizens come to know themselves, are open spaces of possibility for affirmative intervention, the very ground of constitutive criminology, and suggest the possibility for change through this text. Here we are coproducers of meaning in whatever capacity—whether critic or viewer, producer, scholar, or critic. We argue that citizen Jernigan, via body donation, is the constitutive technology animating an imagined stability or optimism through the logic of sacrifice and recognition. Whether the viewer identifies with Jernigan, or body donation specifically, is less important than the pedagogical identification with the logics of sacrifice and recognition. At issue is how the ideals of social change become embodied in a site of consent that is recognized to have articulated particular legitimating practices for social stasis. As scholars we have to ponder how or whether it is the "bare" act itself that registers such optimism, or the collective constructions that might animate the process, both prior to and after the execution.

The main thesis of this chapter is that by melding the work of constitutive rhetorical theory and constitutive criminology, we are able to further elaborate on the conditions of possibility of the decentered subject. This combined constitutive analysis enables us to explore the coproduction of social reality and of subjectivity, and in exploring the prospects for possible directions for humanistically oriented social change. Critics (e.g. Croall 1997; Thompson 1997) have targeted constitutive criminology's affirmative agenda as overly optimistic and relativistic, particularly in its seemingly nonmaterialist understanding of the subject.[3] Our analysis intervenes by emphasizing the subject's conditions of possibility and its range of effects, rather than depicting the subject as a simple or fixed notion of legality or effects. The contributions of constitutive rhetoric in tandem with those of constitutive criminology provide a way to challenge comprehensive and static universalities, including that of the subject or its effects. As Butler (1988, 392) notes, these are always constituted by the "fully embedded organizing principles of material practices and institutional arrangements . . . those matrices of power and discourse that produce me as a viable subject" and make its effects legible. Interrogation maintains a sense of agency by considering the conditions of possibility without "tak[ing] it for granted as an a priori guarantee" (Butler 1988, 392). In short, the body is constituted as subject through the process of repetition, in collective recognition of its accommodation to the normative order.

First we review the ideas of constitutive theory before applying these to the significance of this body donation case, and then placing this case in the context of popular cultural meaning and the anthropology of the gift.

Constitutive Rhetoric and Constitutive Criminology

The work of constitutive rhetoric examines how social identity or the self is constructed, normalized, and disciplined through discursive and social practices. Besides the subject of rhetoric, whether discursive or symbolic, the analysis considers contextual factors that point toward the governing logics and range of possibilities involved, including power, truth, individual agency, and the potential for productive resistance and transformation. Some of the same theoretical developments have influenced the work of constitutive criminology, and constitutive penology (Bosworth 1999; Milovanovic and Henry 1991; 2005). All draw on the symbolic and socially constructed nature of meaning and together they offer a stereoscopic analytical partnership attuned to explore a range of practices and possibilities in matters of violence, discipline, and resistance. In this section of the chapter we briefly summarize the foundations of constitutive rhetoric and constitutive criminology and explore potential intersections and insights each may offer to the analysis.

Constitutive rhetoric provides a theoretical framework that works to understand how subjects are constituted, or created, through various texts. In this view, discourse and social practices work to produce various subject positions that interpellate the audience, normalizing a particular response. Put another way, through constitutive rhetoric a subject is embodied or created and marshaled toward particular practices and normalizations or unquestioned responses. In contrast to the more familiar sender/receiver model of communication that fixes a sender and an audience in a discursive location and privileges the sender, the static nature of the message, and the passive nature of receiver, constitutive rhetoric and constitutive criminology work from a process model that supports a circulation of knowledges and meanings. In this sense, "reality" is constructed and a text is interpreted in a coproduced form whereby the message is returned in inverted form. The gift giver, for example, returns as a recipient of the gift-giving s/he initiated.[4] The momentary completion (iteration) jointly produces meaning/interpretation and forms, which reinforce more hidden discursive forms—drawing on a range of socially held assumptions and ideologies on the one hand, and spinning out the possibility of countless unintended meanings on the other (e.g., the free play of the text).

From the perspective of constitutive rhetoric, discursive practice can create political subjects and discrete forms and assert a collective identity and affirm that identity. Our direction, drawing from Kenneth Burke's notion of identification, moves away from traditional notions of rhetoric as mere persuasion; for persuasion presumes a preexisting audience and the "existence of an agent who is free to be persuaded" (Burke 1969, 50) ignoring the unconscious influences or "discursive effects that induce human cooperation" (Charland 1987, 133), which occur prior to persuasion. Put another way, no one is completely free from socially constructed norms or ideologies that work on the identity, whether one conforms to or resists the expected practices.

In the process of constitution through discursive production an audience is called into being and through its investment of energy reproduces ideology. Althusser's (1970) work exploring Ideological State Apparatuses, ISA's, called this process a hailing, or interpellation, and posited that humans are transformed into subject positions as the "always already" subject recognizes her or himself, simultaneously producing the ideology and the subject (hence, the spoken subject). Recognition works as a ritual of reinforcement of the ideology. Althusser's own example cites a pedestrian who passes by a police officer walking in the other direction, then hears a voice behind calling or hailing, "Hey, you!" In the moment of recognition, even before a turning to verify the subject being addressed, one is subjected or interpellated, by conforming to the ideological foundation of authority constructed through making social meaning.

While Althusser's work was a useful beginning to constitutive rhetoric, the role or even the possibility of individual agency or dissent, remained unclear—a point directly addressed in Charland's developments of constitutive rhetoric. According to Charland, "the identity of a 'people' as a rhetorical construct is not even agreed upon by those who would address it" (Charland 1987, 136). The rhetoric of socialization allows a range of legible or appropriate positions that still naturalize the significance of the hail. In his own example, an audience of Quebecois was called into existence in the interests of political sovereignty. Both supporters and opponents to a particular subjectivity are constituted even as they "seek to justify their position on the basis of what they assert is a will intrinsic to their version of the peuple's [sic] very being" (1987, 136). Consider, too, gender, race, and class effects (and their intersections) in the interpretive processes of the hailed. Also, pointing toward a range of possible responses within the subject position, Foucault's work on the disciplinary function of power specifically notes how the procedures of exclusion provide the mechanisms or techniques for control that allow power to be practiced rather than possessed (Foucault 1976, 101–2). McGee's (1975) work draws on Foucault's notion of pastoral power—the ideology that demands care for the common good—and examines how individual subjects come to privilege and support a collective identity. McGee argues that the process begins out of dormant arguments that represent what the people could possibly become. Next, "specific problems . . . in specific situations" create a willingness to privilege collective concerns over individual identity for the sake of a dream, based on willingness to support a collectively held political myth or ideology. Then, according to Charland (1987), the audience's sense of understanding positions the subjects toward political, social, and economic action. Not only does the understanding shape a narrative that calls the subjects to act but also it does so while maintaining the illusion of freedom. This normalizing effect echoes the subject and ideological conditions, as discussed by both Althusser and McGee, in the unquestioned appropriateness that the act positions itself to produce. For example, the American ideology of "freedom," by itself "pregnant" with meaning, even while remaining a concept without concrete or prescriptive attachments, can be stirred toward specific domestic or international concerns, working in such a fashion that to act in any other way would be simply un-American and unthinkable. In *The Virtual Corpse*, the donor's body is stirred or made legible through the rhetoric of gift-giving, legitimizing the public spectacle of corporeal decimation—which may in turn be animated toward more quotidian public practices like blood donation, and so forth, and may contribute to the support of other political or ideological myths.

Laclau and Mouffe (2001) develop this "stirring" and argue that identities are articulated together and modified toward new ends. This assemblage combines linguistic phenomena along with institutions, rituals, and the like—in an unfixed arrangement of positions. At the perimeter of this social arrangement an "antagonism" constitutes the limits of society, producing a social "identity crisis" that challenges that which stabilized the field of dispersion. In short, otherwise relatively stable discursive formations, anchored signifiers, and identity formations with their underlying supportive rhetoric, undergo slippage, or dislocation allowing new articulations in the social formations.

Constitutive criminology also develops the subject's interpellation and ability to act. According to Henry and Milovanovic (1996; 1999; 2001) constitutive criminology posits that human agents, acting in a sociopolitical context, are the active coproducers and reproducers of their worlds. Put differently, constitutive theory, like constitutive rhetoric, works from the perspective that while discourse and social practices coproduce normative subject positions, the governing logics, including traditional penological apparatuses, still provide a range of legible responses, including oppositional or deviant practices. The coproductive nature of constitutive criminology puts an emphasis on active human agency that is invested in the condition of both human subjects and social structures. Within these practices of power exists an important space for redirecting normalized views. Constitutive criminology looks toward social justice as a governing logic necessary in redistributing social control, both inside and outside the official formal penological apparatus. The arena of discourse, this socially constituted production of subjectivity, works on or disciplines the subject, sanctioning particular performances of appropriate subjectivity, but simultaneously its production is transformed by the subject in its own making. In this sense, constitutive criminology recognizes a mutuality, a resonating coproduction, between human agency, human subject, discursive practices, and structural product (see Ferrell et al. 2001).[5]

The frameworks of both constitutive rhetoric and constitutive criminology understand not only the social production of identity, but also the nonexistence of some concrete (read conspiratorial) animating body of the state or politics that functions "behind" all of this. The socially created subject is constructed, normalized, and disciplined through discursive and social practices, yet, because of breaks, discontinuities, dislocations—in short, singularities—in repetitive iterative practices, still holds the ability to participate as an active and even transcendental creator of his or her social subjectivity and structural product. Whether a specific local act can be recognized as a subject's exercise of agency, we must also consider how the contours of legibility are experienced by those across the social formation. In the next section we draw on constitutive rhetoric/criminology to analyze the body donation of *The Virtual Corpse* as a site of discursive production.

The Case of Jernigan: A Body Bequeathed

To track how Jernigan's body donation might be read, and how it might inform our understanding of the human subject, we first note some of the conditions that contributed to the current context of American body bequeathment programs. In the Middle Ages, human dissections were forbidden, but by the seventeenth century, they were considered public sport, attracting large crowds who jeered and told obscene jokes. Grave-robbing and even murder supplied anatomical "donors" for much of the eighteenth and nineteenth centuries (Roach 2003), but by the twentieth century, human cadaver dissection was both a legally and socially sanctioned portion of requisite training for medical students (Zuger 2004), supplied largely through voluntary programs of body bequeathment. Unclaimed bodies are also made available as property of the state for accredited teaching and research programs but for the past several decades, voluntary donation has provided virtually all programs' cadavers that support the teaching and research programs of universities and hospitals. At this time, there are approximately 110 sanctioned national programs that solicit donor and family support by affirming the voluntary generosity of the donor and the respect due this "indispensable contribution," or what may be called, an economy of recognition on the one hand, and redefinition on the other.

Because body donation programs currently depend almost exclusively on voluntary participation, the medical community works hard to establish a sense of respect, clearly coding the practice as both an important personal decision and a vital part of enhancing the possibilities of the future. Support for such programs partners the interests, expectations, and values of the medical community, the individual donor, and the surviving family or legal representatives whose cooperation is not only important but often essential. In most instances for example, even if the donor has authorized body donation prior to death, the donor's wishes are only followed if the surviving family members agree with this decision. The body donation programs support and expect this normalized understanding of the body as a site of personal ownership and right, initiated via personal application that authorizes the act of donation.

The Body and the Human Subject

The "I own my body" logic fits with phenomenological explanations of the self that social agents constitute or create social reality through symbolic social signs. This perspective presumes an act, such as the decision to participate in a body donation program, proceeds from a "stable identity or locus of agency" (Butler 1990, 140). In constitutive rhetorical theory, like constitutive criminology, however, the social agent is an effect, an "identity tenuously constituted in time—and constituted through a stylized repetition of acts" (1990, 140). While the body is often taken to be a natural, biological substance, constitutive theory conceptualizes the body as a constituted social temporality. This perspective does not deny the material existence of the body but attempts to note how the material body is separate from the cultural meanings and possibilities of identity. In this sense, the work of Deleuze and Guattari and Grosz indicate the distinction of the body to the "mind" (Grosz 1994; Deleuze and Guattari 1977; Patton 2001). For Grosz, for example, it is the model of the Mobius strip that connects the outside (body) with the inside ("mind"), the idea being that they are continuous, each a part of the other. The text of Jernigan's body donation is a useful tool to explore the discursive terrain of social possibility (that is, its territorialization, deterritorialization, and reterritorialization—the libidinal economy underlying discursive practice; including the disciplinary mechanisms that are its determinant—see Foucault 1977). Standing at the precipice of dichotomies of good or evil, alive or dead, criminal or hero, how might we read Jernigan's legibility as a subject?

Before making the decision to donate his body and because of his location as an inmate on Death Row convicted of murder, Jernigan's might conventionally have been seen as having a wasted life. Through his decision to donate his body, however, he might be understood to have redeemed his life, having done some good deed toward the benefit of humanity and the capacity of scientific knowledge, and particularly so in light of his prior subject position of criminal, in spite of "correctional" intervention. In terms of penology, we could even view this enactment as some iteration of successful reentry. Regardless, however, what is read as productive or recognizable about Jernigan's donation is ciphered only in relation to the site of optimism, the hope of scientific discovery and progress made possible by the project and its future applications. This is a competing alternative collective reconstruction. In the video's testimony, the project director enthuses over the "body's quality" and the ability for the project to "recreate a virtual life." The chaplain said Jernigan admitted he felt like a failure as a person, a husband, a mechanic, and welder, but wanted to do something good by donating his body, adding that Jernigan was the only death row inmate to have requested communion.

Justice in Death

In order to get a further grasp of the underlying constitutive factors in the understanding of Jernigan's donation as opposed to noncriminal donors, we can look at Derrida's notion of the gift (1991; see also Caputo 1997, 140–51). For Derrida, a true gift is where there are no expectations of reciprocity. The gift is an end to itself. However, at the point the recipient says "thank you," an entirely new process takes place in which an obligation to reciprocate (a debt) is brought into play. As Derrida (1997, 18) tells us: "A gift is something that you cannot be thankful for. As soon as I say 'thank you' for a gift, I start canceling the gift, I start destroying the gift, by proposing an equivalence, that is, a circle which encircles the gift in a movement of reappropriation." This is a constitutive process in which the definition of the gift is coproduced by the giver and receiver in the background assumptions of gift giving. This process, too, according to Derrida, institutes an "economy"—the receiver of the gift is caught up in a background expectation of replying in kind. This entails calculation, notions of equivalency, of balanced equations. The gift-economy dyad is analogous to the justice-law dyad, where justice is never attainable. It is a duty to recognize the other, but only an unattainable goal, since, for Derrida, it is not something you expect in return, whereas law is a system of rigid rules, determinant and, ultimately, acts of discursive violence, a fictional construct activated by force (Derrida 1986; 1991). The two couplets must always be recognized in their incompatibility: economy and law, on the one hand, provide a fictional stability; the gift and justice provide an unstable future, infinite possibilities, and the horizon for transformative practices, never attainable, but providing the possibility for the "people yet to come." Since the completion of the circle (giver of the gift, reappropriation by the receiver) entails a coproduced cycle, it is also an act of repetition supportive of normativity. Constitutive theorists would see, however, that it is in the gap between the gift and economy, justice and law, where singularities arise, a space within which redefinitions and new discursive articulations may arise. Jernigan's narrative works as a parable whereby we observe, in contrast to the repetition that is entailed with donors who had not been sentenced to death (honorary rituals for the departed), Jernigan's act as the ultimate gift has few if any of these repetitive rituals. There is no expectation of reappropriation. Indeed, we see very few opportunities provided to rejoice Jernigan's gift. His is the ultimate gift in death. It would seem that collective understanding of this ultimate gift must return to the act that precipitated Jernigan's confinement, sentence, and execution; never mind his ultimate statement of reform and call for redemption—it fell on deaf ears. But, an uneasy space has been created between the gift and economy, between justice and law, a space within which alternative understandings of the gift and justice may be articulated. It is a moment of the subversion of repetition for Butler (1990, 142–49), a moment of madness for Caputo (1997, 144). Perhaps our best hope is the call to the poet for its possible articulations.

The Contemporary Cultural Meaning of Body Donation

Jernigan's donation is imbricated in the articulated relationship between his donation and the social logics of the day. Jernigan's body donation, and by proxy Jernigan himself, can appear as virtuous and sacrificial precisely not because he wanted it to be so or said it was, but rather because such a practice exceeds contemporary social understandings of the body, personal responsibility, and ultimately, the nature of the gift. As Tierney (1999) notes, contemporary notions of personal existence have placed self-ownership and self-preservation at the "very top of the moral scale" (234), but it was not always so. In premodern tradition, truly virtuous people were regularly expected to be willing to give up their lives in both military and nonmilitary circumstances.[6] Because, today, one is "expected and encouraged to embrace (the body's) corporeal existence and to be overwhelmingly concerned with the highly differentiated economy of earthly temporality" (234) often only for a "prolonged and pleasant earthly existence" for the self, it might seem that sacrificial acts might not even register as such in a contemporary economy, nor be conceived as an ultimate gift in the act of death. On the contrary, it is precisely because the contemporary recognition of body donation is deployed through the seeming "selflessness" and agency of a single self that this practice may be read as a potent moment of sacrifice. Put differently, if the "truly virtuous" (body donors) were the majority, if the disposition had already become the normalized expression of citizenship, the practice of body donation would be read merely as an obligatory gesture—that which virtuous people "do." Instead, putting aside pleasure, Jernigan may be recognized to have performed honorably because body donation remains a seeming extravagant offering. But only extravagant in so much that the gift, in our collective background assumptions, is a coproduced definition that entails a full cycle for its completion; gift entails a responsive gesture, which thereby annuls the very act. And, once again, this very enigma provides a space within which questions of giving, offering, and return can be traced to conceptions of justice itself. It is a moment of rearticulation of the possible.

In our best efforts to understand or apply theory to specific circumstances, however, we may dismiss the way our ethical commitment colors our perspective. While we, as meaning-making coparticipants in whatever capacity, want to believe the best of our own motivations and judgments, we may neglect understated aspects of the social production of violence and misuse of power. Specifically in the Jernigan case, it is possible that in the very moment we analyze or applaud Jernigan's contribution, we cover over our complicity in the violence of deprivatizing his death and decimating his corpse. We connive in the ongoing production of gift-with-expectation-of-return, we place a debt on the receiver of the gift. Literally carved and placed on display for others' purposes, how might Jernigan be also understood as emptied out as a subject and merely put to use in the service of some fantasy of wholeness or integrity? Here we track how respect, ethical understandings, and pedagogical technology work in the production and reading of this text concerning Jernigan's body donation.

Respect

Though Jernigan did consent to donate his body to "advance medical science and education," he never knew of the scope and impact of the project or its publicity, nor did his family, who neither gave consent for the donation or the disclosure of his identity and personal history articulated and circulated as a part of this historical development of technology. The Visible Human project has reached across the globe with staggering amounts of academic data, over 800 licenses, a host of products, and even two documentaries (Kasics n.d.).

While stories of Jernigan's role in the project have been investigated from a number of perspectives (see Waldby 2000; Murray 2002; Kasics n.d.; etc.), here we are concerned with Jernigan as re-presented through *The Virtual Corpse*. This account frames Jernigan's story through interviews with family members, the Texas prosecutor, and Jernigan's defense and appellate attorneys. Jernigan had been charged with two burglaries prior to the robbery and murder of an elderly rural Texan man. Interrupted by the homeowner while attempting to take a microwave oven, Jernigan murdered the homeowner to avoid being identified by this witness. Jernigan's wife said she turned him in after assurances from law enforcement officials that he would not get the death penalty, aided by the promise of a conjugal visit that was never allowed. After 12 years of appeals, Jernigan's death sentence was upheld.

Though Jernigan's brother was allowed to observe his execution, he says the family, even his mother, was not allowed to touch, hug, or say goodbye to her son, but allowed only a brief opportunity to touch his dead body in the morgue before the corpse was hurried out so they could freeze and transport him to the project headquarters in Colorado. In her interview, Jernigan's widow says she's been told of important medical interventions made possible by Jernigan's body donation, including a baby who got CPR while still in the womb and a man whose arms were cut off who received a better quality of artificial limbs.

This protocol, bypassing family permission and neglecting gestures that facilitate family closure, stands in marked contrast to most body donation appeals in which the virtue of the donor and the value of the gift—gestures of respect and acknowledgement (recognition)—are prominently featured and include extensive gestures to affirm both the donor's and the family's role and need for respectful regard. We will discuss each of these briefly.

In body donation websites, for example, prospective donors are repeatedly framed as generous and caring souls whose body donation is a "most unique and caring gift." The critical role body donation plays in sustaining medical teaching and research is emphasized, reminding donors that what they do makes it possible for anatomical coursework, one of the "first and most foundational courses" in medical training. The donor is informed of the host of medical professionals that rely on donors to properly train. Besides medical doctors, dental, nursing, and physical therapy students also participate in the program, and each anatomical course component offers "new and innovative ways" to help other patients. The gift is said to multiply far beyond the classroom and present time and circumstances; as Dean Mueller, one program coordinator, says, donors' bequeathments benefit everyone for they "give back to society and give a student a chance to learn something that can influence generations to come" (Mueller 1999). Emphasizing the urgency, scope, and purpose of the donation, Mueller says "all [donations] are needed and must occur for medical education and science to advance well past the twenty-first century."

Besides explaining the value and purpose of the contribution, body donation discourse extensively details procedures and protocols involved in body donation. Question and answer sections address concerns prospective donors may have and emphasize the commitment to the dignity and respect of the donors throughout the process. Donors are told that once the body is transferred to the program center, a rigorous protocol for proper handling of the body is carefully followed. For example, Wayne State University's mortuary science website says each cadaver is "treated with the utmost of care and respect" and "maintained in a clean restricted area permitting only medical students faculty, staff, and students of health related professions" (Body Bequest Program n.d.). Other universities have similar explanations, and one even promises that students wear white clothing.

Family members' participation is an important part of most donors' body donation process and several specific gestures are designed to include them as well. Once the teaching or research process is completed—a process of up to three years in some institutions—the university cremates the remains and either returns them to the family, if requested, or holds an annual interment ceremony at a local cemetery to honor the donors from that year's program. Practices vary from university to university, but family members are invited to attend the service and bring flowers, and some universities have medical students attend or write letters to acknowledge the value of the gift. One university program notes that cremated remains are buried in "individual urns" (Willed Body Program n.d.), and another urges family and friends to attend to "share memories and begin the healing process" (Anatomical Donations Program n.d.). In this way, the possibility for recognition continues long after the physical death of the body. These services, despite being held two to three years after the death, continue to work on constituting the value and identity of the person and their family members.

While we might expect shifts in protocol under particular circumstances, the normalized understanding of appropriate respect toward the donor, the body, and the surviving family stands in shocking contrast to the testimony by Jernigan's family. Jernigan's widow's comments speak to the absence of even the most general kinds of information or concern for the respect or recognition of how, for the family at least, Jernigan's identity might be tied into his body:

> "We've never even had a memorial for him to lay him to rest and where's the body? We need to close this. What he did was so much wrong but he's a human being and we need to put him to rest [pause] somewhere, and no one's ever done that. I keep wondering where's his body? After they sawed him up and sliced him up, where's the body at?" (Kasics n.d.)

The ultimate gift remains nameless, recedes in the background; the confrontation with the ultimate act of self-transformation by a killer questions our own complicity to the normative order of gift-giving without acknowledging another more selfless form, an understanding which could indeed lead us to ultimately question the form of justice we so dearly collectively hold. In short, repetition is subverted; but, in its subversion, a space is generated for novel imaginary and discursive practices. Of course, vigilance must exist to counter the expression and stabilization of unquestioned forms that further reify or disenfranchise.

Ethics

The need for respect works in conjunction with the need to mark the donation with value or a sense of good. Alain Badiou argues that most versions of contemporary human ethics, like human subjectivity, depend on an a priori knowledge. Much of Western ethics specifically relies on a natural or Kantian foundation that subscribes to ethics as an a priori ability to discern evil. This idea presupposes that humans think we naturally know evil when we see it—whether we suffer or judge it—and know that evil must be stopped "by all available means" (Badiou 2002, 9). While such ethics appear self-evident, in Jernigan's case, like so many others, such a standard is inconsistent and incapable of consensus. To address this disparity, Badiou calls for an "ethic of truth" where subjects are constituted through their engagement in the specificity of a truth process. Key in this process is the subject's willingness to engage the event, or void, with a commitment to linger in uncertainty—even to the point of brokenness in this sea of singularities and uncertainties. This renunciation of the certainty of self is a willingness to embrace the tension of fragmentation and multiplicity in the specificity of each circumstance.[7] Says Badiou, "The Good is Good only to the extent that it does not aspire to render the world good. Its sole being lies in the situated advent of a singular truth. So it must be that the power of a truth is also a kind of powerlessness" (2002, 85). Such powerlessness seems contrary to the agenda of identity politics and the matter of respect.

Pedagogical Technology

In addition to the matters of respect and ethics, it is important to note the possibility of the text as pedagogical technology. Through this text, we have noted the range of possible legibility, a sense of public recognition concerning Jernigan's act of body donation. The text also works as a constitutive technology animating an imagined stability or optimism through the logic of sacrifice and recognition. It is not a question of whether the viewer identifies with Jernigan or body donation specifically as "the" affirmative intervention, but more a question of how the experience of viewing and pondering this text, and particularly its emphasis on sacrifice and the gift, may work to alter the meaning making in other situations. Put differently, as this particular text is considered to mean—perhaps exemplary or perhaps irrelevant—can articulate, challenge, or rupture particular partnered texts. To work through this portion of the argument, we turn to a recent work by Lauren Berlant concerning American sensibilities.

In her essay "Uncle Sam Needs a Wife," Berlant (2002) details a shift in Western affiliation and optimism about the good life. While collective cohesion once settled around such political investments like voting, contemporary affiliation is manifest through a feeling structure, and specifically, recognition of empathetic identification. In this climate, national sentiment attaches to post–political emotional events like the death of Princess Di or John Kennedy, or even the post–9/11 patriotism that validate the "I" and the "we" that recognizes an event and each other through our coproduced response. As Berlant argues, the collective witnessing of a violent and premature end to an optimistic, even sacred, possibility grants a pseudo-intimacy and teaches us meaningfulness and cohesion only through empathetic identification. Such witnessing both directs our attention toward and away from other spaces of mattering.

Critical here is what gets to count as worthy and through what mechanisms. Beyond the mere practice itself, the relationship in this political form includes consideration of affect structures, authorizing fantasies (like citizenship), the range of effects and recognizability, and the public investment as well as how certain sites secure the intelligibility of a universalist national culture while others seem ordinary or anonymous, speaks to how normative understandings manage privilege and "humanness." The authorizing—even utopic—fantasies of citizenship, care for others, and the good life are fueled by emotional identification with others through particular logics.

Contemporary body donation discourse works as a technology of productive power to constitute recognizable citizens deemed worthy or valuable on the basis of virtue or goodwill. While most prospective donors are repeatedly framed as generous and caring souls whose body donation is a "most unique and caring gift," this sense of recognition does not extend equally to all, and here, Jernigan's position as a convicted murderer certainly jeopardizes that status. Contemporary cultural understandings of the body mark the identity of the body and who the "real" person is as consubstantial, or same, while recent identity politics matters have continued to challenge and question the possibility of the Lockean ideal of equality—for how the identity is known includes more than merely the convictions or preferences of the self. Charles Taylor (1994) argues that the commitment to human equality, the Lockean notion that underwrites much of the logic of contemporary multiculturalism, fails to consider how the need for recognition or respect participates in the constitution of a person's identity. The way in which the identity of the person is known and/or conferred always includes more than the material conditions, including the corporeal body. As in the Jernigan case, what marks the body (and beyond) as recognizable comes from different fragments or multiplicities of subjectivity as constituted by the arrangement in the social formation of discourse. Additionally, efforts to confer dignity toward a person or group on the basis of simply being human or alive is an inadequate gesture, for this homogenizing attempt negates the distinctiveness of identity. As Taylor notes, for marginalized groups, the lack of recognition may continue to work on the group even after the formal and material mechanisms of discrimination and confinement are removed, for the identity remains inadequately recognized. Here, we echo Taylor, emphasizing how the need for personal recognition is an integral and oft-neglected aspect of identity formation that exceeds the material, corporeal body as a site of identity and distinction. Recognition, the longed-for acknowledgement of value and virtue that contributes to the citizen's self-identity, is precariously but potentially productively placed in the contingent social arrangement.

In the example of *The Virtual Corpse*, neither Jernigan nor any institution or text is fully able to manage the possibility or prevention of his recognition as sacrificial giver and his death as gift or not. But this does not foreclose the possibility of optimism. Instead, we must more diligently track the potential spaces of possibility in this configuration of polysemy or multiple meaning making.

Examination of such a potentially formidable rhetorical force mandates attention to the potential space for both resistance and the transformative practice of individual agency.[8] According to Foucault, "the problem of truth, the problem of power, and the problem of individual conduct . . . can only be understood in relation to each other, not independently" (Foucault 1985, 2). As Foucault has noted, "one needs to investigate historically, and beginning from the lowest level, how mechanisms of power have been able to function" (1976, 100). The analysis of power comes not through whom or with what intention power works, but rather through investigation of the specific capillaries, that is regional or local practices of power.[9] These examples, what Foucault would call fragments of genealogies, gesture toward important local practices that function at the margins of exclusion, "gestures that defy translation, throw sense off track, and thus short-circuit the system through which sense is made" (Biesecker 1992, 357) and enact the "can-doness" of the individual, holding the potential to redistribute the governing logics in a particular context. Here, constitutive criminology places particular emphasis on what makes the capillaries flow and to what effect, and to potential practices of subversion, such as "social judo," which do not add to overall violence in society (Henry and Milovanovic 1996).

It is important to underscore that such "regional or local" gestures including Jernigan's body donation have the capacity to be read as affirmative social change beyond the parameters of even intention. In this very precarious space, the conditions of possibility are able to transform understandings of subjectivity in keeping with constitutive criminology's aim to track the "emergent, contingent, and revisable notion of human subjectivity" (Henry and Milovanovic 1996, 12). The seemingly "dispensable body of the condemned" (Murray 2002) may be marked by optimism of attachment extending far beyond the local gesture. Indeed, we may question the nature of the gift-economy and the justice-law dyads and search within the gaps and dialectics of both elements of these dyads in negotiating singularities that provide the potential for alternative discursive constructions, alternative notions of subjectivity, and alternative notions of a more humanistically oriented society. It is not that "economy" and "law" must be dismissed; in fact, in Caputo's (1997, 147) read of Derrida, "Give economy a chance; let a little chance and gift make its way into our economies. Lighten up. Loosen up the circle." Law is not justice, law is not a gift.[10] It is the gap between the two that provides a space for the possible.

In the political technology of individuals, Foucault says the "reason of state" (art of government) has been normalized as a discursive formation with the state's function to reinforce itself, creating a political marginalism that recognizes individuals only in relation to their potential for change, either positive or negative, in the interests of the state. Again in this example, the creation of subject positions allows procedures of exclusion that allow delinquency to be "controlled, pursued, punished, and reformed" (1976, 102). Toward this goal, the state intervenes in all aspects of individual behavior—as happiness, once posited as the effect of a successful government, is now instead a necessary commodity for the survival of the state. In other words, subjects who believe themselves to be happy are essential for the state to strengthen, expand, and protect itself. It may be in this context that the gift has stabilized into a relentless iterative circle, repetition, whereby it is ongoingly provided with energy investment, collectively in our unexamined gift-giving establishing the debt for the other. Jernigan provides a disruption in the normative practices, a subversion of repetition.

Conclusion

How the political rationality that allows the "reason of state" to be practiced with the competing rationality of individualism is an important arena for exploring how we recognize and identify ourselves. This is particularly so because, according to civil service author Delamare, how the individual is called up for the interests of the state may necessarily be correlated in that "what is superfluous for individuals can be indispensable for the state, and vice versa" (Foucault 1994, 413), provides an important tension between person and state utility. Even while believing in democracy's lure of individual agency—we instead reify sovereignty's rules of right and perpetuate disciplinary norms. Yet even in the production of truth Foucault reminds us that power circulates and functions—people undergo and exercise power (not just a target), remaining the vehicles of power, not its points of application.

The space for productive resistance and transformation acknowledges competing rationalities between state and agency and a perception of the power or force in the "reason of state." Foucault clearly gestures away from juridical power as a motivator or as a tool of resistance/change. In the "Political Technology of Individuals," Foucault (1982) makes a clear distinction between a law (juridical) system and an order (administrative) system—the state's order as maintained through police practices. He points to this division as necessarily irreconcilable, with reconciliation possible "only in the form of an integration of law into the state's order" (Foucault 1994, 417). In subscribing to the function of the juridical rules of right and their interpretation and application, the subjects reify the sovereignty's rules of right, returning to a repressionary view of power. Together, "the right of sovereignty and a mechanism of discipline . . . define . . . the arena in which power is exercised" (1976, 106). While these mechanisms have nothing in common, they function and work in a dialectical exchange in a society of normalization. Their apparent incompatibility is the very site of a necessary arbitrating discourse, even while accompanied by the usual dangers of reifying the right of sovereignty. What's left? The possibility of a new discursive formation that must be antidisciplinarian and liberated from the principle of sovereignty—a vague and complicated site of resistance that leaves more questions than answers but clearly endorses neither the juridical reification of the sovereign nor the disciplinary function. Or, as Caputo (1997, 151) tells us: "Just as we always find ourselves *between* the gift and economy, so we find ourselves always between justice and the law, always trying to interrupt the authoritative voice of the law with the soft sighs of justice, to relieve the harsh strictures of the law with the gentleness of a gift."

What does this mean for the examination of constitutive rhetoric and constitutive criminology? The matter must be explored at the local and "extreme points of its exercise, where it is less legal in character" according to Foucault—the arena of discourse that disciplines the citizen through performance of good citizenship. Here again, Jernigan's body donation is a useful ground of consideration. While someone could easily argue this as a Foucauldian model of pastoral power with the disciplined subject (Jernigan) trying to recover their soul, not doing so here helps underscore the complications of too tidily tying the act to the effect. A sudden surge in body donation is unlikely (although see Mullen 2005), but perhaps science is legitimized toward new ends or perhaps sacrifice is taken up as a moral code of citizenship—but what is important is that the future effect spills beyond its original borders. Jernigan is desirable to the project and science's future only as a corporeal body, but the identity of what else is Jernigan continues to complicate what is distinct or "real" about Jernigan the body as well.

Notes

1. See Henry and Milovanovic 1996; 2000; 2001; Milovanovic and Henry 2001.

2. A particularly intriguing development is the plastination technique invented by German anatomist Gunther von Hagans in 1977, which he has recently expanded into an art exhibit containing "Body Worlds" that has now been seen by some 16 million people worldwide. The exhibit has elicited 6,500 body donations for future exhibits, from donors who give consent so that their remains will be put to "good use" in educating the public. Hagans is reported to have said that his exhibit represents the "democratization of anatomy," the liberation of death from the medical industry (see Mullen 2005).

3. Although see Henry and Milovanovic (1999; 2003), who argue that neither materiality nor idealism is prioritized in their analysis; they are both coproductive forces.

4. This may be understood as similar to a Mobius strip, which has only one surface but with a twist in it, such that ants would be able to walk on it indefinitely without crossing a boundary as depicted in M. C. Escher's famous drawing of ants moving in a figure eight. For an application to the "dangerous mentally ill," see Arrigo (2004, 159–66). It was named after mathematician and astronomer August Ferdinand Mobius, who invented the strip in 1858.

5. These authors have, for example, shown how the activity of BASE-jumping can undergo various coproductive dimensions in the constitution of the "reality" of this activity in the context of Bridge Day.

6. Dragan Milovanovic recalls his days in Vietnam as a combatant where there were many an instance of internal resolutions that if a hand grenade were to fall among his fellow grunts, there would be no doubt about jumping on the grenade to save the fellow grunts' lives.

7. See also Giddens (1991) and Beck's (1992) notion of late modernity (post-1980s) and the emerging "risk-society" and its attendant ethics.

8. We must always be attentive to the reemergence of hegemonic normative orders, or discursive structures and ideologies embedded within them that introduce new, be they hidden and/or inadvertent hegemonic forms, whether at the micro, or macro level of occurrence.

9. Consider, following Foucault's insights, our legal freedoms (e.g., Constitutional Rights) during nonwork hours compared to their gross limitations with the new disciplinary mechanisms at the workplace engendering limited free expression, association, privacy, right against unreasonable searches and seizures, and so forth.

10. As Caputo (1997, 150) says, "The law is a calculated balance of payments, of crime and punishment, of offense and retribution, a closed circle of paying off and paying back."

References

Althusser, L. 1970. "Ideology and Ideological State Apparatuses." Pp. 239–50 in H. Adams and L. Searle, eds., *Critical Theory since 1965*. Gainesville: University Presses of Florida.

Anatomical Donations Program. n.d. Ann Arbor: University of Michigan website. Retrieved February 4, 2005, <www.med.umich.edu/anatomy/donors/>.

Arrigo, B. 2004. "The Inside Out of the Dangerous Mentally Ill." Pp. 150–73 in E. Ragland and D. Milovanovic, eds., *Lacan: Topologically Speaking*. New York: Other Press.

Badiou, A. 2002. *Ethics: An Essay on the Understanding of Evil*. New York: Verso.

Beck, U. 1992. *Risk Society*. London: Sage.

Berlant, L. 2002. "Uncle Sam Needs a Wife: Citizenship and Denegation." Pp. 144–74 in R. Castronovo and D. D. Nelson, eds., *Materializing Democracy: Toward a Revitalized Cultural Politics*. Durham, NC: Duke University Press.

Biesecker, B. 1992. "Michel Foucault and the Question of Rhetoric." *Philosophy and Rhetoric* 25: 351–64.

Body Bequest Program. n.d. Detroit: Wayne State University website. Retrieved February 4, 2005, <www.med.wayne.edu/anatomy/BEQUEST/>.

Bosworth, M. 1999. "Agency and Choice in Women's Prisons: Toward a Constitutive Penology." Pp. 205–26 in S. Henry and D. Milovanovic, eds., *Constitutive Criminology at Work: Applications to Crime and Justice*. Albany: State University of New York Press.

Burke, K. 1969. *A Rhetoric of Motives*. Berkeley: University of California Press.

Butler, J. 1988. "Performative Acts and Gender Constitution: An Essay in Phenomenology and Feminist Theory." Pp. 392–402 in A. Jones, ed., *The Feminism and Visual Culture Reader*. New York: Routledge.

———. 1990. *Gender Trouble: Feminism and the Subversion of Identity*. New York: Routledge.

———. 1992. "Contingent Foundations: Feminism and the Questions of 'Postmodernism.'" Pp. 3–21 in J. Butler and J. W. Scott, eds., *Feminists Theorize the Political*. New York: Routledge.

Caputo, J. 1997. *Deconstruction in a Nutshell: A Conversation with Jacques Derrida*. New York: Fordham University.

Charland, M. 1987. "Constitutive Rhetoric: The Case of the People Quebecois." *Quarterly Journal of Speech* 73: 133–50.

Croall, H. 1997. "Crime: Understanding More and Condemning Less?" *Reviewing*

Sociology 10, no. 3. Retrieved February 6, 2005, <www.rdg.ac.uk/RevSoc/archive/volume10/number3/10-3a.htm>.

Deleuze, G., and F. Guattari. 1977. *Anti-Oedipus*. Minneapolis: University of Minnesota Press.

Derrida, J. 1986. "Declaration of Independence." *New Political Science* 15: 7–17.

———. 1991. *Given Time*. Trans. P. Kamuf. Chicago: University of Chicago Press.

———. 1994. "The Force of Law: The Mystifical Foundation of Authority." Trans. M. Quaintance. In D. Cornell, ed., *Deconstruction and the Possibility of Justice*. New York: Routledge.

———. 1997. "The Villanova Roundtable: A Conversation with Jacques Derrida." In J. Caputo, ed., *Deconstruction in a Nutshell: A Conversation with Jacques Derrida*. New York: Fordham University Press.

Ferrell, J., C. Milovanovic, and S. Lyng. 2001. "Edgework Media Practices, and the Elongation of Meaning." *Theoretical Criminology* 5, no. 2: 177–202.

Foucault, M. 1976, January 7. "Lecture One." Pp. 78–108 in C. Gordon, ed., *Power/Knowledge: Selected Interviews and Other Writings 1972–1977*. New York: Pantheon Books.

———. 1977. *Discipline and Punish*. New York: Pantheon.

———. 1984. "On the Genealogy of Ethics: An Overview of Work in Progress." Pp. 340–72 in P. Rabinow, ed., *Foucault Reader*. New York: Pantheon Books.

———. 1985. "Final Interview." *Raritan* 6, no. 2. As cited in B. Biesecker (1992), "Michel Foucault and the Question of Rhetoric." *Philosophy and Rhetoric* 25: 351–64.

———. 1994. "The Political Technology of Individuals." Pp. 403–17 in P. Rabinow, ed., *The Essential Works of Foucault, 1954–1984*, vol. 3. New York: The New Press.

Giddens, A. 1991. *Modernity and Self Identity*. Cambridge: Polity.

Grosz, E. 1994. *Volatile Bodies*. Bloomington: Indiana University Press.

Henry, S., and D. Milovanovic. 1996. *Constitutive Criminology: Beyond Postmodernism*. London: Sage.

———. 1999. *Constitutive Criminology at Work: Applications to Crime and Punishment*. New York: State University of New York Press.

———. 2000. "Constitutive Criminology: Origins, Core Concepts, and Evaluation." *Social Justice* 27, no. 2: 268–90.

———. 2001. "Constitutive Criminology." Pp. 50–51 in E. McLaughlin and J. Munci, eds., *The Sage Dictionary of Criminology*. London: Sage.

———. 2003. "Constitutive Criminology." Pp. 57–69 in M. D. Schwartz and S. Hatty, eds., *Controversies in Critical Criminology*. Cincinnati: Anderson Publishing.

Kasics, K. (director). 2000. *Blue End* (motion picture). Switzerland. Available from First Run Icarus Films, 32 Court Street, 21st floor, Brooklyn, NY 11201.

———, (producer, director). n.d.. *The Virtual Corpse* (television documentary). HBO.

Laclau, E., and C. Mouffe. 2001. *Hegemony and Socialist Strategy*. 2nd edition. New York: Verso.

McGee, M. C. 1975. "In Search of 'the People': A Rhetorical Alternative." *Quarterly Journal of Speech* 61: 235–49.

Milovanovic, D., and S. Henry. 1991. "Constitutive Penology." *Social Justice* 18: 204–24.

———. 2001. "Constitutive Definition of Crime: Power as Harm." Pp. 165–78 in S. Henry and M. M. Lanier, eds., *What Is Crime? Controversies over the Nature of Crime and What To Do About It*. Boulder, CO: Rowman & Littlefield.

———. 2005. "Constitutive Penology." Pp. 154–57 in M. Bosworth, ed., *Encyclopedia of Prisons and Correctional Facilities*. London: Sage.

Mueller, D. A. 1999. "What Is Anatomical Donation? Why Do Families Request It?" *Michigan Funeral Directors Association Journal* 59, no. 4: 5.

Mullen, W. 2005, February 5. "Exhibit Gives Cadavers New Life of Their Own." *Chicago Tribune*: 1, 18.

Murray, S. 2002. "Review of the book *The Visible Human Project: Informatic Bodies and Posthuman Medicine*." *Reconstruction* 2. Retrieved February 10, 2005, <www.-reconstruction.ws/021/revVisibleHP.htm>.

Patton, P. 2001. *Deleuze and the Political.* New York: Routledge.

Roach, M. 2003. *Stiff: The Curious Lives of Human Cadavers.* New York: Norton.

Taylor, C. 1994. *Multiculturalism: Examining the Politics of Recognition.* Princeton: Princeton University Press.

Thomson, A. 1997. "Post-modernism and Social Justice." Retrieved February 6, 2005, <http://ace.acadiau.ca/soci/agt/constitutivecrim.htm>. A shorter version was published in *Canadian Journal of Sociology* 23 (1998): 109–13.

Tierney, T. F. 1999. "The Preservation and Ownership of the Body." Pp. 233–61 in G. Weiss and H. F. Haber, eds., *Perspectives on Embodiment.* New York: Routledge.

Waldby, C. 2000. *The Visible Human Project: Informatic Bodies and Posthuman Medicine.* New York: Routledge.

Willed Body Program. n.d. Lansing: Michigan State University website. Retrieved February 4, 2005, <www.rad.msu.edu/ANATOMY/pages/willed/default.htm>.

Zuger, A. 2004, March 23. "Anatomy Lessons, a Vanishing Rite for Young Doctors." *New York Times.*

Index

About the Editors and Contributors

Shahid Alvi is Professor of Criminology, Justice and Policy Studies at the University of Ontario Institute of Technology. He is author or coauthor of numerous articles and book chapters and four books, including the recently released *Deviance and Crime: Theory, Research and Policy* (with Walter DeKeseredy and Desmond Ellis). He is also the 2002 recipient of the Critical Criminologist of the Year Award from the American Society of Criminology's Division on Critical Criminology.

Bruce A. Arrigo is Professor of Crime, Law, and Society in the Department of Criminal Justice at the University of North Carolina, Charlotte. His research and teaching interests include critical and philosophical criminology, criminal and legal psychology, and crime and social justice policy. He has authored more than 125 articles, book chapters, and scholarly essays. Recent books include *The French Connection in Criminology: Rediscovering Crime, Law, and Social Change* (coauthored with Dragan Milovanovic and Robert Carl Schehr; State University of New York Press, 2005); *Criminal Behavior: A Systems Approach* (forthcoming from Prentice Hall, 2006); and *Philosophy, Crime, and Criminology* (coedited with Christopher R. Williams; forthcoming from the University of Illinois Press, 2006). He is a Fellow of the American Psychological Association and a Fellow of the Academy of Criminal Justice Sciences.

Gregg Barak is Professor of Criminology and Criminal Justice at Eastern Michigan University and was the 2004 Visiting Distinguished Professor and Scholar, College of Justice and Safety at Eastern Kentucky University. He is author or editor of eleven books, his most recent being *Violence and Nonviolence: Pathways to Understanding* (Sage, 2003). Dr. Barak is a Fellow of the Academy of Criminal Justice Sciences and the recipient of the Critical Criminologist of the Year, 1999, awarded by the American Society of Criminology's Division on Critical Criminology.

Elaine Barclay is a researcher in rural social issues at the Institute for Rural Futures, University of New England, Armidale, New South Wales. She is also Director of the Centre for Rural Crime, Safety and Security, which is an international research centre located within the Institute for Rural Futures. Over the past seven years, Dr. Barclay has developed an extensive program of research in rural crime in collaboration with Professor Pat Jobes of the University of New England and Professor Joseph Donnermeyer of Ohio State University. Dr. Barclay has also conducted research in farm succession and inheritance as well as studies in information technology, welfare services for farm families and biosecurity in rural communities. Elaine has a degree in Social Science, postgraduate qualifications in Psychology and a Ph.D. in Rural Sociology/Criminology, which focused upon property crime on farms.

Julie Borkin is a rhetorical studies doctoral student at Wayne State University's Department of Communication, where she is completing a dissertation on contemporary calls for civic commitment and public sacrifice.

Michelle Brown's research explores the intersection of culture, punishment, and risk. She is working on a monograph exploring the meanings of U.S. imprisonment in cultural practice while serving as Assistant Professor and criminologist in the Department of Sociology and Anthropology at Ohio University. She is coeditor of *Media Representations of September 11* (Praeger, 2003).

Kimberly J. Cook is Professor of Sociology at the University of North Carolina, Wilmington. Her book *Divided Passions* (Northeastern University Press, 1998) explores public opinions on abortion and the death penalty. More recently, she was a Senior Scholar Fulbright (2001) recipient at the Australian National University, where she conducted the research framing the analysis of her coauthored chapter in this book. Her current research examines the postprison experiences of death row exonerees in the United States (with Saundra Westervelt). When not working, she spends her time with the most enchanting dachshund and partner ever made!

Walter S. DeKeseredy is Professor of Criminology, Justice and Policy Studies at the University of Ontario Institute of Technology. He is author or coauthor of eleven books and over fifty refereed journal articles. In 2004, he and Martin D. Schwartz jointly received the Distinguished Scholar Award from the American Society of Criminology's (ASC) Division on Women and Crime. In 1995, he received the Critical Criminologist of the Year Award from the ASC's Division on Critical Criminology.

Joseph F. Donnermeyer is Professor in the Rural Sociology program, College of Food, Agricultural and Environmental Sciences, Ohio State University. From 2001 to 2005, he was the Program Area Leader for Rural Sociology and Chair of the Rural Sociology Graduate Studies Committee at Ohio State. He currently serves as the International Research Coordinator of the Centre for Rural Crime, Safety and Security at the University of New England in Australia, where he has been a visiting academic on two separate occasions. Dr. Donnermeyer's major field of study is criminology, with a special focus on rural and agricultural crime. He received his M.A. and Ph.D. degrees in Sociology from the University of Kentucky, and his B.A. degree in Sociology from Thomas More College, a small liberal arts college located near Cincinnati. He holds a lifetime Honorary Membership in the Ohio Crime Prevention Association and regularly conducts leadership training on social change and community for police organizations.

Judith Grant, whose specialization is in the area of women, addiction and recovery, teaches in a tenure-track position in the Department of Sociology, Anthropology and Criminology at Missouri State University in Springfield, Missouri. Previously, she taught for four years at Ohio University in Athens, Ohio. Dr. Grant received her Ph.D. in Women's Studies from York University, Toronto, Ontario. Her research interests include drugs and gender; crime, justice and gender; women, addiction and recovery; violence against women; public policy issues; community activism and community-academic alliances.

Stuart Henry is Professor of Social Science and Chair of the Department of Interdisciplinary Studies at Wayne State University. He is author and co-author (with Dragan Milovanovic) of numerous articles and books on post-modern criminology, most notably, *Constitutive Criminology* (Sage, 1996) and *Constitutive Criminology at Work* (State University of New York Press, 1999).

Pat Jobes has written extensively on rural communities, social change, and social problems in Australia, the United States, Romania and Pakistan. Dr. Jobes served until recently as a fellow to the Criminology Research Council in Canberra, Australia, coming to the Council as Associate Professor on the faculty at the University of New England, Armidale, New South Wales. Although he is now retired, he continues to write and conduct research on rural crime. He has held professorial positions at the University of Colorado, Boulder, and at Montana State University and visiting faculty appointments as Senior Fulbright Fellow at the University of Bucharest, the University of

Oregon, New Mexico State University, Utah State University and the University of Agriculture, Faisalabad. In 2002 he was elected to a four-year term as President of the Section on Deviance, RC-29, of the International Sociological Society. Dr. Jobes received his B.A. (Psychology) and M.A. (Corrections) degrees at the University of Colorado, Boulder. His Ph.D. (Sociology) was conferred by the University of Washington.

MaDonna R. Maidment is Assistant Professor in the Department of Sociology and Anthropology at the University of Guelph. Her publications and research interests focus in the areas of feminist criminologies, sociology of punishment, and wrongful convictions. Her most recent work with criminalized women (forthcoming with the University of Toronto Press) is titled *Doing Time on the Outside: Deconstructing the Benevolent Community.*

Dragan Milovanovic is Professor of Justice Studies at Northeastern Illinois University. He has authored numerous books and journal articles in the area of postmodern criminology, law, and social justice. His most recent books are *Critical Criminology at the Edge* (Criminal Justice Press, 2004) and *An Introduction to the Sociology of Law* (Criminal Justice Press, 3rd edition, 2003). He is also the editor of the *International Journal for the Semiotics of Law.*

Stephen L. Muzzatti (Ph.D., York University) is Assistant Professor of Sociology at Ryerson University in Toronto, Canada, where he teaches courses in deviance, media and popular culture. He has written on such diverse topics as crimes of globalisation, criminological theory, Marilyn Manson, youth, street racing and motorcycle culture. He is the editor (with Vince Samarco) of the anthology *Reflections from the Wrong Side of the Tracks: Class, Identity, and the Working Class Experience* (Rowman & Littlefield, 2005). Stephen is a member of the American Society of Criminology's Division on Critical Criminology and coeditor of the *Critical Criminologist* newsletter.

Barbara Perry is Professor of Criminology, Justice and Policy Studies at the University of Ontario Institute of Technology. She has written extensively in the area of hate crime, including two books on the topic: *In the Name of Hate: Understanding Hate Crime*, and *Hate and Bias Crime: A Reader*. Most recently, she has conducted interviews with Native Americans on their experiences of hate crime. She is also completing a British Home Office project on antiracism programming in England and Wales. Her work has been published in journals representing diverse disciplines: *Theoretical Criminology*, *Journal of Social and Behavioral Sciences*, *Journal of History and Politics*, and

American Indian Quarterly. Dr. Perry continues to work in the area of hate crime and has begun to make contributions to the limited scholarship on hate crime in Canada. Here, she is particularly interested in anti-Muslim violence and hate crime against Aboriginal people.

Chris Powell has written and lectured widely on various aspects of social (or, increasingly, antisocial) control. His best-known work addresses the ideological role of humor and the criminalisation of "gypsy" populations. He has held academic posts at Swansea Institute and the Universities of Sheffield and Bangor in the U.K. In a futile attempt to evade the highly oppressive nature of bureaucratisation in the British system he moved to the U.S. to take up his present post as Associate Professor of Criminology at the University of Southern Maine. He is now considering going freelance! The move did, however, enable him to be with his delightful coauthor and their equally delightful dachshund.

Martin D. Schwartz is Professor of Sociology and Presidential Research Scholar at Ohio University. He has written or edited eleven books, more than sixty refereed journal articles, and another forty book chapters, government reports, and essays. A former officer of several organizations, he received the Lifetime Achievement Award from the American Society of Criminology's (ASC) Division on Critical Criminology. In 2004, he and Walter S. DeKeseredy jointly received the Distinguished Scholar Award from the ASC's Division on Women and Crime.